Mythical Beasts

MYTHICAL
BEASTS

Edited by
JOHN CHERRY

Published for the Trustees of the British Museum by
BRITISH MUSEUM PRESS

ACKNOWLEDGEMENTS

The idea for this book came from Nina Shandloff, a Senior Editor at British Museum Press, and her enthusiasm in commissioning and inspiring the authors, carrying out the initial editing and picture research and compiling the glossary were invaluable. Subsequent editing was carried out by Colin Grant, with picture research assistance from Rona Skene, design by Behram Kapadia and production by Susanna Friedman. In addition the authors would like to acknowledge the help of Ruth Baldwin, Morris Bierbrier, Claude Blair, Richard Blurton, John Boardman, Lucilla Burn, Timothy Clark, Dominique Collon, Barrie Cook, Stephanie Dalley, Elizabeth Foy, Kate Garratt, George Hart, Virginia Hewitt, Nigel King, Robert Knox, Carol Michaelson, Susan Montgomery, Emma Owen, Richard Parkinson, Mavis Pilbeam, Venetia Porter, Sarah Posey, Stephen Quirke, Robin Seager, Patsy Vanags and Susan Youngs. The authors are grateful to both Celia Clear and Emma Way of British Museum Press for their encouragement.

The quotation on p. 71 from *Sonnets to Orpheus* in *Poems 1906–1926* by Rainer Maria Rilke, translated by J. B. Leishman and published by Chatto & Windus in the UK in 1936 and by New Directions Publishing Corporation in the USA, is reprinted by permission of the Estate of the translator and New Directions Publishing Corporation; and the quotation on pp. 164–5 from 'Siren Song' in the collection *You are Happy* by Margaret Atwood is reprinted by permission of the author and Oxford University Press Canada.

British Library Cataloguing in Publication data
A catalogue record for this book is available from the British Library

ISBN 0 7141 1737 4

Designed by Behram Kapadia
Typeset in Linotron Bembo by
Rowland Phototypesetting Ltd
Bury St Edmunds, Suffolk
Printed in Italy by Imago Publishing Ltd

HALF-TITLE PAGE Head of the gorgon Medusa on an Athenian red-figured *hydria* (water jar), from Tarquinia, about 500–480 BC.
FRONTISPIECE Two kirins, Japanese ivory netsuke, 18th century (left) and 18th–19th century (right).
TITLE PAGE Sphinx among stylised plants, Phoenician ivory openwork plaque, from Nimrud, Assyria, 800–700 BC.

Contents

Introduction

What is a mythical beast? For the purposes of this book, a mythical beast is not simply a beast which has myths attached to it. Lions, horses and dogs all have myths attached to them, but this does not make them mythical beasts. A mythical beast is one which never existed in reality, but is an invention of the mind. It may be composed of parts of different animals, such as the head and wings of an eagle and the body of a lion, so making a griffin. It may be created by multiplication, like a many-headed hydra. Some beasts combine the human with the animal, such as the centaur, the mermaid or the minotaur. By combining the parts of different animals the mythical beast emphasises the differences between them. Mythical beasts may be distinguished from demons which are evil spirits, sometimes in two-legged form, or monsters which are sometimes merely misshapen animals. This book describes and illustrates the diversity of the human imagination which created mythical beasts.

It is true that such beasts are often remarkable for their repetition. Nature indeed embodies a greater variety than the imagination. As the writer Jean Luis Borges commented in his preface to *The Book of Imaginary Beings*, 'The zoology of our dreams is far poorer than the zoology of the Maker.' Yet it is the attention, often extending to devotion, that some imaginary animals have inspired that makes them worthy of our interest. Many of the beasts discussed here could be examined at far greater length, but this study is aimed at introducing readers to this menagerie and suggesting where to hunt them further.

How were these particular beasts selected for this book and why were some given longer treatment than others? It was those mythical beasts with an interest and resonance transcending cultural boundaries that have attracted the authors, even though the meaning given to them in different

Beast of the Apocalypse with many heads, from an Apocalypse manuscript painted between 1320 and 1330, probably in East Anglia.

cultures may vary widely. Dragons are perhaps the most widespread mythical beast. The unicorn and the griffin share an origin in the ancient world and a parallel development in the Middle Ages. The sphinx links the ancient world of Egypt with the modern. A chapter on birds was considered, but the phoenix, the barnacle goose and others do not easily flock together. Gods and goddesses have generally been excluded, as have real animals. The beasts chosen here are important not only for their stories but for their underlying meanings and symbolism too.

The geography of mythical beasts appearing in this book ranges from the ancient Near and Far East to present-day Europe, and includes (in the Glossary) some from Africa, Australia and the Americas. An important aspect is the transmission of form and meaning between different areas and cultures. Distance itself could lend an air of mystery, illustrated by the assumption, both in the ancient world and in the Middle Ages, that such animals originated or lived in distant parts. For instance, the phoenix was thought to come from Arabia, an idea that itself went back to ancient Egypt, and medieval writers believed that dragons had their breeding-places in India and Ethiopia.

There is often a close association between the genesis of mythical animals and the myths of creation. For instance, in the Mesopotamian *Epic of Creation*, Tiamat is the personification of the sea. She creates a troop of ferocious monsters to aid her in her struggles against the god Ea, who knows everything, and Ea's son Marduk, the Hero. These monsters include a horned serpent, a scorpion-man, a fish-man and a bull-man. Eventually Marduk kills Tiamat in single combat and captures all the other demons that she has created. Marduk then cuts Tiamat in half to make the sky and the earth, and proceeds to organise the rest of the universe. This accomplished, he creates man. The Greek Creation myth similarly includes the birth of monstrous creatures; Typhon, a grisly monster with a hundred dragons' heads, who was the son of Gaea, the mother of the Olympian gods, marries his sibling Echidna to produce Cerberus, the Chimaera, and many others. Even Christian scenes of God creating the birds and animals include such mythical beasts as the unicorn and griffin, because the Bible was thought to provide spiritual authority for their existence.

The characteristics of the mythical beast often included the possession and control of natural forces, such as fire and water. Dragons which breathe fire are commonplace, but the idea of a water monster breathing fire, such as the description in the Book of Job of Leviathan breathing fire from his mouth and smoke from his nostrils, is more unusual. Chinese dragons were generally beneficent, since they controlled the weather and provided rain at the proper seasons. In early Hindu mythology the dragon Vritra, whose home was in the clouds, was more evil. It approached on the wings of the monsoon holding in its body vast reservoirs of water, which were only released when Indra, the thunder god and lord of the elements, attacked it with a bolt of lightning. Then the dragon burst and the land was watered.

Representations in art, and particularly sculpture, can show us how mythical beasts have been viewed in the past. Just as they often mark the border between two different creatures, so they were often used to mark important borders and sacred boundaries and to guard entrances. This is clearly shown by the colossal stone figures of winged and man-headed bulls and lions that flanked the entrances to the great Mesopotamian palaces of Kalah and Khorsabad and astonished the first discoverers of those civilis-ations. In more recent times, figures of lions and griffins were used to

God creates the animals. In this scene from the early 14th-century Queen Mary psalter the unicorn and the griffin are shown placed before the throne of God.

guard Romanesque portals in Italy, which in turn influenced usage in other countries. In Greek mythology dragons and serpents also appear as guardians, notably the python at Delphi, or the dragon Ladon who assisted the three sisters known as the Hesperides to guard the golden apples which Hera had received as a marriage gift.

Sometimes the death of mythical beasts results in their rebirth. The most

The reverse of the 'Phoenix' jewel shows the emblematic device of the phoenix rising from the flames, the monogram of Queen Elizabeth I and a crown beneath heavenly rays. This English jewel, with its portrait bust of the queen on the obverse, was made about 1570–80.

obvious example of this continuity is the phoenix, which arises from the ashes of the fire that consumes it. Other births occur at the death of monsters: Pegasus, the winged horse, springs from the blood of the Greek Gorgon Medusa, after she is killed by the hero Perseus. There is also the concept that beasts die and are resurrected in a perpetual process. Such an example of death and rebirth is the daily pursuit of the sun by the Egyptian serpent dragon Apep, leading finally to a deadly night-time conflict in which Apep is slain and dismembered but fortunately is reconstituted in time for the next day.

Some mythical beasts, like the creations of Tiamat, were embodiments of the power of evil. In the Near East the serpent or dragon was, in particular, a symbol of the principle of evil. In Egypt Apophis was the great serpent of the world of darkness vanquished by Ra. In the Old Testament, the dragon is the source of death and sin, a conception which was adopted in the New Testament and so passed into the Christian mythology of the Middle Ages, when the dragon was seen as representing the devil and all his works. In particular it served as a symbol of heresy. The creation of the knightly order of the vanquished dragon by the Holy

Roman Emperor Sigismund in 1418 celebrated the victory of orthodoxy over the heretic John Hus.

One of the most important functions of some mythical beasts was to provide the hero with an opponent in his victorious fight against evil. Notable examples of this struggle between heroes and the forces of evil are the fights between Bellerophon and the Chimaera, St George and the dragon, and Sigurd and the dragon Fafnir. Occasionally the struggle with the animal is presented as an overwhelmingly impossible task. For instance, in the history of Bel and the Dragon in the Apocrypha, Daniel has to slay the dragon without staff or sword, a task that was believed impossible. Daniel manages it by ingeniously stuffing pitch, fat and hair down the dragon's throat. Likewise Hercules found it difficult to kill the many-headed dragon known as the Lernaean Hydra, since every time a head was struck off two more grew in its place. He eventually solved this problem by setting fire to a neighbouring forest so that he could cauterise the neck stumps as each head was cut off – a fine example of heroic lateral thinking. But the death of the mythical beast is not always the end of the matter.

Conquered by heroes, some beasts became themselves emblems of valour. The qualities of the mythical beast that led to this interpretation are clearly stated by the seventeenth-century writer, Sir Thomas Browne, in

Hercules and the Lernaean Hydra shown on a red-figured jar attributed to the Geras painter. Made in Athens about 480–470 BC.

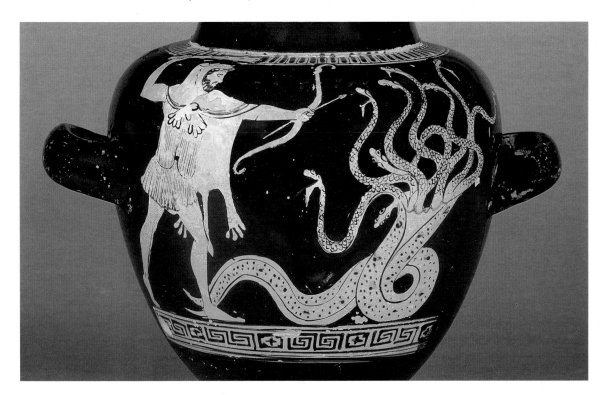

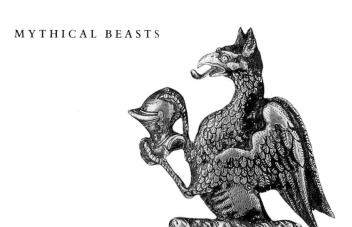

An English silver griffin of about 1600, which served as a livery badge for the retainers of the Cholmondeley family of Cheshire.

his definition of the griffin: 'So doth it well make out the properties of a Guardian, or any person entrusted; the ears implying attention, the wings celerity of execution, the lion-like shape courage and audacity, the hooked bill reservance and tenacity. It is an emblem of valour and magnanimity, as being compounded of the eagle and the lion, the noblest animals of their kind; and so it is applicable unto Princes, Presidents, Generals and all heroick Commanders; and so it is also born in the Coat-arms of many noble Families of Europe.'

One of the most notable survivals of the mythical beast into modern times is in heraldry, both on a shield and also as a supporter holding up the shield. Agamemnon may have started the fashion since he had on his shield, besides the gorgon's head, a blue three-headed serpent. The dragon as a warlike symbol was taken from the conquered Dacians by the Roman Emperor Trajan to be the emblem of the cohort, an infantry unit of the Roman army. The dragon on a standard was an emblem of the Anglo-Saxon kings of England before the Normal Conquest and, as late as 1245, was displayed by Henry III when he went to war against the Welsh. The fashion for using mythical beasts in coats of arms, as opposed to banners or standards, appears to have started in France and Germany in the late fourteenth century and spread to England as a result of the French wars. Frequently mythical beasts show their fierce guarding role as the supporters at the side of shields. Two of the most famous of these are the lion and the unicorn on either side of the English royal arms. And to the present day mythical beasts continue to be used by chemists, banks, insurance companies and others as a symbol assuring their customers of their security.

The strength and demonic energy of many mythical beasts would suggest that they could never be harnessed, and so the ability to control them was a certain indication of heroic status or strength. For example, Bellerophon tried to tame Pegasus but found it impossible, until the goddess Athena gave him a magic bridle. Some mythical beasts were even harnessed to draw triumphal chariots, a service particularly performed in the Middle Ages in Italy where, for example, the griffin draws the triumphal

The symbol of the griffin as currently used by the Midland Bank. This version was designed by Wolf Olins in 1988.

car of the City of God in Dante's *Purgatory* and the unicorn is often depicted drawing the chariot of Chastity.

As guardians of borders and crossing-places, mythical beasts had an important role in controlling the border between life and death. The entrance to the Greek underworld was guarded by Kerberos (Cerberus), a three-headed hound who admitted anyone who wanted to enter, but devoured anyone attempting to leave. Another way of crossing this boundary was to be transported by a harpy, a bird-woman, who flew with the soul of the dead to Hades. The early fifth-century Lycian funerary pillar known as the 'Harpy Tomb' shows them in flight.

The monsters of the ancient Near East sprang from the concept of a cosmic struggle between gods and demons as the determiner of human fate. By the European Middle Ages they were seen very differently. To the medieval Christian monks these nightmare visions of ferocious beasts were transmuted into symbols of the earthly passions and supernatural powers that assailed them in their own struggle for spiritual perfection. With the advent of modern psychology they have become symbols of the unconscious mind, especially its desires.

For example, the unicorn was proud, noble and fiercely courageous, but also gentle and serene. He could only be captured by a virgin girl, who could then lead him to the palace of a king. On one hand the unicorn was seen as a symbol of Christ, while on the other he was seen as a symbol of worldly love. On the caskets sometimes exchanged between lovers in the later Middle Ages, the unicorn represents the lover and the virgin girl his beautiful, sweet beloved.

The seductive attractions of the mythical beast provoked St Bernard of Clairvaux in the twelfth century to rail against the use of beautiful deformity in the carvings of the cloister in his denunciation of the art that was fostered by the monks of the Burgundian monastery of Cluny. 'To what purpose are those unclean apes, those fierce lions, those monstrous centaurs, those half men, those striped tigers, those fighting knights, those hunters winding their horns? Many bodies are here under one head, or again many heads to a single body. Here is a four-footed beast with a serpent's tail; there a fish with a beast's head . . . so many and so marvellous are the varieties of shapes on every hand that we are more tempted to read in the marble than in our books.'

Mythical beasts are creatures of the imagination, living as symbols and never dying. They have continued to exist through succeeding generations, societies and civilisations, although often with changed meanings and associations. The trail of such beasts is marked by the evidence of both literature and art. The contributors of this book have drawn upon the variety and richness of surviving art and antiquities to illustrate the continuing life and changing perceptions of these strange beasts.

Dragons

Where and when were dragons born? Did they spring full-grown from an artist's hand or a bard's lips? In the absolute sense, both these questions are unanswerable. Artefacts depicting dragons in one form or another appear as early as the fourth millennium BC. Yet, in the absence of texts of the same date, the meaning and intention of these dragon objects remain obscure. When written language begins to accompany visual imagery, the place of dragons in myth becomes clear. Yet the form of the dragon at times developed independently of its meaning. For example, a dragon whose shape derived from a Chinese model carried very different connotations in fifteenth-century Iran from those of its Ming Chinese counterpart. Although the idea of the dragon is at times as slithery and elusive as the actual beast, the chapter which follows will attempt to present dragons in their visual and literary manifestations from prehistoric times until the present. Needless to say, many dragons will evade inclusion here, but their essential nature, if not their localised idiosyncrasies, should be evident in the discussion of their cousins.

Antiquity

The creature we identify today as the dragon – a scaly reptile with a snake-like body, crocodilian head, four feet, horns, wings and fiery breath – evolved in form from several strains. In ancient India and Egypt dragons were identified with (or embellishments of) snakes, though the Indian makara certainly derived from a crocodile. The earliest Chinese dragons resemble either lizards or composite beasts with the tails of snakes and the heads of other animals. Ancient Near Eastern dragons, while scaly, represent a thoroughly made-up creature, in which reptilian and mammalian attributes are both present but neither is dominant.

OPPOSITE 'The crow addresses the assembled animals', watercolour from a book of fables, possibly *Anwar-i Suhayli* of al-Kashifi. This scene may illustrate a variant of the episode in this book when the crow addresses the birds to rally their support against the leader of the owls. Real animals are here combined with a simurgh, or phoenix (top right), a snaky Chinese-style dragon (middle right) and a crocodilian Indian makara (lower left). Attributed to Miskin, India, Mughal, *c.* 1610.

Excavations in Pakistan and China have uncovered artefacts, either decorated with snakes or in the form of composite beasts related to dragons, that predate the invention of writing by hundreds of years. While a cylinder seal from Bannu dating to the late second millennium BC may be an early example of snake-worship, a long-lived phenomenon in the subcontinent, the Chinese pig-dragon, remains an enigma. Comparable pieces, complete with their curved, scaly tail, have been found in Neolithic sites in Liaoning province, north-east China. Dating from the fourth millennium BC, they are associated with burials. In one case a pair of such jades was found placed back-to-back in the chest cavity of a body. Whether this indicates a ritual use or simply the value accorded to objects fashioned of jade remains a mystery. Equally unknowable is whether such pieces were considered to be dragons at all and, if they were, what they symbolised to their fourth-millennium owners.

With the advent of writing in the third millennium BC the mythical significance of dragons becomes somewhat clearer. The *Epic of Creation*, an early second-millennium Babylonian work, details the struggle of the gods Apsu, god of the primordial waters under the earth, and his consort, Tiamat, the sea, against Ea, their son, the all-knowing. Having killed Apsu, Ea took over his domain and with his own lover created Marduk, a god-hero. Meanwhile, at the urging of her children, Tiamat plotted her revenge. To help her in her war she begat

> giant snakes/sharp of tooth and unsparing of fang [?].
> She filled their bodies with venom instead of blood.
> She cloaked ferocious dragons with fearsome rays
> and made them bear mantles of radiance, made them god-like,
> [*chanting this inscription*]
> 'Whoever looks upon them shall collapse in utter terror!
> Their bodies shall rear up continually and never turn away!'
> She stationed a horned serpent, a *mušhuššu* – a dragon, and a *lahmu* – hero,
> . . . Bearing merciless dragons, fearless in battle.

BELOW This cylinder seal impression of *c.* 2000–1500 BC from Bannu in the North-West Frontier region of Pakistan reveals an early instance of the symbolic importance of snakes in the subcontinent. The snakes and birds on this seal may refer to the earth and sky. The lone snake at the left is an impression of the round end of the seal.

LEFT In its original state this Chinese jade pig-dragon of *c.* 3500 BC would have had a scaly tail but it is not certain whether creatures such as this were thought to be dragons. It is believed, but not proven, that the pig-dragon derived its form from jade earrings found in burials of the Hongshan culture, *c.* 3800–2700 BC.

Despite Tiamat's efforts and her initial success in deterring her enemies, Marduk challenged her to single combat and defeated her. To do so, he forced wind into Tiamat which distended her belly and enabled him to pierce her with an arrow, Marduk then split her down the middle, put up one of her halves as a roof for the sky to hold back the waters, 'so that they could not escape', and laid down the other half to form the surface of the earth. As for the mušhuššu dragon, he and Tiamat's other monsters were captured and submitted to Marduk. When Marduk accepted the trappings of kingship from the other gods, the mušhuššu dragon took its place at his feet.

Even in this epic, where the dragon is not central to the narrative, its ambivalent significance is evident. As a member of Tiamat's army of monsters, it is ferocious and evil. Yet, subdued by Marduk, it is tamed and has been transformed into a guardian servant of the King of the Gods. Not only is the association of the dragon with water – in this case Tiamat, personification of the sea – a consistent characteristic of dragons, but also the role of guardian, first of the gods but later of treasure, is established very early. Moreover, as is clear from the *Epic of Creation* text, snakes are differentiated from dragons. By contrast with Egypt, where snakes in myth perform many of the functions of dragons, the symbolism of Babylonian snakes is separate from that of dragons.

Although the physical attributes of the Babylonian dragon were not adopted by the Egyptians, a Sumerian version of the *Epic of Creation* may be the origin of one version of the Egyptian myth of the defeat of Apophis, the sea-snake and enemy of the sun-god Re. Here the god Seth, later reviled as the enemy of Osiris, overcomes Apophis in a fashion which parallels Marduk's victory over Tiamat. Not only does this contest represent the victory of light over darkness but it also symbolises the defeat

RIGHT This impression of an Akkadian cylinder seal of *c.* 2300–2200 BC shows a bearded god, named as Iba'um in the inscription, above a dragon of the mušhuššu type. As with the mušhuššu of the god Marduk, this dragon is placed at the god's feet. Another bearded god holds a rope coming from the dragon's neck and leads a worshipper by the hand.

of chaos and the renewal of life. In Egyptian religion darkness and light, death and life, Osiris and Re were seen as a continuum. Because of the Egyptian emphasis on the afterlife, snakes figure largely in accounts of Re's progress through the underworld.

According to Egyptian belief Re travelled through the underworld, Duat, each night. By the fifteenth century BC Re's progress was detailed in the *Book of What is in the Underworld*, or *Am-Duat*, and illustrated on the walls of the tombs of Tuthmosis III (1425 BC) and Amenhotep II (1401 BC). The journey is divided into twelve hours called Scenarios. In the Fourth Scenario Re reaches a passageway to the tomb of Osiris with two open doors guarded by snakes, some of which have a human head and four legs or three snake-heads and wings. These dragon-like creatures act only as guards and do not harm Re. In the Seventh Scenario Re observes from his solar boat the victory over Apophis, the giant serpent, symbol of chaos, who tries to swallow Re. Apophis is depicted incapacitated by knife wounds. Again, in the Twelfth Scenario a snake appears as the body into which the solar boat is towed and out of whose mouth Re merges as Khepri, the scarab beetle. Re in the form of Khepri then sails up from the East to shine as the sun for the next twelve hours.

In an analogous but somewhat later account of Re's underworld journey, the *Book of Gates*, each of the twelve hours is entered through a gateway guarded by a snake. Fire-breathing cobras crown the towers of the gate. In the Second Scenario Apophis the giant snake, enemy of Re, is again vanquished. The Third Scenario boasts the Lake of Cobras which guards Re's flame and the huge coiled serpent Hereret, flanked by goddesses who swallow whatever evil issues forth from Hereret. Again, in the Fifth Scenario Apophis appears, defeated and giving up his human victims to be received by Re. Variations on the defeat of Apophis occur in the Ninth, Tenth and Eleventh Scenarios, culminating in the chaining of the serpent.

The dragon or serpent in this vignette Egyptian papyrus has a bearded human head and a jackal-headed tail. In the 11th–10th centuries BC papyri were increasingly produced with iconography that was idiosyncratic and not standard. The dragon here reflects the theme of resurrection and solar rebirth and is depicted against a starry night sky. From a papyrus of Henut-tawi, Twenty-First Dynasty, 11th–10th centuries BC.

Despite the Egyptian adherence to the form of the snake in depictions of Apophis and other serpents of the underworld, the function of these snakes is decidedly dragonish. In addition to the evil, dark, chaotic properties of Apophis, the denizens of the Lake of Cobras act as guardians of Re's precious fire. The guardian snakes above each gate breathe fire, presumably to immolate enemies of Osiris and Re or those who should not pass through the underworld. Once again the serpent-dragons possess the potential for good, especially when they are in the service of gods such as Re. However, their role as guardians implies their capacity for destruction through fire, venom or constriction. Additionally, the association of serpents with the underworld, a clear allusion to snakes living underground, and their connection with death and rebirth, also presumably related to snakes' ability to 'regenerate' through shedding their skins, are common threads in the mythology of dragons worldwide.

Both snakes and dragons figure in the Old Testament, and neither had positive connotations. The snake who tempts Eve to eat the apple in the Garden of Eden is the classic symbol of the devil. This episode is also an example of the association of snakes with trees, a phenomenon found in Greek myths and in present-day India where sculptures of snakes are placed under trees. In India the snake is also associated with the Hindu god Siva; according to Kramrisch, *Manifestations of Shiva*, 'Serpents can raise themselves, they are symbols of power; serpents can kill, they are symbols of death; serpents can shed their skin, they are symbols of rebirth. They resemble the phallus and sexual connotation always accompanies their image. Ancient, uncanny powers, serpents (nāgas) were made into images in their own right.' As with so much of Hindu symbolism, the same creature embodies opposing ideas.

Whereas the snakes of Hindu mythology remain free of the trappings of traditional winged dragons, the snake in the Garden of Eden is sometimes depicted as a winged devil-headed dragon. However, the serpents who guard trees in Greek myths are shown, until medieval times, as snakes, not as winged dragons. The interchangeability of dragons and snakes in the Bible and Greek myth most probably stems from a linguistic source:

The fire-breathing and non-fire-breathing serpents shown in the central register of this sarcophagus of the Thirtieth Dynasty, *c.* 345 BC, are part of the pantheon of the Egyptian underworld as described in the text *Am-Duat*. The sarcophagus itself was never used by its owner Nectanebo II because he fled to Nubia following the Persian invasion of 343 BC.

LEFT In this woodcut, *The Whore of Babylon* (1498), Albrecht Dürer has illustrated in unstinting detail the lines from *The Revelations of St John*, '. . . and I saw a woman sit upon a scarlet coloured beast, full of names of blasphemy, having seven heads and ten horns'. She holds a gold cup 'full of abominations and filthiness of her fornication'.

ABOVE RIGHT This plaque of uncertain date (AD 1000–1900), showing a five-headed cobra, or *nagakal*, is of a type placed under trees in the Deccan region of India. As it has no obvious symbols of the god Shiva, with whom cobras are often associated, this piece is most probably connected with general serpent worship, which has been continuous in India since prehistoric times.

the Greek word *drakon* meant 'large serpent' as well as 'dragon'. It also reveals the consistent iconography of dragons and snakes as guardians of the valuables kept in the tree, be they apples or the Golden Fleece, and as evil obstacles to the forces of good.

With Greek myths we encounter gods as well as men, albeit superhuman heroes, in combat with dragons. Unlike the myths of ancient Egypt or

Mesopotamia, those of the Greeks have remained current in art and literature until very recently. Depictions of serpents/dragons on ancient Greek objects convey how the Greeks thought of dragons in visual terms, but later renditions of the same stories reveal the development of the dragon form in the west.

In his twelve labours Hercules had to combat two dragon-like beasts. A many-headed serpent, the Hydra, dwelt under a tree at the source of a river and stalked the swamps near Lerna. Each time Hercules managed to chop off one of its heads, two grew in its place. In order to overcome the monster, Hercules enjoined his nephew, Iolanus, to burn the stump of the Hydra's neck after each decapitation to deter regrowth. When they finally overcame the Hydra, Hercules dipped his arrows in its venomous blood and made them poisonous.

In his final labour Hercules was sent to the end of the earth to fetch the Golden Apples of the Hesperides, a source of eternal youth. Tended by nymphs called the Hesperides, the tree on which the apples grew was guarded by the serpent, Ladon. In one version of the story Hercules fought and killed the snake before taking the apples of immortality back to King Eurytheus, who had ordered all of the twelve labours. To commemorate his triumph Hercules henceforth brandished the image of the dragon on his shield.

RIGHT Part of a red-figured amphora showing a Hesperid, one of the daughters of the Evening Star, approaching the tree that bears the Golden Apples, while the serpent Ladon guards it. On the other side of the jar, Hercules supports the heavens as Hera watches. Attributed to the Owl-Pillar Group, Italy, Campania, *c.* 450–430 BC.

The popularity of Hercules lasted well into the late antique period. As late as the fifth century AD the dragons Hercules overcame continued to be depicted as snakes. Even renderings of Typhoeus, or Typhon, the last Titan whom Zeus conquered with great effort, are not faithful to the written description of a gigantic monster with a hundred dragons' heads springing from his shoulders, each with fire-spitting eyes, and a body covered with feathers, a head and face covered with bristles, and more snakes sprouting from his thighs. Classical artists tended to single out some of the attributes of Typhoeus – his snake-infested thighs or the flames spitting from his eyes – as identifying characteristics of the creature. Again, despite the description of the dragons emanating from his shoulders, classical artists persisted in representing them as snakes.

The long life of snake-as-dragon representations in classical art attests to the firm establishment of a canon of imagery in classical Greece which was maintained in ancient Rome and into Byzantine times. Unlike other composite monsters of Greek myth, such as the sphinx and the harpy, classical dragons owe nothing, in form at least, to foreign influences. Only with the advent of the Middle Ages and the introduction of new ideas from the east by returning Crusaders did the iconography of the dragon begin to change in Europe. As for the meaning of dragons in classical antiquity, they symbolised evil and, in the case of Typhoeus, chaos. Unlike the dragons of the ancient Near East and Egypt, those of ancient Greece were destroyed, not tamed, by the heroes who overcame them. Although medieval European artists did not borrow the classical form of the dragon, they and their literary counterparts certainly continued to believe in dragons as the incarnation of evil, darkness and the other negative connotations ascribed to the beast in antiquity.

China

From its origins in prehistoric China, the dragon developed in form and meaning so that in oracle bones of the Shang and in the divinatory text, *I Ch'ing*, the dragon, or *long*, had fairly well-defined characteristics. Whereas in oracle bones the various forms of the written character, *long*, are generally reptilian, the dragon is not yet specifically connected with rain. By the time of the *I Ch'ing*, however, composed over many hundreds of years during the second and first millennia BC, this connection was established. Although through the centuries Chinese dragons diversified, falling into numerous categories and adopting various attributes, their association with rain, clouds and the sky remained fixed.

In the *I Ch'ing* a series of diagrams and their reading according to patterns formed by throwing special sticks provide the basis for divining the future and choosing the correct action. Originally the advice must have been connected with agricultural matters – when to plant, when to harvest, etc. Thus in 'Heaven', the first diagram, the lowest line reads: '"First, nine: a dragon hidden in the water is useless"' and has been interpreted as meaning 'the heavenly giver of the fertilising rains is still useless to mankind'. Perhaps as a result of increased control or understanding of agriculture, later commentators understood this line to mean that one should refrain from action. Four of the following five lines of the diagram mention or allude to the dragon. On the second and fifth lines the dragon is seen, first in the rice fields then in the sky, and in both 'a great man will be seen'. Not only is the sighting of the dragon, symbol of rain, understood as an advantage, it is also an omen of the birth or appearance of a great man, often an emperor or a wise and holy man. The final, top line of the diagram reads: '"The dragon exceeding proper limits. There will be regret."' If the dragon flies too high, the rain will not reach the earth. Also, if the dragon is the symbol of the great man, he will regret acting immoderately. The inclusion of the number nine refers to a 'fullness of *yang*', the male principle, of which the dragon is an exemplar.

While some lines in other *I Ch'ing* diagrams simply repeat the ideas expressed in the first one, others refer to dragons as the producers of thunderstorms: '"Dragons fighting in the open field; their blood is dark . . . and yellow."' Along with snakes, dragons hibernate in winter, sleeping in pools. In summer, when the rains come, the dragons rise to the sky. Other ancient texts mention azure dragons, symbols of spring, drawing the carriage of the emperor, which was adorned with banners showing two entwined dragons. The sighting of the azure dragon announced the arrival of spring thunderstorms and the awakening of animals from hibernation.

The recognition of the dragon's special and benevolent powers led to its symbolic association with the emperor, as one of the 'spiritual beings' or symbolic figures which decorated the imperial robes or lived in or near the imperial palace. In addition to emperors' outer garments painted with the dragon and other mythical beasts, a remarkable processional banner of the Han Dynasty (1206 BC–220 AD) recently found draped over the tomb of the Marquis of Dai in excavations at Mawangdui, Changsha, confirms the early ritual significance of dragons. At the top of the T-shaped banner two confronting, three-toed dragons have been painted in great detail. On the bottom of the banner other dragons are entwined through a jade disk. Other auspicious beasts such as qilins and tortoises appear in the composition as well as small human figures engaged in various sedentary activities.

This banner and many other objects attest to the maturity of dragon imagery by the time of the Han Dynasty. The essential attributes of the dragon now included a scaly body, four legs with clawed feet, a long upturned nose, whiskers, long horns and hairy ears. On the Han robe the

The dragon as guardian or protector is used to good effect in this Chinese sword guard. By the time this lacquer guard consisting of two confronting dragons was produced in the 3rd or 2nd century BC during the Zhou-Han Dynasties, dragons were ubiquitous in the Chinese decorative vocabulary. The sword was most probably ceremonial since lacquer would not have been an effective deterrent in battle.

dragons' eyes are round, perhaps a development from the round-eyed taotie and dragons on Chou bronzes, but this remains an established trait of Chinese dragons. In fact, Chinese dragons were thought to embody resemblances to parts of nine different creatures, as explained by Qiguang Zhao in 'Dragon: Symbol of China': 'the head of a camel, the horns of a deer, the ears of a cow, the neck of a snake, the abdomen of a clam, the scales of a fish, the claws of an eagle, the eyes of a devil, and the paws of a tiger.' As the dragon's form became more specifically defined, its role as a pseudo-historical creature expanded. Various annals of Chinese history from the Han Dynasty onward detail specific appearances of dragons or dragon fights in certain pools which resulted in floods or fogs. Although Chinese dragons usually portended good, the death of a dragon or its appearance in the wrong place or at the wrong time could be a very bad omen.

Not all Chinese dragons fit the description of that composed of nine other animals. The horse-dragon, a river-dweller, had the four legs and hooves of a horse and was said to have had curly hair on its back '"like a map of starry dots"'. The dragon-horse emerged from the Yellow River and presented the legendary emperor Fu Xi with this 'River Map' from which the diagrams of the *I Ch'ing* were derived. The winged beast could walk on water as well as fly. Although it was essentially a river-spirit, its horse and dragon components underscore its significance as a symbol of Earth and Heaven.

Numerous factors have contributed to the long life of the dragon in China. Just as the nāga has been incorporated in the imagery of various religions and cults in India, so the dragon has figured in legend as well as religion in China. The nāgas of Indian Buddhist jatakas and sutras become dragons in the Chinese context. Chinese geomancy, the system of determining auspicious sites for houses, temples and graves naturally incorporated in its rules consideration for the dragon. Not only does the Azure Dragon represent east; dragons also symbolise water, and the contours of many mountains and hills resemble the undulating form of sleeping dragons.

By the time of the Ming (AD 1368–1644) and Ch'ing (AD 1644–1912) Dynasties, dragon lore and artistic imagery proliferated. The auspicious nature of the beast ensured its appearance on gateways and roofs, imperial banners and garments, and a myriad other objects in daily use. In keeping with a general trend toward categorisation, writers enumerated all the attributes of dragons, from their organs used for medicinal purposes to their sex lives. One thing leads to another, so naturally the offspring of dragons were the subject of some treatises, such as the *Wuh tsao tsu*, written around 1592. Here nine dragon young used as ornaments are listed. They include *p'u lao*, dragons which like to cry, used as handles of bells; *sze-niu*, music-lovers, decorating musical instruments; *ch'i-wen*, which like to swallow, adorning ridgepoles of roofs when they swallow evil influences; *chao-jing*, more leonine than dragon-like, which prefer heights, situated at the four corners of roofs; *ai-hwa*, which like killing, used to decorate sword-grips; *hi-pi*, a variant of the qilin, literature-lovers who appear on grave ornaments; *p'i-han*, a litigious beast used above prison gates as guards; *swan-i*, which like sitting and are depicted under the feet of Buddhas and Bodhisattvas; and finally the *pa-hia*, tortoises which carry heavy objects, are placed under grave-monuments.

This scene of a man with a hoof-shaped foot standing and writing on a tablet in front of a dragon with horse's hooves, a great mane and three rocky peaks on its back may depict the legendary ruler Fu Xi. He received the trigrams of the *I Ch'ing*, or 'Book of Changes', from a horse-dragon that emerged from the Yellow River. The string of money in the foreground may be auspicious 'dragon-horse money'. Ink and colours on paper, from Cave 17, Dunhuang, Tang Dynasty, 9th century AD.

Not all of the dragon young are dragons themselves, a factor attributable to the dragons' ability to couple with creatures of different species. Thus, various Chinese mythical beasts are thought to have been sired by dragons. Moreover, certain Chinese emperors claimed descent from dragons which impregnated their mothers in dreams or when disguised as men. The power of dragons to transform themselves into different shapes accounts for many unusual or miraculous events said to have been caused by dragons.

Among the best-known images of the dragon are two which may appear to be related. The first consists of the giant paper dragon chasing a red ball in Chinese New Year processions, on the fifteenth day of the first month. Although the orb has been interpreted as representing thunder belched out by the dragon, its association with a specific time in the year may have an astronomical basis. In this scenario the dragon would represent the constellation Draco, which nears the point of the setting sun until at the New Year it rises exactly where the sun sets. Thus, the dragon could be seen to be confronting or even devouring the sun. A variation on this interpretation equates the ball with the moon which appears before the rising of the dragon star, thus heralding the arrival of the New Year. The idea of the dragon chasing the ball and swallowing it may symbolise the disappearance of the moon behind or into the clouds and may be intended to bring on the rains of spring.

The second familiar device is that of the dragon and the pearl. While the imagery certainly had Buddhist connotations of the precious pearl which 'grants all desires', the pearl may also symbolise the moon. Chinese Buddhist texts describe the Great Hall of the Fa(h)-yü-sze temple in which eight dragons carved in joists or ribs of the roof stretch their claws toward a gilt glass ball, 'the pearl of perfection', suspended from the ceiling. The writer M. W. De Visser has suggested that the representation of the ball as red may allude to this golden orb. However, it may still be a reference to the moon, which does appear red at certain times of the year. Most

The dragon chasing a pearl is a favourite motif of the Chinese Ming ceramicists. In addition to its auspicious symbolism the motif of a dragon in clouds pursuing a pearl is highly dynamic and enhances the circularity of the cup on which it appears. Copper-red and white painted slip porcelain stem-cup, Ming Dynasty, *c.* 1401–50.

probably, the red ball and pearl, sometimes adorned with spiral designs or flames, combine a variety of meanings that incorporate Buddhist and Taoist beliefs and accommodate the generally auspicious iconography of the Chinese dragon.

Unlike the dragons of the west, those of China, Japan and South-East Asia continue to this day to possess potent meaning in many facets of life. Although the form of the dragon stabilised in the Ming Dynasty and ceased to change dramatically, its use as a decorative ornament did not abate. Imperial edicts decreed that only the robe of the emperor and the heir apparent could bear the three-clawed dragon, and four-clawed dragons could appear on the garments of high officials at the court. Other official documents concerning ornamental dragons underscore their powerful symbolism and the extent to which they stood for the emperor and his possessions. Nevertheless, dragons in China were rarely tamed, even by emperors. They still appeared in the sky, fighting and bringing rain, and their spirit lives on in Asia.

Japan

With its legacy of indigenous Shinto beliefs and Buddhism imported from India by way of China, Japan developed its own distinctive dragon lore. Although Japanese belief in dragons predated the advent of Buddhism in the sixth century AD, Chinese dragon symbolism and Buddhist nāga imagery rapidly fused with Japanese ideas. The Japanese also adopted the classical physical form of Chinese dragons. Nevertheless, the geography of Japan, with its mountains, pine forests and lakes, its island climate and the Japanese love of fantastic tales, led to notions about dragons that developed independently of their Chinese models.

Before the acceptance of Buddhism in Japan, a dragon, formed from a third of the body of the fire-god Kaguzuchi, produced rain and snow in answer to men's prayers. As in China and India, river-gods in Japan took the form of dragons and were thought capable of bringing rain. Likewise the sea-dragon, or wani, appeared first in an ancient Japanese legend, but with the introduction of Chinese and Indian dragons and nāga-rajas, the wani became identified with them. According to one story, the sea-god Toyotama hiko no Mikoto, or Abundant Pearl Prince, and his daughter lived in a palace at the bottom of the sea. When the princess noticed the face of a beautiful youth reflected in the well near the palace gate, the sea-god invited him into the palace. Then the princess and the youth married. After three years in the palace the youth returned to earth and the pregnant princess followed. The youth built a 'parturition house' for her beside the sea and she beseeched him not to look while she was giving birth. Unable to resist the temptation to peek, the youth saw that the princess had become a wani, or dragon. In her shame and anger the princess abandoned her child and returned to her father's palace. In some versions of the story the sea-god is called a sea-snake, and in some depictions the sea-god and his daughter are shown with dragons over their heads like Indian nāgas.

While the dragon river-gods of Japan possessed the power of bestowing and stopping the rain, another dragon sea-god held the pearl of ebb and the pearl of flood. With these he could dry up the seas and make them rise. Although a connection may exist between the pearl chased by Chinese dragons and these pearls, a more likely analogy is with the treasure hoards of Indian nāgas.

By the eighth century AD Buddhist priests and shrines had begun to replace or at least parallel the function of Shinto priests and temples as the most effective intermediaries and sites for inducing the dragon-gods of rivers or ponds to bring rain. Whereas Shinto priests had prayed and sacrificed animals and even humans to dragon-gods of the rivers and sea, Buddhist priests took other approaches. One of the most famous locations for seeking rain was the pond in the Shinsenan or Sacred Spring Park. Here, priests came and recited sutras to frighten the dragon and make him rise to the sky. If that did not work, the pond in which the dragon lived was emptied while bells were rung and drums were beaten in order to force the dragon through discomfort and fright into the heavens. Tantras or magical formulae were also used both to bring rain and, in the case of the priest Shubin, to catch dragons and shut them up in a water-pitcher. Out of hatred for the emperor and a rival priest, Shubin's imprisonment of the dragons caused a three-month drought. Finally, the dragon-king Zennyo had to be brought from India, and he earned the eternal gratitude of the whole country by causing it to rain for three days. Many additional legends are connected with this dragon and others which inhabited ponds. While most of the stories centred on the rain-giving or rain-stopping talents of the dragons, other tales concern their role as auspicious or transformational beasts.

As in China, the sighting of a dragon was often an omen of a successful reign or simply an abundant harvest. Nevertheless, despite courtiers' opinions to the contrary, the dragon-horse presented to the fourteenth-century emperor Godaigo appears to have boded ill for his reign since a schism of the northern and southern courts occurred a few years after he accepted the gift. However, the sudden death of the dragon-horse in the year preceding the schism may have been the real cause of the rift.

The protean quality of dragons meant both that they could transform themselves into humans and that people could be reborn as dragons. One such dragon, the reincarnation of the Buddhist priest Genko, lived in the Cherry-Tree Pond (Sakura ga ike), where twice a year people with a special

wish would come to pray. The supplicants would make an offering of hard-boiled rice in a bucket. If they later found the bucket empty, the dragon would have accepted their offering and heard their prayer (De Visser). If the rice was untouched, the prayer would not be answered. The priest Genko had wished to become a dragon because the life of a man was too short for learning the Buddhist doctrine. In order to make the transition from man to dragon, he had sat in meditation with one drop of water in his hand until clouds and rain formed and he flew up into the sky and then to the pond. There he meditated until his death and transformation to dragonhood. Not only does this story reaffirm the Buddhist role

In this painting, *Storm Dragon*, Tani Buncho (fl. 1765–92), a leading Japanese artist of the Edo school, has depicted dragons in wet clouds, reminding the viewer of their ability both to hold the heavenly waters in and release them.

of dragons but it also reminds us of one of the universal traits of dragons, their longevity.

In addition to many tales of dragons themselves, numerous mountains, rivers and ponds in Japan are named after them. While dragons inhabited many mountains and rivers, some of these sites must have been given their names because of their resemblance to dragons sleeping or in motion. In Japan dragons were also associated with the will-o'-the-wisp, natural occurrences of fleeting phosphorescent light. These lights, called dragon-lanterns, rose from the sea to the mountains where they settled in pine trees near temples. They were considered gifts from the dragons who lived in the sea to the gods, Buddhas or Bodhisattvas worshipped in the nearby shrines. Although the earliest literary evidence for dragon-lanterns dates from the fourteenth century, innumerable legends chronicle their appearance. Of the appearance of a dragon-lantern at the Manju or Manjusri temple at Ama no hashidate, one sixteenth-century text details its course from the gate of the dragon-palace under the sea to the temple where it stayed in the top of a tall pine tree for about half an hour. This sight was visible only to believing Buddhists.

A final noteworthy phenomenon associated with Japanese dragons is that of dragons' eggs. These were thought to lie dormant a thousand years in the sea, a thousand years in the mountains and a thousand years in a village in the form of a stone containing a tiny snake. Attracted by the beautiful colours of these stones, people would bring them home. The stones had the added attraction of constantly sweating water, and thus they were useful as inkstones. However, these stones had one serious drawback. At the end of three thousand years, the stone would split, enabling the small snake to emerge. Immediately it would begin to grow at an alarming rate until it smashed its way through the roof of the house and ascended to the sky amid thunder and lightning as an enormous dragon. In some cases the stone remained intact but for a hole produced by the emerging snake. As with most Japanese dragon legends, various highly dramatic versions of the dragon's egg tale exist in literature. These reaffirm not only the association of the dragons with the sea and the thundery skies but also the Japanese penchant for specific and highly graphic legends to illustrate dragons in all their manifestations.

Islam

With the advent of Islam in the early seventh century and the Muslim conquest of the lands from Spain to Central Asia by the mid-eighth century, a spectrum of diverse cultures came nominally under the control of a leadership centred first in Damascus and later in Baghdad. The realignment of borders that took place following the Muslim ousting of the

Byzantine Christians from Egypt and the Levant and the Sasanian Zoro-astrians from Persia allowed for an east–west exchange of goods and ideas that eventually produced new artistic styles. In this environment dragons continued to exist, at first embodying symbolism inherited from pre-Islamic Persian, Indian and Greek traditions and later reflecting strong Chinese influence. In Arab literature dragons had definite astrological and astronomical connotations, whereas in Persian literature they figure in scientific texts and in numerous tales of heroes' victories over evil.

In the Islamic world astronomy and astrology were considered closely related sciences. Nevertheless, the chain of textual transmission from pre-Islamic to Islamic authors determined the iconography of the symbols used to illustrate each type of text. Dragons appear in both astronomical and astrological texts, but they vary as much according to the prototypes on which they were based as according to their particular function in the text.

One of the most commonly represented dragons in Islamic art is the constellation Draco. In fact, it appears in the earliest extant Islamic manu-script of *Suwar al-Kawakib al-Thabitah*, or 'The Figures of the Fixed Stars', by 'Abd al-Rahman b. 'Umar al-Sufi (AD 903–86). This manuscript, now in the Bodleian Library, Oxford, was copied and illustrated in 400 AH/ AD 1009–10 by al-Husain b. 'Abd al-Rahman b. 'Umar b. Muhammad, supposedly the son of the author. While the treatise itself was based on the *Almagest* of Ptolemy and Arab astronomical writings, the illustrations were probably copied from a celestial globe. The costumes, drapery, jewel-lery and hairstyles of the human figures adhere to the prevailing style of Arab painting of the period, whereas the animals are more faithful to late antique prototypes. Draco thus follows the classical norm in which dragons were depicted as snakes. Like the constellation Serpentarius, Draco is shown with his mouth open, baring four or five fangs above and below a long forked tongue. His scaly body twists twice and then bends up before tapering down to his tail. The only concession to the creature's identity as a dragon is the long curving lock that extends from its eye to its lower jaw. This may indicate eastern – that is, Persian – influence.

In the early and medieval Islamic world a dragon far more ubiquitous than Draco was Jawzahr, a so-called pseudoplanet, which was responsible for lunar and solar eclipses and comets. Jawzahr figures in the astrological system which ascribes the maximum power or exaltation of each planet to the moment when it stands in a particular sign of the zodiac. When the planet travels through the opposite sign, its power is at a minimum and it is in its dejection. The word *jawzahr* implies the head and the tail of the dragon, which were taken as symbols of the two points of intersection or nodes of the moon's orbit with the ecliptic, the imaginary circle around the sun. These two points travel over a period of years through the signs of the zodiac, causing eclipses to occur at different times of the year.

This coin of 1202–3, showing a dragon-tailed Sagittarius, comes from the mint at Mardin, the capital of a Turkish dynasty, the Artuqids, who ruled in northern Iraq, Syria and southern Turkey from the 12th to the 15th centuries. Unlike the majority of Islamic coins, which are exclusively epigraphic, copper Artuqid coins include a whole range of astrological, princely and mythological symbols, copied from both contemporary and ancient sources.

Since many ancient cultures believed eclipses to be the result of a giant snake or dragon devouring the sun or the moon, the symbol of the cause of these eclipses was the dragon. According to the Indian myth, which certainly influenced Islamic astrology, Vishnu cut the dragon Rahu in half but his tail continued to live independently and both halves were the eternal enemies of the sun and the moon. Not only were the two halves of the dragon responsible for eclipses but the tail also caused comets. In both Hindu and Islamic astrology the head and the tail of the dragon represent the ascending and descending nodes of the moon. The exaltation of the head took place in Gemini, while that of the tail also occurred in Sagittarius. As numerous representations of Sagittarius with a dragon-headed tail attest, this symbolism was generally accepted. Additionally, the dragon's tail often exhibits a knot, which itself symbolises the actual node of the moon. Literary references date from at least the ninth century and artistic versions are known from the eleventh or twelfth centuries onward.

Aside from dragons representing the exaltation and dejection of the moon's nodes in Gemini and Sagittarius, they are also found threatening the sun and moon when those planets are shown with Leo and Cancer. This form of representation had nothing to do with the function of the pseudoplanet Jawzahr. Rather, it demonstrates the strength of belief in the dragon's ability to devour the sun and the moon. By the twelfth century, examples of dragons devouring the sun or moon proliferated in Islamic art. An outstanding example, sadly now destroyed, was the Talisman Gate at Baghdad. Here, in the spandrel above the gate, two dragons were carved with heads near the centre, open-mouthed and threatening a child who sat between them cross-legged and holding their tongues. Below, at the springing of the arch, lay two lions. The artfully coiled bodies of the dragons were each knotted twice, a reference to the nodes of the moon. They have well-defined scales, wings, horns and legs, recalling composite beasts of the ancient Near East. The child is said to symbolise the new moon, and the lions, as the astrological sign Leo, have a clear solar connection. Thus, the whole ensemble must allude to the eclipse. However, since eclipses were considered bad omens, the presence of this type of symbolic grouping above the Talisman Gate and on numerous other gateways and doors suggests that they were intended to ward off evil and protect the inhabitants within the city walls.

With the Mongol invasion of Iran and Iraq in the first half of the thirteenth century, the form of the Chinese dragon supplanted that of the more snaky Near Eastern creature. Although dragons such as those on the Talisman Gate exhibit some of the characteristics associated with Chinese dragons, the shape of their wings and the curves of their bodies differ markedly from those of their Chinese cousins. Lively, sinuous Chinese-style dragons are found on Persian fifteenth-century blue and white cer-

amics in imitation of Chinese prototypes, but the most thorough repertoire of sinicised Islamic dragons inhabits the pages of Persian, Turkish and Mughal Indian manuscripts of the fourteenth to the seventeenth centuries.

Persian epic literature, in particular the *Shahnameh*, or 'Book of Kings', abounds with stories of heroes outwitting and slaying dragons. Compiled around 1010 by the poet Firdausi, the *Shahnameh* consists of the legendary history of Iran down to the historical period of the Sassanian kings and ending with the Islamic period. From the epoch of legendary kings, Rustam stands out as the most courageous, long-lived and celebrated of Persian heroes. His superhuman feats against the Turanians, the perennial enemies of the Iranians, and innumerable demons, witches and beasts included a successful combat against a dragon, one of seven challenges he met as he traversed Mazandaran on a mission to rescue his king, Kay Kavus. One night Rustam slept, unaware that he had chosen a dragon's lair. As the dragon approached and tried to attack the hero, Rakhsh, Rustam's miraculous horse, whinnied loudly and ran to protect his master. When Rustam awoke, the dragon disappeared. The next time this happened, Rustam threatened to punish the horse if he should disturb him again. The third time the dragon emerged, Rakhsh roused Rustam in time. Together they defeated the beast, and Rustam cut off its head.

Not only are Rustam's challenges paralleled in the *Shahnameh* by those of Isfandiyar, but kings of the historical past such as Alexander and Bahram Gur also tested their mettle against dragons. Their feats were celebrated by the twelfth-century poet Nizami in his *Khamseh*, or 'Five Tales'. As in most instances in Persian literature, the dragons represent evil and at times guard treasure, which passes rightfully to the embodiment of good, the heroic king.

Although dragons, painted and described, proliferate in the *Shahnameh* and the *Khamseh*, the most often illustrated Persian texts, they also populate other works such as the collection of fables, *Kalila wa Dimna*; the biographies of religious figures, such as the *Qisas al-Anbiya'*, which describes the lives of the Prophets from Adam to Muhammad; or the *Khavarannameh*, the fictional life of 'Ali, the son-in-law of Muhammad; and books about the wonders of the world, such as Qazvini's *Aja'ib al-Makhluqat*, the 'Wonders of Creation'. An occasional 'good' dragon, such as the Iranian Shah Faridun in disguise, slithers across the pages of Persian literature, as do multi-headed dragons and the devil himself in the form of a dragon. In general, these dragons lived on land, often in caves, from which they emerged to do battle.

Persian and Turkish artists from the fourteenth century onward incorporated a set of features in their depictions of dragons that reveal the influence of Chinese prototypes combined with the stylistic variations one would expect of different periods and places. The hornless slug or simple

In Ottoman Turkey dragons inhabiting foliage were not only incorporated in the decorative borders and bindings of books and all manner of decorative arts but they were also a favourite subject of artists producing drawings, like this mid-16th century example, in the so-called 'saz-leaf' style. These drawings do not illustrate texts, so the specific meaning of the dragons in them, if it existed, remains elusive.

serpent descended from classical prototypes gave way to a long, undulating creature with horns and whiskers on its long head. Usually four-footed, Islamic dragons spout fire from their front and rear shoulders and often breathe it as well. Their backbones are jagged and flame-like or rimmed with a thick ridge. Their bodies are scaly, though often their skin is painted in a brilliant colour with spots of a contrasting hue to denote scales. While numbers of teeth and claws, shape of tongue and other details vary enormously, Islamic dragons are immediately recognisable. Despite their evil connotations, they decorate any number of objects, from Persian jade cup handles and Turkish sword hilts to bookbindings and carpets. They gambol in foliage and roar at the phoenix-like simurgh; they oblige heroes by almost never winning a battle; and in their sinuous, rhythmic motion they are as lively and continuous as the Islamic arabesque.

Christendom

The starting point for any study of dragons in the Christian context is the Bible. In both Old and New Testaments dragons represent evil and often specifically symbolise the devil, whom God will ultimately destroy. As mentioned above, the serpent in the Garden of Eden has on occasion been depicted as a dragon, but Old Testament dragons usually inhabit the sea. They are distinguished from the monster, Leviathan, as in these verses from Psalms 74:13–14:

Thou didst divide the sea by thy strength: thou brakest the heads of the dragons in the waters,
thou brakest the heads of Leviathan in pieces, and gavest him to be meat to the people inhabiting the wilderness.

Although dragons are mentioned in the Old Testament books of Psalms (74:13–14, 89:10), Isaiah (27:1, 51:9) and Job (7:12, 26:12–13), they are not described. By contrast, the New Testament Revelation of St John the Divine, Chapter 12, portrays the dragon graphically and in action:

1. And there appeared a great wonder in heaven; a woman clothed with the sun, and the moon under her feet, and upon her head a crown of twelve stars:
2. And she being with child cried, travailing in birth, and pained to be delivered.
3. And there appeared another wonder in heaven; and behold a great red dragon, having seven heads and ten horns, and seven crowns upon his heads.
4. And his tail drew the third part of the stars of heaven; and did cast them to the earth: and the dragon stood before the woman which was ready to be delivered, for to devour her child as soon as it was born.

The woman gave birth to a son who was protected by God, and she took refuge in the wilderness.

7. And then there was war in heaven: Michael and his angels fought against the dragon; and the dragon fought and his angels,
8. And prevailed not; neither was their place found any more in heaven.
9. And the great dragon was cast out, that old serpent, called the Devil, and Satan, which deceiveth the whole world: he was cast out into the earth, and his angels were cast out with him.

While those in heaven could rejoice, 'the inhabitants of the earth and the sea' now had the devil to fear.

13. And when the dragon saw that he was cast unto the earth, he persecuted the woman which brought forth the man child.
14. And to the woman were given two wings of the great eagle, that she might fly into the wilderness, into her place, where she is nourished for a time, and times, and half a time, from the face of the serpent.
15. And the serpent cast out of his mouth water as a flood after the woman, that he might cause her to be carried away of the flood.

Here the Archangel Michael is depicted spearing Satan in the form of a dragon. The owner of the cameo may have worn it for its amuletic powers of good over evil. Blue-glass paste, Venice, 14th century.

The earth swallowed up the dragon's flood and he determined to make war with her offspring. Then a beast with several heads, ten horns with crowns and 'the name of blasphemy' on its heads rose from the sea. Its body like that of a leopard, its feet those of a bear and its mouth that of a lion, this beast could heal itself immediately and derive its power from the dragon. This and another beast which 'had two horns and spake as a dragon' were worshipped for their ability to heal and do miracles. Essentially, they symbolise the false prophets and unbelievers that dissuade men from the true faith. They are the mouthpieces of Satan, represented by the dragon. Later (Rev. 16:13–14) false prophets are described as 'unclean spirits like frogs' that come out of the mouth of the dragon.

Such vivid imagery lent itself to pictorial representation, and in medieval Europe many renderings of these horrific dragons can be found. Once the dragon is cast out of heaven, he resumes his natural habitat in the sea, from which he emerges to do battle. The fact that the woman grows wings in order to fly from the dragon may ultimately derive from the Indian concept of the combat of the nāga and garuda (fabulous bird). Despite the explicit biblical description of the multi-headed dragon, scenes of St Michael and his angels expelling it from heaven show it with one head as often as with seven. The variation in iconography may have been the result of the dual system of depicting saints in action and as devotional images with their attributes.

In medieval Europe Christian literature centring on the lives of the saints burgeoned. Not only were the miraculous feats and gruesome martyrdoms of the saints detailed in the Apocrypha, but also Jacob da Voragine's immensely influential thirteenth-century text, the *Golden Legend*, did much to popularise the lives of the saints. In fact, despite the efforts of the late fifth-century Pope Gelasius to repudiate the sainthood of many well-known figures, their legends survived. The Crusades saw the restitution of many previously discredited saints, especially those who overcame dragons. In keeping with this trend, dragons came to symbolise paganism which was vanquished by the warriors of Christ.

Perhaps the most famous of those repudiated but much-loved saints is St George, patron saint of England. Although his identification with a fourth-century bishop of Cappodocia seems unlikely, he did come from the Near East, perhaps Syria. The scene of his momentous battle with the dragon is most often placed in Selene in Libya. Near this city a dragon inhabited a lake or marsh and preyed upon the flocks belonging to the residents. To keep the dragon at bay, the people decided to feed him two sheep daily. Eventually, having exhausted their supply of sheep, they were forced to sacrifice two children a day, chosen by lottery. Finally, the sorry lot fell to the king's only daughter, Cleolinda, and after much resistance he was compelled to send her to her fate. As she approached the dragon's lair, St George was riding by and, noticing her, asked her why she was weeping. When she explained, he insisted on rescuing her by combating the dragon. A terrible battle ensued.

Often St George is depicted having broken his lance but about to strike the final blow with his sword. Rather than kill the dragon on the spot, St George bound the beast with Cleolinda's girdle. She then led it to her city, where St George told the terrified citizens to have no fear since belief in God had enabled him to subdue the dragon. They then accepted Christianity and all were baptised in one day. Only after this mass conversion did St George slay the dragon and cut off his head. While he appears not to have encountered other dragons, he did continue to champion the faith, ultimately dying a martyr's death in Lydda, Palestine.

During the Third Crusade in Palestine King Richard I invoked St George as the special protector of his army. St George was named patron saint of England in 1222 and later of the Order of the Garter, founded in 1348. Portrayals of the saint show him standing, lance in hand, with the dragon at his feet, or in full combat with the dragon. In medieval and later renderings of this episode the dragon does not always conform to one type. Some artists portrayed it as a two-footed lizard without wings and with small, rounded ears instead of horns. Most European examples, however, have wings like those of a bat, with pronounced ribs and stiff, pointed ears or horns. They have either two or four legs, clawed feet and snaky tails. Unlike the dragons of China or Korea, the form of European dragons varied broadly from the types mentioned to beasts that most resemble lions, those with birds' wings and segmented serpents' tails, and yet others with heads most resembling Chinese *fu* dogs. As long as the saints had the proper attributes, artists could exercise their ingenuity in producing the most horrific dragons imaginable.

In addition to St George, many other saints are known for their encounters with dragons. St Philip the apostle found that the people of Hieropolis in Phrygia worshipped Mars in the form of a dragon. As he held up the cross, he ordered the dragon to leave the temple of Mars, which it did. However, its poisonous breath killed many people, and the priests of the temple were so enraged at Philip's action that they crucified him. Historically, this exorcism may have been an attempt to convert a cult of snake-worshippers. Despite Philip's role as one of Christ's apostles, depictions of his life are rare.

At least two women, Sts Margaret of Antioch and Martha, overcame dragons. Imprisoned for refusing to marry a pagan, St Margaret was devoured by a dragon in her cell, but the cross she held punctured the dragon and she emerged unharmed. For obvious reasons, she is revered as a patron saint of childbirth. St Martha, the patron saint of housewives, travelled to France where she defeated a dragon at Tarascon by sprinkling

This 14th-century icon of St George and the dragon was used as a window shutter in Archangel'sk, Russia, before the British Museum acquired and conserved it, leading to the discovery of the icon beneath layers of overpainting. The icon has been dubbed the 'Black George' because of the rarity of images in which St George is depicted riding a black horse.

it with holy water. Both saints are portrayed trampling the dragon but Margaret sometimes holds it by a cord and Martha carries a water-sprinkler. On rare occasions in the west saints such as Clement of Metz tamed dragons, but far more often they vanquished and then killed them.

The use of dragon legends extended beyond the bounds of religious instruction. As a symbol of evil, dragons were an excellent means of allegorically describing local ills and the struggle to overcome them, rather than actually naming names. Thus, according to Janet Hoult, the account of Sir Richard de Waldegrave and his friends driving a dragon into a marsh near Bures, Suffolk, in 1405 may in fact refer to the expulsion of a person rather than an actual beast. As late as the seventeenth century, English heroes such as More of More Hall were delivering their countrymen from fearsome dragons, in this case the fire-breathing, child-eating dragon of Wantley, but even this tale may allude to the outwitting of an evil man.

In the Middle Ages the biblical and legendary accounts of dragons were augmented by 'scientific' descriptions in bestiaries. These popular compendiums explained many of the real flora and fauna of the medieval world as well as fantastic creatures. Animals were viewed in terms of Christian morality so that some were considered symbols of good while others were evil incarnate. To their Latin and ultimately Greek prototypes the writers of medieval bestiaries added a Christian interpretation which placed more emphasis on symbolic content than on empirical observation. Needless to say, dragons and their various snake cousins epitomised evil and sin.

The dragon of bestiaries is commonly depicted strangling an elephant. Considered the largest of snakes, dragons in Romanesque-style bestiaries have two feet and wings like those of a bird. By contrast, the basilisk, the king of snakes, had either two or four feet, a cock's head and the wings of a swan, and killed by a look or with its breath. Although the stories connected with vipers, asps and hydras vary, their physical typology is remarkably uniform. They are often winged, with two or four feet, and have pointed ears. Oddly, they only resemble real snakes in their long, scaly, coiled bodies. Presumably, the illustrators of medieval bestiaries were more concerned with adhering to visual prototypes that ultimately descended from a late antique source than with rendering snakes as they actually appear.

Because of its symbolic nature the dragon was well suited to the practice of alchemy, the pseudo-science that attempted to transform base metal into gold. Medieval alchemists were highly secretive, in part because they were distrusted and persecuted as charlatans. Thus, they developed misleading terminologies to dissuade the curious and keep necessary but uninitiated helpers in the dark. Simply stated, the dragon symbolised 'matter in its imperfect unregenerate state'. The slaying of the dragon would reduce metals to a non-metallic state. Extremely complex recipes, enumerated in the arcane language of alchemical texts, attribute different characteristics to different types of dragon. A dragon eating its own tail represented the alloy of copper and silver warmed with mercury for three weeks until all traces of copper and silver were invisible. A winged dragon symbolised the volatile element, while the wingless version was the fixed element. Accompanying the treatises describing alchemical processes were illustrations in which the dragons for the most part conform to the European winged type described above, though at times they lack wings and have more than one head. Clearly in the late Middle Ages (the fourteenth to sixteenth centuries), the heyday of alchemy, the symbolic power of dragons persisted and proved useful in maintaining the secrecy of alchemical processes.

A final category of European dragons is the type portrayed on the heraldic device. Although dragons had appeared on shields in Ancient Greece – for example, Hercules adopted the emblem – the high art of heraldry and hereditary heraldic symbols did not develop until the thirteenth century. Dragons had long adorned standards, intended to frighten the enemy with their ferocity and strength. Yet only in the reign of Henry VII (1485–1509) did the red dragon of Cadwallader become a supporter of the shield bearing the royal arms. According to Welsh legend, two dragons fought; the red one signified Wales and the white one the Saxons. Cadwallader was the last native ruler of Britain descended from the sixth-century King Maeolgwn. Thus the incorporation of the red dragon as a supporter of the royal shield signified the unity of Britain.

Although the Stuarts inserted the Scottish unicorn in place of the red dragon in 1603, the latter continued in use on royal seals and insignia and on buildings and bridges in various royal parks and precincts. Not until the nineteenth century did the formal association of the red dragon and Wales revive. In 1807 the red dragon was declared the king's badge for Wales, and in 1907 King Edward VII added the red dragon to the badge borne by the Prince of Wales. In 1911 King George V decreed the inclusion of a small shield bearing the red dragon on the Prince of Wales' larger shield in order to place more emphasis on Wales. The form of the present shield of the Prince of Wales derives from a 1953 order giving the red dragon greater prominence and adding the Welsh motto to the edges of the shield: Y DDRAIG GOCH DDYRY CYCHWYN – The Red Dragon Gives Impetus.

Assorted dragons

Myths and artistic renderings of dragons are in no way limited to those detailed here. One need only consider the Norse myth of Sigurd or examine Celtic and Viking carvings to be reminded of the widespread European

The coat of arms of the City of London acquired dragon supporters in the 17th century. The shield contains the cross of St George and the sword of St Paul, and a shield and fan surmount it. Pencil and watercolour on paper, 18th century.

occurrence of dragons. Even in cultures untouched by Chinese or European civilisation, dragons and their cousins flourished. Whereas dragons figure as lake spirits in various Native North American creation myths, in Central and South America the primary form of dragon is the plumed serpent.

Rather than embodying only negative meaning as in most European dragon myths, the pre-Columbian American dragons encompass both good and evil. The composite bird and snake, called Quetzalcoatl in Mexico, incorporated the symbolism of earth (snake) and sky (bird). Called Kukulkan by the Maya, this bird/serpent was thought to rule the four quarters of the earth. Perhaps for this reason various Mayan and Aztec kings added 'Quetzalcoatl' to their names and the deity came to be considered the divine manifestation of the first king. The god could take many forms, including the sun and the planet Venus. Reminiscent of Chinese and Islamic dragon myths in which the moon or sun is swallowed by a dragon, Quetzalcoatl as Venus is depicted being engorged by a serpent, symbol of the earth.

When depicted without feathers, serpents may have two heads at either end of an undulating body. Such images apparently symbolise eternity and, as such, have links with the belief in other cultures that snakes were immortal because they could shed and grow new skins. The use of turquoise mosaic for such renderings also had religious significance. Under the Aztecs, turquoise was graded in three classes according to its level of fineness. The most valuable, *teoxiuitle*, was reserved for ritual use as it was considered the property of the gods. This brilliant stone was thought to

This brooch consists of two dragonesque heads at either end of one body. With curious ambiguity the heads can be viewed either as having bird-like beaks and top-knots or as having long, knobby amphibian snouts and large ears. Enamelled bronze, Romano-British, 2nd century AD.

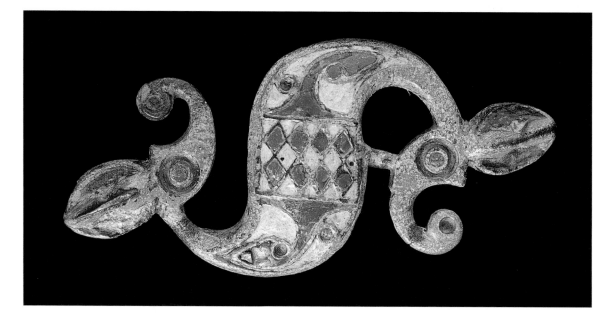

A remarkable double-headed serpent, thought to have been worn as part of the headdress ensemble of a participant in a ritual. It would have been produced by Mixtec artists working at the Aztec royal court and may have been among the gifts presented to Cortes by Montezuma II in 1519. Turquoise mosaic over wood, red shell, and white shell, Mexico, 1400–1521.

exhale smoke, a fitting attribute for the greatest god of the Aztec pantheon, Xiuhtecuhtli, and one of his manifestations, Xiuhcoatl, the fire serpent, also known as the turquoise serpent. Although the iconography of the double-headed serpent differs from that of Xiuhcoatl, the use of turquoise for both may well indicate related, if not identical, symbolism.

Conclusion

The preceding pages have highlighted only a few of the best-known dragons from an international galaxy of such beasts. To the rational thinkers of the modern era, they are mythical creatures, relegated to a superstitious past. Yet, in modern fiction and art worldwide, dragons survive. Whether negative or positive, dragons remain potent symbols of nature beyond man's control.

Unicorns

For such a rare mythical beast, the unicorn has inspired a remarkable intensity of belief and symbolism. With a body sometimes like that of a horse and sometimes like that of a goat, its primary distinguishing characteristic is its single horn. Straight, occasionally wreathed and more rarely saw-toothed, the horn enabled it to defend itself and kill its opponents, but also to purify streams and pools of any poison. Of all the mythical beasts, the unicorn is one of the most elusive and secretive – impossible to capture except with the aid of a virgin.

Seen from the side, any animal with two horns may appear to have only one, and this experience may have provided the initial inspiration for the idea of the unicorn. Another source was, undoubtedly, the Indian rhinoceros which is the only real animal that possesses a single horn. Whatever its origin, however, belief in the unicorn gained great strength, particularly in Europe during the Middle Ages, and its mysterious qualities only seemed to encourage attempts to seek it out. Although appearing as a curiosity in classical literature, the unicorn only became firmly established in allegory and myth through Christianity. The capture of the unicorn was first seen to be a peaceful affair. Only later in the Middle Ages does it develop into the cruel killing of a deluded beast. The concept of the death of the unicorn, which took strong hold in Germany in the Middle Ages, was interpreted as symbolic of the death and sacrifice of Christ. The hunting of the unicorn was even seen as an allegory of the Annunciation of the birth of Christ by the Angel Gabriel. During the Reformation, there was a reaction against such symbolism, and this, together with the rational approach of the new learning, diminished the strength of the myth. The creature survived in medical and heraldic usage, however, and belief in the unicorn is even documented as late as the nineteenth century. It is this continuity, along with the complexity of the myth, that gives the unicorn its contemporary interest.

The naming of the animals by Adam, from a Dutch bible illuminated about 1440. He blesses the unicorn while Eve stands behind him in an attitude of prayer.

Classical literature

The unicorn was first described in literature by Ctesias, a Greek physician at the Persian court of Artaxerxes and Darius II, around 400 BC. His account of India (which he called Indica) is the original source for many fabulous stories of the east, which include such strange creatures as headless men (with faces between their shoulders), the sciapods (who have a single foot which they use as an umbrella against the sun) and the cynocephali (men with dogs' heads who can only bark). Among the animals he describes are the manticora, griffins and unicorns. These he describes as:

> . . . wild asses as large as horses or even larger. Their bodies are white, their heads dark red, and their eyes dark blue. They have a horn in the middle of their forehead that is one cubit [about 18 in/45 cm] in length; the base of this horn is pure white . . . the upper part is sharp and of a vivid crimson, and the middle portion is black. Those who drink from these horns, made into drinking vessels, are not subject, they say, either to convulsions or the falling sickness. Indeed they are immune even to

45

poisons if, either before or after swallowing such, they drink wine, water, or anything else from these beakers. This animal is exceedingly swift and powerful, so that no creature, neither the horse nor any other, can overtake it. There is no other way to capture them in the hunt than this: when they conduct their young to pasture, if they are surrounded by many horsemen, they refuse to flee, thus forsaking their offspring. They fight with thrusts of their horn; they kick, bite, and strike with wounding force both horses and hunters; but they perish under the blows of arrows and javelins, for they cannot be taken alive.

This early description already includes some of the essential character- istics of the unicorn – the single horn, the magical quality of repelling poison, the fleetness and fierceness, and the fact that it can only be captured by devious methods. Megasthenes, however, an ambassador to India in about 303 BC, whose treatise survives in the work of a number of authors such as Pliny, provides the most comprehensive early report of India. Pliny's work, finished in about AD 77, was the most popular classical text on natural history during the Middle Ages. It is a vast, uncritical collection of miscellaneous material, extending to some forty-seven books. India was particularly abundant in wonders. Following Ctesias and Megasthenes, he says that the Orsaean Indians hunt many wild beasts, the fiercest of which is the 'monoceros, with a body like a horse, head like a stag, feet like an elephant, and a tail like a boar; it has a deep bellow, and a single black horn two cubits [3 ft/90 cm] long projecting from the middle of the fore- head. They say that it is impossible to capture this animal alive.' This horn is about twice as long as that described by Ctesias.

There are other classical references to one-horned animals. Julius Caesar, in his *Gallic Wars*, reported the existence of a one-horned animal in the forests of Germany: 'It is known that many kinds of animals not seen in other places breed therein . . . There is an ox, shaped like a stag, from the middle of whose forehead, between the ears, stands forth a single horn, taller and straighter than the horns we know.' Another writer on the nature of animals, Aelian (about AD 170–235), provides further evidence of the one-horned animal of India: 'The horn is not smooth but has spirals of quite natural growth, and is black in colour'; and 'From these variegated horns, I am told the Indians drink, and they say that a man who has drunk from this horn is free from incurable diseases; he will never be seized with convulsions . . . nor be destroyed by poisons.' The interest of Aelian's comments is that he gives the first hint that the fierceness of the unicorn is abated by female influence. 'It likes the lonely grazing grounds where it roams in solitude, but at the mating season, when it associates with the female, it becomes gentle and the two even graze side by side.'

The lack of direct contact between India and Europe in the early Middle

Ages meant that, for centuries, Europeans' knowledge of India continued to be dependent on the words of Ctesias and Megasthenes. Their unicorn does seem, in fact, to have been the Indian rhinoceros, since in India and China people still attribute to the horn of this animal the power of protection against poison.

The unicorn played only a very minor part in classical mythology and was not commonly represented in classical art. However, in a watercolour that probably represents a lost Roman wall painting from Rome, the huntress-goddess Diana was represented as she was worshipped at the great Temple of Diana at Ephesus on the western coast of Asia Minor: the lower half of her body is shown as a column of prancing animals, at the top of which are unicorns. In contrast to this association of the unicorn with a clearly pagan goddess, the first patriarchs of the Christian church gave the unicorn its popularity in the medieval world by interpreting it in the language of religious allegory, which was gradually widened and deepened.

The Christian world

Progressive translations of the Hebrew Old Testament provided the authority for the Christian interpretation of the unicorn. In Alexandria in the third and second centuries BC the original Hebrew text was translated into Greek, a translation commonly referred to as the *Septuagint* from the seventy-two translators involved in the work. The beast called in Hebrew *re em* became the Greek *monoceros*, that is, unicorn. In the Vulgate, the Latin translation of the Bible made by St Jerome from the original languages in the fourth century AD, *re em* was given in some cases as *rhinoceros* and in others as *unicornus*. The Vulgate was the Latin version of the Bible most widely used in the west. When the Latin Vulgate was translated into the vernacular, the name was translated, for instance, as unicorn in the English translation made in 1611 and authorised by King James I of England. So in the King James version, the unicorn appears in the Book of Job (39: 9–11) as a creature of great strength and power:

> Will the unicorn be willing to serve thee, or abide by thy crib? Canst thou bind the unicorn with his band in the furrow? Or will he harrow the valleys after thee? Wilt thou trust him, because his strength is great?

Given divine sanction by its appearance in the Bible, the unicorn was adopted as a Christian symbol in the fourth century. In particular St Basil (*c.* AD 330–79), who was Bishop of Caesarea and a learned man of great holiness, played a major part in this development. Taking the passage quoted above from Job, he comments that Christ 'will be called the Son of Unicorns, for, as we have learned in Job, the unicorn is irresistible in might and unsubjected to man.' Since the horn in the Bible often denotes glory and salvation, he declares: 'Christ is the power of God, therefore he is called the unicorn on the ground that he has one horn, that is, one common power with the Father.'

The unicorn acquired even greater popularity through its inclusion in a collection of stories and legends, which interpreted the habits and characteristics of animals in a way that could provide lessons for Christians. Written anonymously between the second and fourth centuries AD, it is sometimes known as the *Physiologus*, since in each chapter 'Physiologus' (meaning the scientist) is cited as the source. Originally written in Greek, probably in Alexandria, the text contains descriptions of mythical and fanciful creatures. Each account concludes with the moral lessons to be learned. The *Physiologus*, which was translated into Latin in the fifth century, was an immensely popular book in the Middle Ages. Translated into other languages, many of the descriptions were expanded and new creatures added. By the twelfth century this, as well as other sources such as the *De Animalibus* of Isidore, Bishop of Seville, in the seventh century, were brought together in the compilations known in western Europe as bestiaries, which were usually illustrated. It is here that the full religious symbolism of the unicorn may be found. To quote the description of a unicorn from a bestiary in the Cambridge University Library, as translated by T.H. White:

Unicornis the unicorn, which is also called rhinoceros by the Greeks, is of the following nature.

He is a very small animal like a kid, excessively swift, with one horn in the middle of his forehead, and no hunter can catch him. But he can be trapped by the following stratagem.

A Virgin girl is led to where he lurks, and there she is sent off by herself into the wood. He soon leaps into her lap when he sees her, and embraces her, and hence gets caught.

Our Lord Jesus Christ is also a Unicorn spiritually, about whom it is said: 'And he was beloved like the Son of the Unicorns'. And in another psalm: 'He hath raised up a horn of salvation for us in the house of . . . David'.

The fact that it has just one horn on its head means what he himself said: 'I and the Father are One' (John 10:30). Also according to the Apostle: 'The head of Christ is the Lord'.

It says that he is very swift because neither Principalities, nor Powers, nor Thrones, nor Dominations could keep up with him, nor could Hell maintain him, nor could the most subtle Devil prevail to catch or comprehend him; but, by the sole will of the Father, he came down into the virgin womb for our salvation.

It is described as a tiny animal on account of the lowliness of his

A drawing in Queen Mary's psalter of the early 14th century, showing a unicorn fighting an elephant.

incarnation, as he said himself: 'Learn from me, because I am mild and lowly of heart'.

It is like a kid or scapegoat because the Saviour himself was made in the likeness of sinful flesh, and from sin he condemned sin.

This provides the basic elements for the medieval interpretation of the unicorn, since here the unicorn is compared to a goat, a much smaller creature than the horse or ass of Ctesias or Pliny. The smallness of his size is compensated for by his swiftness which makes him impossible to capture. Christ could not be captured but, just as the unicorn is tamed by a virgin maiden, so Christ, by the will of the Father, surrenders his divine nature and becomes human, through the Virgin Mary, for the salvation of mankind. In a tenth-century *Physiologus* in Brussels, the scene of the capture of the unicorn by a maiden is shown beside a scene of Christ addressing two disciples. His words, which are often quoted in the *Physiologus*, are written behind: 'Learn of me, for I am meek and lowly in heart' (Matthew 11: 29). This is one of the very few pictorial demonstrations of the identification of the unicorn with Christ.

Only in the *Physiologus* is it mentioned that the death of the unicorn occurs while he rests his head in the virgin's lap, and this provides the basis for many of the medieval illustrations of the unicorn. In some medieval versions the virgin uses a mirror, perhaps symbolising pride or vanity, to bewitch the animal. A delightful illustration of this use of the mirror occurs on the enamelled medallion from the monastery of Sauerschwabenheim in Rheinhessen, now in the Bayerisches Nationalmuseum, which was probably made in Paris in the third quarter of the fourteenth century.

In other scenes the unicorn suckles at the breast of the virgin before his death. The symbolism of the virgin who entraps the unicorn was sometimes extended to a parallel with the milk of the Virgin Mary. For just as the milk of the Virgin Mary was associated with her powers of intercession,

A unicorn in silver against an enamelled background from the lower band of enamelling on the Savernake Horn. This ivory horn, for long associated with the tenure of the forest of Savernake in Wiltshire, has two bands of enamelling which were added in the mid-14th century and show the creatures of the forest.

so it could be used to tame and still the unicorn. This connection is revealed in the early fourteenth-century English poem, perhaps written by the Franciscan William of Shoreham, which invokes Mary under her various titles and includes a verse referring to the unicorn:

> that unicorn that was so wild
> aleyd is of a cheaste;
> thou has it itamed and istild
> with milke of thy breste.

The capture of the unicorn through the agency of a virgin was, in the twelfth century, symbolically connected with the birth of Christ and used to illustrate the virtue of purity. In the twelfth-century Floreffe Bible, now in the British Library, the scene of the capture of the unicorn is shown on the same page as the Nativity (fol. 168). This theme was used by preachers in their sermons, particularly by Honorius of Autun, a popular early twelfth-century theologian from southern Germany. His widely read writings had a considerable effect on medieval art. Although not an original thinker, he wrote simply and clearly and placed great emphasis not only on the literal and historical, but also on the symbolic and legorical, methods of interpreting the scriptures. He used the bestiaries with their fantastic animals to typify the world, the flesh and the devil. In his *Scala Coeli* he creates a theory of knowledge based on the way objects are seen. After discussing normal vision, he explains how through spiritual vision man sees objects similar to existing forms through the working of memory or imagination and also sees unknown forms which are accepted as real, such as unicorns or griffins, as well as fabulous monsters such as the Chimaera.

In the thirteenth century, the idea that the capture of the unicorn represented the Incarnation was developed into an elaborate allegory of the

The hunt of the unicorn shown on a tapestry altar frontal in the Marien-kirche, Gelnhausen, Germany. The hunter is the angel Gabriel who greets the Virgin Mary with the words '*Ave gratia plena dominus tecum*'. The Virgin sits in the enclosed garden with the unicorn. Middle Rhenish, about 1500.

Annunciation of the forthcoming birth of Christ to Mary. Known as the chase of the unicorn or the mystic hunt, it was particularly popular in Germany and north-eastern Europe. The Virgin is often shown in fifteenth-century engravings and woodcuts seated inside an enclosed garden, the *hortus conclusus*, surrounded with symbols of her inviolate virginity. Sometimes the unicorn is shown in her lap, at other times he is shown breaking into the enclosed garden. The hunter, the Angel Gabriel, sometimes sounds his horn outside the garden and sometimes breaks in to pursue the unicorn. He is frequently accompanied by dogs, usually four, which often represent the four Virtues: namely Mercy, Truth, Peace and Justice.

The end of the Middle Ages saw the greatest popularity of the unicorn as both a secular and a religious symbol. However, in 1563 the Council of Trent, which reformed Catholic spiritual belief and church organisation in the light of the spread of Protestantism, forbade the use of the unicorn as an allegory of the Annunciation in Christian art. From this moment it disappears from the symbolism of Christianity, yet its popularity continues in the worlds of literature, art, heraldry and medicine.

The secular medieval interpretation

The secular interpretation of the unicorn myth in the Middle Ages was just as strong as the religious. Indeed, if a late medieval lady is shown cradling the head of a unicorn in her lap, one cannot be sure whether the triumph of religious or secular love is being celebrated. It is this ambiguity that makes the unicorn one of the most fascinating of all mythical beasts. It is often only the surrounding context that indicates whether the scene is to be interpreted in a secular or religious manner. The capture of the unicorn in the lap of the maiden was widely portrayed in the bestiaries as a secular theme. Sometimes fierce, well-armed hunters pursue the animal. Sometimes the lady appears welcoming and soft, at other times she is hard and severe. She is usually clothed but occasionally appears nude, as in a bestiary in the British Library where she invites the hunter (clad in chain-mail and armed with a spear) to draw near. The unicorn, with a long straight horn, lies quietly, his head against the naked body of the maiden, unaware of his impending capture.

In the thirteenth century, the French writer Richard de Fournival wrote a bestiary that gave a secular rather than a religious interpretation of the animals. In this, known as the *Bestiaire d'Amour*, the unicorn symbolises the lover, beguiled by the virgin who represents his beloved. The hunter who kills the unicorn is none other than Love. In his book Richard describes how he was attracted to his beloved by her odour:

Florentine engraving of *c.* 1465–80 showing an Italian maiden, known as Marietta from the name on her cloak. She is about to fasten a collar, which is attached to a tree by a chain, onto the neck of her unicorn.

. . . just as the unicorn falls asleep under the influence of a maiden's fragrance. For this is the nature of the unicorn, that no other beast is so hard to capture . . . that no one goes forth against him except a virgin girl. And as soon as he is made aware of her presence by her scent, he kneels humbly before her and humiliates himself as though to signify that he would serve her. Therefore wise huntsmen who know his nature set a virgin in his way; he falls asleep in her lap; and while he sleeps the hunters, who would not dare approach him while awake, come up and kill him. Even so has Love dealt cruelly with me; in my pride, I thought never to see the woman whom I should care to possess . . . But Love, the skilful huntsman, has set in my path a maiden in the odour of whose sweetness I have fallen asleep, and I die the death to which I was doomed.

This very secular portrayal of the symbolism of the unicorn and the maiden is reflected in the way the scene is shown on late medieval enamels and ivories. The significance of the scene is often to be understood by the surrounding events. An example is on an ivory casket produced in Paris in the mid-fourteenth century and now in the British Museum. On the lid is the scene of the assault on the castle of Love, which is defended by the winged figure of Love and ladies armed with roses. The centre of the lid shows ladies watching a tournament, while to the right a lady gives the key of the castle to the knight kneeling before her. On the right-hand end of the casket the unicorn lies in the lap of the maiden holding the mirror while the huntsman, his eyes fixed upon the maiden, kills it with his spear. Next to this scene, Tristan and Isolde converse and their eyes meet. They are watched by Isolde's husband King Mark, who hides in a

LEFT A unicorn is killed in the lap of a naked virgin by a warrior in chain mail, carrying a buckler. The unicorn's horn is like a narwhal's tusk, straight, sharp and spiralled. From a 12th-century English bestiary.

BELOW A unicorn is killed by a huntsman with a spear while he rests in the lap of a virgin. From the side of an ivory casket carved in Paris in the second quarter of the 14th century showing scenes of love and romance.

tree and whose face is reflected in the pool beneath. The last two scenes both show reflected images, but they may also show the contrast between the pure love of the huntsman for the maiden as he kills the unicorn with the passionate and lustful love of Tristan and Isolde. It is also ironical that King Mark witnesses the faithlessness of Isolde his wife, just as the hunter witnesses the maiden's betrayal of the unicorn. The ivory casket was certainly conceived as a gift between lovers, and may even have been a marriage gift. The unicorn is often represented on painted panels, prints and tapestries, and so became a popular symbol of betrothal and marriage.

A symbol of chastity

It is one of the contradictions of the myth that the unicorn can serve as a symbol of chastity as well as of marriage. Since it was only through a virgin that the unicorn could be captured, the unicorn was never shown beside a lady with sexual experience. Thus the unicorn came itself at the end of the Middle Ages to symbolise a pure and chaste life. One of the most beautiful examples of this is the appearance of the unicorn on the medal made by Pisanello for Cecilia Gonzaga, the daughter of Gianfrancesco I, Marquess of Mantua, in 1447. It was particularly appropriate to

Unicorns pulling a triumphal cart, portrayed by Piero della Francesca (1410/20–92) in the painting, *The Triumph of the Duchess of Urbino*, in the Uffizi Gallery, Florence.

Cecilia since she ended her life in a convent. The medal shows on the reverse a rocky landscape lit by a crescent moon, while a semi-nude female figure is seated on the left with her left hand placed on the head of a goat-like unicorn. Chastity as a virtue is sometimes represented as a lady holding a standard on which is depicted a unicorn with its head in the lap of a virgin.

One of the finest representations of the unicorn as chastity occurs in the pictorial representations of the poems known as the *Triumphs*, written by the fourteenth-century Italian poet Petrarch. He wrote six poems forming a sequence of Triumphs. First Love triumphs, but is conquered by Chastity, who succumbs to Death. Fame triumphs over Death, Time over Fame, who submits to Eternity – the final Triumph. These poems had a very wide influence on pictorial art. All six have invariably been represented by scenes in which the main element was the triumphal chariot, although Petrarch only described it in the Triumph of Love. It has been suggested that there was a great pageant, probably in Florence in the middle of the fifteenth century, in which the six Triumphs were enacted, and that this pageant contributed to the diffusion of the representation of the Triumphs with chariots drawn by different animals. The triumphal car of Chastity was often shown drawn by unicorns, and this is well illustrated by the painting by Jacopo del Sellaio of the Triumph of Chastity. Here a pair of white unicorns attended by virgins draw the triumphal car of Chastity, on which Chastity stands in triumph over Cupid.

Unicorns, by their wild and uncontrollable nature, are rarely harnessed or ridden. There is, however, a fifteenth-century heraldic manuscript in Munich where Chastity is personified as a knight in full armour who rides upon a unicorn.

The medal for Cecilia Gonzaga of Mantua by Pisanello (*c.* 1395–1455), struck in 1447.

The medical use of the horn

From the time of the Ctesias the horn of the unicorn was thought to have particular medical and amuletic properties. The ability to purify water is first mentioned in the *Physiologus*, and the unicorn is often portrayed dipping its horn into a stream. Indeed, it was said that the other beasts of the forest would not drink from a pool until the unicorn had dipped his horn in it to confirm its purity. This association of the unicorn with the purity of water was taken further in the Middle Ages, as is demonstrated in the French manuscript of *c.* 1470 known as the *Wharncliffe Book of Hours*. Here a unicorn kneels in the virgin's lap and gazes into a mirror, while beside the pair a fountain spouts water into a stream which surrounds the island on which both are placed. The fountain was also associated with the Virgin Mary because of the purity of its waters. The Virgin is sometimes described as the mirror without blemish, the fountain of gardens, and the well of living waters.

A unicorn dips his horn into a river to rid it of poison in an engraving from the series devoted to the hunt of unicorn by the French engraver Jean Duvet, about 1562. These were intended to honour the love of the French King Henri II for his mistress Diane de Poitiers.

It was not only the horn that was highly valued in the Middle Ages. St Hildegard of Bingen, a twelfth-century German nun, thought that an ointment made of unicorn's liver and egg yolks was valuable for the healing of leprosy, that the wearing of a belt made from unicorn's skin would ward off plague or fever, and that the wearing of shoes made of unicorn's hide would ensure healthy feet. In the *Romance of Parzifal*, written by Wolfram von Eschenbach in the early years of the thirteenth century, the heart of a unicorn and the carbuncle which grew under its horn were among the various remedies which were used to heal the wounds of Anfortas, King of the Grail. This, however, was romance and, even in the Middle Ages, some writers were more circumspect. Albertus Magnus (1193–1280), who wrote so much on the properties of metals and stones, says little of the horn's magical virtues, merely stating that they should be investigated further.

Since the unicorn's horn could detect poison it was of great use in testing food and drink before feasts. Only kings and princes possessed a whole unicorn's horn. Sometimes it was simply set on the table before the guests so that any change in its appearance might instantly be seen. More commonly, however, a fragment of unicorn's horn was used to touch the food and drink before the meal began. Henry VI of England (1421–71) had a fragment of unicorn horn set in a pendant for him to put into his drink. The story is told of James I of England (1566–1625) that in order to test the efficacy of a horn he gave one of his servants poison mixed with the powder of the horn and, when the man fell dead, declared that he had been deceived, for clearly the horn was not genuine unicorn. The practice of using the horn as a proof for poison continued in the court of the Kings of France until the Revolution there in 1789.

Belief in the purifying quality of the horn led to the extension of its use to beakers or cups. It was not easy to shape beakers from horns of such small diameter, so cups were fashioned which included only a piece of the horn. Among the objects once belonging to Queen Elizabeth I that were given by James I to his Queen was 'a little cup of unicorn's horn, with a cover of gold and set with two pointed diamonds and three pearls pendent'. There are many references to similar cups, with a piece of unicorn's horn, used as a proof against poison. Almost all belonged to rich and well-born owners, clearly demonstrating the aristocratic associations of the horn, for the horn was very expensive and it was the powerful who most feared poison.

Fragments of unicorn's horn were sometimes worn as jewellery either as a pendant, set in jewels, or in finger rings. For instance, Margaret of Denmark, wife of James III of Scotland, had in 1488 'a serpent toung and one unicorne horne set in gold', and King Martin of Aragon had in 1410 'a piece of unicorn mounted in a collet of gold with its own red lace'.

The belief in the medicinal value of the unicorn's horn led also to the adoption of the unicorn as a symbol of the apothecary. Two unicorns were chosen as the supporters of the arms of the Society of Apothecaries of London in 1617, and the most usual sign for an apothecary's shop in the seventeenth century was a unicorn, or at least its head and horn. Today, particularly in Germany, many pharmacies trade under the sign of the unicorn.

ABOVE Unicorn used as a pharmacy sign in Gelnhausen, Germany.

The horn in treasuries and in collections

Many 'unicorn horns' were kept in treasuries and churches where they were listed in inventories in the late fourteenth and fifteenth centuries. In England Westminster Abbey and the church of St Paul in London each had one before the middle of the sixteenth century, when they were probably sold. One of the best-known horns was kept at St Denis, near Paris. In the seventeenth century John Evelyn described it as 'a faire unicorne's horn sent by a King of Persia, about 7 foote long'. The church of St Mark in Venice now possesses three, and on one of these the spiral ridges have been worn away by scraping for powder for curing illness. The Council of Ten at Venice decreed that, because of these scrapings, the 'horns were to be decorated with silver from the points to the silver-gilt handles so that the marks of former scrapings may be concealed, and they are to prohibit any further scrapings except in cases allowed by unanimous vote of the Council of Ten'. Most of these, as well as the horns now preserved at the Cluny Museum in Paris and in the church of St Bertrand de Com-

RIGHT This English narwhal horn of the second quarter of the 12th century has alternating carved and plain bands and was probably used as a ceremonial staff.

minges in France, are the horns of the narwhal, or Arctic whale, which possesses a long straight horn, often with spiral grooves. An example of such a narwhal horn which has the alternating grooves decorated with Romanesque carving is in the Victoria and Albert Museum. A very similar example was sold at Christie's in 1994, and it has been suggested that the two may originally have been produced for Lincoln Cathedral.

Unicorns' horns were also valued additions to royal treasuries. A unicorn's horn in the English royal treasury was kept beneath the chapter house at Westminster Abbey in the reign of Edward I. There was a notable robbery here in 1303, when Edward was away in Scotland, and the unicorn's horn was discovered under the bed of one of the main conspirators. In the inventories of the French kings, the earliest reference is to a horn in the collections of Charles VI in 1388. The Duc de Berry, brother of Charles V, possessed a whole unicorn's horn. Such horns were considered great rarities, and were occasionally mounted to stand on the table. Many horns came into the collections of princes. The horn of Philip the Good, Duke of Burgundy (died 1467), eventually passed into the Imperial Treasury at Vienna.

Seeking the unicorn became a feature of the exploration of the New World in the sixteenth and seventeenth centuries. So many new animals and species of plants were being discovered that it must have seemed quite possible that one day the unicorn would be found. This is illustrated by the great 'Horn of Windsor' which the German traveller Hentzner saw in 1598 and which he valued at £100,000. This horn was picked up on 22 July 1577 on an island in Frobisher's Strait, and when it reached England it was 'reserved as a jewel by the Queen's Majesty's commandment, in her wardrobe of robes'. It was, of course, a narwhal horn.

It was in 1638 that the Danish zoologist and antiquarian Ole Worm gave a public reading of his dissertation on the origin of unicorns' horns that proved they were really tusks of the narwhal. However, throughout the seventeenth century some writers continued to believe in the existence of the unicorn; one such was Edward Topsell, who wrote the *Historie of Foure-Footed Beastes* and who said that 'God himself must be traduced, if there is no unicorn'.

In England, other scholars were sceptical about the existence of the unicorn. Sir Thomas Browne, the Norwich physician comments in his book *Pseudodoxia Epidemica* that there is little agreement among those who describe the animal about either its size or nature. The horn is differently described and the horns that exist are of different natures. He concludes:

Since, therefore, there be many unicorns: since that whereto we appropriate a horn is so variously described, that it seemeth either never to have been seen by two persons, or not to have been one animal; since though they agreed in the description of the animal, yet it is not the horn we extol the same with that of the ancients; since what horns soever they be that pass among us, they are not the horns of one but several animals: since many in common use and high esteem are no horns at all; since if they were true horns, yet might their virtues be questioned: since though we allowed some virtues, yet were not others to be received; with what security a man may rely on this remedy, the mistress of fools hath already instructed some, and to wisdom (which is never to wise to learn) it is not too late to consider.

Some unicorns' horns ended up in the collections of curiosities that were to develop into museums. For instance, there was a horn of a unicorn in the Sloane collection which was to become the foundation collection of the British Museum. It is described as 'the head of a staffe of unicorns horn'.

Heraldry

By comparison with the griffin, the unicorn is rather shy as a heraldic creature, despite his fierceness and courage. He is not common in English but appears more frequently in medieval German heraldry. His earliest appearance there is on the town seals of Gmund in Swabia in the thirteenth century. The unicorn is seen more often on family shields in German heraldry. In the Manes manuscript of ballads, the first written example of which dates from the first third of the fourteenth century, a silver-grey beast rampant on a blue ground is allocated to the minnesinger Dietmar of Aist, who came from Thurgau where many families are identified by this bearing. Another German poet who used the unicorn on his arms was Friedrich von Schiller (1759–1805), not since he was a physician or because of the poetic nature of the unicorn, but for the reason that it had already long been used in his family.

The unicorn appears more often as the supporter of the shield or on the crest that surmounts the shield than on the shield itself. This supportive role is very clearly shown in the most famous depiction of the unicorn in art, the 'Lady with the Unicorn' series of six tapestries, in the Cluny Museum in Paris. Woven in the late fifteenth century, they show the five senses, Taste, Hearing, Smell, Touch and Sight, and the final one shows a tent, in front of which a lady replaces a necklace in a casket. The role of the unicorn, whose depiction is one of the most appealing features of these tapestries, is to display the arms of the Le Viste family. On five of the tapestries he holds up the standard of the family, on two he wears a shield around his neck, and on one he wears a cloak around his neck with the shield of the family. Only in the tapestry devoted to Sight is he relieved of his burden, for here he gazes into the mirror that the lady holds to reflect his face. In the last tapestry the lion and the unicorn, as well as displaying the arms of Le Viste, hold up the sides of the tent, of which the lady is clearly the mistress. The tent has the legend 'A . *Mon Seul Desir* . I' ('My One Desire', with the initials 'A' and 'I') along the top, and it has been argued that by replacing the chain of desire in her casket the lady demonstrates that her sole desire is fulfilled. These scenes are founded on an old French romance known as *Le Romans de la Dame a la Lycorne et du Biau Chevalier au Lyon*. The bridegroom may be represented in the tapestries by the arms of Le Viste, which the unicorn so assiduously displays, and it is likely that the tapestries were made to commemorate the marriage of Aubert Le Viste to Jeanne Baillet in 1470.

In their heraldic function as supporters of the shield, unicorns had a particular association with Scotland from the early fifteenth century. King James I (1406–37) had a herald called the Unicorn Pursuivant in 1426, and the use of the unicorn as a supporter of the Scottish royal arms first appears in the reign of James III (1460–88). He possessed a unicorn's horn set in gold as well as textiles decorated with thistles and unicorns. The gold coins known as 'unicorns' first appeared in Scottish currency in 1486 and were so called because they showed a unicorn holding the royal arms between his front legs. One of the finest early depictions of unicorns as supporters is in an illuminated Book of Hours of King James IV (1488–1513) in Vienna, dating from around 1505, which shows James in prayer before an altar. On the altar frontal is embroidered the arms of Scotland with white unicorns (without chains) on each side. Above their heads is the motto 'In my defense'. An unusual appearance of the Scottish heraldic unicorn is as the pendant to a collar which is shown in the stained glass of the Jerusalemkerk in Bruges in Belgium. The collar surrounds the arms of Anselme Adornes, a leading burgher of the city, who acted as an envoy between James III of Scotland and Charles the Bold, Duke of Burgundy, and the collar was probably a gift from James to Anselme. The negotiations he carried out in 1468 so impressed James that he was knighted and named as a royal councillor of Scotland. The use of the unicorns as supporters of the royal arms of Scotland continued throughout the sixteenth century and Mary, Queen of Scots (1542–87), had two unicorns as supporters on her great seal.

There is some evidence for the heraldic use of the unicorn by the English royal family as early as the first half of the sixteenth century, since it is one of the series of royal beasts that were carved for the bridges at Rochester and Hampton Court to mark the marriage of Henry VIII with Jane Seymour in 1536. Since the unicorn held her arms, it may be considered as one of her beasts. It may even be that the English use of the unicorn as a heraldic beast goes back to Edward III. However, the role of the unicorn as one of the supporters, together with the lion, of the English royal arms

A gold coin of James III of Scotland known as a 'unicorn'. First struck in 1486, these coins show a unicorn with a crown around his neck to which a chain is attached.

dates from 1603, when James VI of Scotland ascended the throne of England as James I, and the arms of Scotland appear on the royal arms together with those of England and Ireland. The joining of the lion and the unicorn in this way may be referred to in a nursery rhyme:

The Lion and the Unicorn
Were fighting for the Crown
The Lion chased the Unicorn
All around the town.
Some gave them white bread
Some gave them brown,
Some gave them plum cake,
And drummed them out of town

After 1603 the unicorn was often shown with a crown on its head, but following the Hanoverian succession to the throne in 1714 the crown was removed. The strife between England and Scotland was resumed and it is also possible that this period may have produced the rhyme, for its earliest recording is found in 1709. There is a most interesting illustration of the lion and the unicorn on either side of a shield carved in the panelling of the Hall at Ightham Mote in Kent. A lion is rampant on one side of the shield, while on the other the unicorn rushes headlong down the other side in flight. Above the shield the crown tips over to one side.

The opposition of the lion and the unicorn actually dates back much earlier since it is found on an Egyptian satirical papyrus dating from the period of Rameses III about 1200 BC. This shows a well-drawn lion and a unicorn, each sitting on a low stool, playing a game with chess-like pieces on a board between them. This opposition of these two beasts, one real and the other mythical, has endured for a remarkably long time. It reappears in sixteenth-century poetry in Edmund Spenser's *The Faerie Queen*, where the imperial power of the lion is defied by a 'prowd rebellious unicorn'. The lion adopts the trick of hiding behind a tree and then slips away to one side, so that the charging unicorn plunges his horn into the trunk of the tree and is unable to release himself. This also explains the way in which Shakespeare uses belief in the unicorn as a mark of easy credulity in *Julius Caesar*, when Decius Brutus says of Caesar:

He loves to hear
that unicorns may be betrayed with trees.

The device of the German printer, Thielman Kerver, in a *Book of Hours* printed in 1504.

The survival of the unicorn as a symbol up to the present day has depended on its quality as a symbol of purity. It was particularly used as a watermark for paper, for here the ability of the horn to test water for poison was used to demonstrate that the paper had been produced in pure water. It was by far the most popular animal represented in papermarks, since some 540 different figures of unicorns are recorded on paper produced between the end of the fourteenth and the end of the sixteenth centuries.

From this, it spread to be used as a printer's symbol, particularly in Germany where the sixteenth-century printer Thielman Kerver used it. In the early part of this century it was used as a publisher's house device by Melchior Lechter in 1908. Its most enduring presence in the modern world is as a symbol of security and so it is often used by savings banks, though here the elusive quality of the unicorn might be seen to be a disadvantage.

The east

The Chinese unicorn, known as the *qilin*, shares some of the characteristics of the western unicorn. (*Qi* refers to the male unicorn while *lin* refers to the female.) This unicorn has the body of a stag, the hoof of a horse and a single horn 12 ft (3.6 m) long springing from the middle of its brow. Unlike the western unicorn, who usually appears white and pure, he is multicoloured. The unicorn is solitary and cannot be caught, and his appearance betokens a most auspicious event. One appeared before the birth of Confucius holding in its mouth a tablet of jade on which the praises of Confucius were engraved. It also appeared shortly before his death. The unicorn is supposed to spring from the centre of the earth. Since in Chinese mythology the phoenix represents fire, the dragon air, and the tortoise water, it is possible that the unicorn originally represented the earth. The horn of the unicorn did not have the same associations for the Chinese as it did in the west. The Chinese were well aware of the difference between the qilin and the rhinoceros. The prophylactic value of the rhinoceros horn was highly valued, since in the Tang dynasty the belts of mandarins were often studded with it.

In Islamic art a four-footed beast with a single long horn was identified in written sources as a karkadann. It was sometimes shown with wings. Descriptions of the karkadann in literature suggest that it was based on the rhinoceros, though sometimes the body is compared with the lion's or the stag's. Its horn is usually straight, though occasionally curved. It has great fierceness and strength and is particularly antagonistic to the elephant. It is interesting that this may be the source of the comment found in western bestiaries that the unicorn often fights with the elephant and uses its horn to wound the elephant in the belly. The karkadann can be tamed through the influence of a hero or an overpowering personality, but there is no suggestion of a virgin being used in the capture of the animal, showing that this variation of the story is entirely western.

The distinction between the eastern and the western versions of the animal can be clearly seen in the account of Marco Polo (1254–1324), who on his journeys to the east described the rhinoceros in Sumatra; its horn immediately evoked associations with the unicorn. He calls the animal a unicorn but states explicitly that this ugly beast has nothing to do with the unicorn which, according to 'our stories', was caught in the lap of a virgin.

The unicorn in art

Three-dimensional representations of the unicorn are unusual in the Middle Ages. It may have been the ability of the unicorn to purify water that led to the shape being used for bronze aquamaniles, since they were used for pouring out wine or water at table. A fine bronze aquamanile, some 10 in (25 cm) high, in the form of a unicorn was sold at Sotheby's in 1983 and is now in an American private collection. Probably made in Lorraine or Saxony in the thirteenth century, it was acquired in the Italian town of Chiavenna in the nineteenth century.

More often, however, the unicorn was used as a decorative motif on a piece of silver. For instance, a unicorn is shown in the lap of a wild woman on the silver beaker made and engraved by the Lübeck goldsmith Hans Timmermans in the early sixteenth century. The exact source of the engraving is known, since it was copied from the engraving made by the German Master ES about 1461 and used for the Queen of the Animals in one of the earliest western European sets of cards. The wild woman was a hairy creature who lived deep in the forest. The popularity of this scene of the wild woman taming the unicorn is shown by the fact that the same source was used for the decoration of an oven tile now in the Zurich Landesmuseum. Wild men, as well as women, were apparently capable of taming unicorns since in a suit of cards engraved by the Master ES in 1463 a wild man controls his unicorn by holding its mane and tail.

A unicorn is captured by a wild woman. One of a series of engravings, showing man's capture by women and the folly of love, on a silver beaker made and engraved by the Lübeck goldsmith, Hans Timmermans, who flourished in the first three decades of the 16th century.

The unicorn defends himself against the hunters. A French tapestry from a series woven around 1500, probably for a member of the La Rochefoucauld family, and now in the Metropolitan Museum, New York.

In the unicorn tapestries in the Cluny Museum the unicorn plays only a subsidiary part, but he is the principal subject of the series now in the Cloisters in New York. This enchanting set, formerly in the possession of the family of La Rochefoucauld, passed, via the Rockefeller Collection, to the Metropolitan Museum in New York. These seven tapestries offer the most extensive surviving portrayal of the hunt of the unicorn. Their inspiration was drawn from the medieval illustrations of the hunting of stags. In the first tapestry the hunters set forth with dogs while a scout sent on ahead beckons them towards their quarry. The unicorn first appears in the second tapestry, dipping his horn in a stream to purify it. Around him are the animals of the forest, while the scene of purification is watched by the huntsmen. After leaping a stream in the third tapestry, the unicorn defends himself in the fourth. Here he wounds a dog with his horn while kicking out with his hind legs at the hunters. In this scene the difference between a stag and a unicorn hunt is shown by the hunter, who bears a sheath inscribed *Ave Regina* and who clearly represents the Angel Gabriel. The hunters are, of course, unable to kill the unicorn, and the fifth tapestry (unfortunately fragmentary) shows the unicorn tamed by the virgin. In the sixth tapestry the unicorn is killed by spear and sword, and its body is brought to the castle of the king. Thus the killing of the unicorn is separated from the scene of the unicorn in the lap of the virgin and is clearly inspired by the death of the stag. The carrying of the unicorn to the castle is based on the carrying of the stag back after a successful hunt. In the final tapestry the unicorn is shown entrapped within a fence chained to a tree. The tree is a pomegranate tree, itself an emblem of fertility.

Like the Cluny tapestries, they were probably woven to celebrate a marriage. All the tapestries in this series have the letters AE linked together by a cord in the form of a bow knot. The significance of this monogram is not clearly understood. At one time it was thought that the tapestries were made for Anne of Brittany to celebrate her marriage to Louis XII of France in 1499, but this is not now generally accepted. The tapestries first appear in the La Rochefoucauld family, and it is likely that they were woven around 1500 for a member of that family.

Another hunt of the unicorn is the sequence of prints by the French

A unicorn, ridden by an amorino (little cupid), is borne on a chariot in another engraving by Jean Duvet (see p. 57), about 1562.

engraver Jean Duvet in honour both of the unicorn and of the love of Henry II of France (1519–59) for his mistress, Diane de Poitiers. Like the tapestries in the Metropolitan Museum, the series combines scenes of the unicorn legend, such as the unicorn dipping his horn into a river to rid it of poison, with the hunt of the unicorn. It is possible that Duvet had seen the Metropolitan tapestries when they were in the possession of the Rochefoucauld family. The concluding scenes of this series show the unicorn borne on a chariot and a final scene of the unicorn in a triumphal procession about to be crowned with a wreath of leaves, which derive their composition from the chariot and procession scenes used to illustrate Petrarch's *Triumphs*.

The continuation of the romantic influence of the unicorn in art into the twentieth century is shown by the popular painting by Arthur B. Davies (1862–1928) in the Metropolitan Museum of Art in New York. Here a herd of three unicorns approaches a kneeling girl on a promontory set against a deep bay, while another girl looks out to sea. The figures of both girls and unicorns are minute compared with the vastness of nature.

The unicorn in literature

The unicorn has had a long life in literature since it is so obviously a symbol of love. It is the appearance of the unicorn in the romances of the Middle Ages that lies behind the tapestries in the Cluny Museum, and it often appears in the finale of an allegorical hunt. In Richard de Fournival's *Bestiaire d'Amour*, as we have seen, the skilful huntsman is Love and the quarry is the unicorn who represents the lover. The connection between the unicorn and love continues into modern literature, notably with Iris Murdoch's novel *The Unicorn*.

At other times the unicorn reflects the quality of tireless strength, as in the Irish poet W. B. Yeats' poem 'The Unicorn and the Stars' where Father John says: 'The unicorns – what did the French monk tell me? strength they meant, virginal strength, a rushing, lasting, tireless strength.'

This sense of a quality of tireless strength was referred to by Aelian when he remarked: 'unicorns are far swifter than any ass or even than any horse or deer . . . To pursue them is, in the language of poetry, to chase the unattainable.' Unicorns symbolise the unattainable and the elusive, and these qualities of the unicorn recur time and again, as is clearly shown in W. H. Auden's poem 'New Year Letter' where he describes childhood among the cedars. In this the unicorn is portrayed as an animal which no magic charm can reveal to the reader, and past childhood is as elusive as the innocent beast.

It is quite reasonable to assume that the unicorn, unlike some other mythical beasts, might have existed. There is nothing inherently improbable about a goat-like animal with only one horn, and while a horse with

Unicorns, painted by Arthur B. Davies about 1906 and now in the Metropolitan Museum, New York.

a horn is improbable, it is not as unlikely as an animal composed of half an eagle and half a lion. The possibility that the unicorn might have existed, together with the fact that it never did, gives it a dream-like quality. For instance, it is only when Sebastian, in Shakespeare's play *The Tempest*, has staggered through the marvels and terrors of Prospero's island that he declares, 'Now I will believe that there are unicorns.' But Lewis Carroll in *Through the Looking-Glass* puts this into reverse when Alice meets the Unicorn, who has always thought of children as fabulous monsters. Here each is only convinced of the existence of the other when they see and talk to each other. In a more amusing way the dangers of disbelief in unicorns are indicated in the American writer James Thurber's short story *The Unicorn in the Garden*.

Finally, the enduring hold that the unicorn has on the imagination of poets and writers is best summed up by the lyric German poet Rainer Maria Rilke (1875–1926). His sonnet in the series *Sonnets to Orpheus* (dated 1923) was inspired by the visual impression of the tapestries in the Cluny Museum, and shows how the appearance of a mythical beast in one work of art can inspire another:

This is the creature that has never been.
They never knew it, and yet none the less
entirely loved it, from its suppleness
to the very light of the eyes, mild and serene.

It never was. And yet their love supplied
the need of being. They always left a space.
And in that clear space they had set aside
it lightly raised its head and felt no trace

of not being real. They did not give it corn,
but fed it with their feeling that it *might*,
somewhere, exist. Were able to confer

such strength, its forehead grew a horn. One horn.
It came up to a virgin once, all white –
and lived on in the mirror and in her.

Griffins

Antiquity

The griffin is a very ancient beast, or rather bird, whose ancestors made their first known appearance more or less simultaneously around 3000 BC in Egypt and Mesopotamia. In Egyptian art, which produced a vast range of composite and half-human animal forms, the early griffin had the head of a falcon, vulture or other bird of prey; the rest had lion-like parts, which were combined with other features of a bird in a variety of ways. Sometimes the head was shown crested, and as a result the griffin came to acquire one of its main characteristics – ears. As a pictorial symbol, the griffin most often stood for the victorious Pharaoh trampling on his enemies, represented by a serpent beneath its claws, but later it came to be replaced by other images of the Pharaoh, such as that of a man-headed sphinx.

In Mesopotamia and Elam the griffin was first portrayed rather as a winged lion, sometimes with a bird's back legs and tail, but the true griffin with the head of an eagle can also be found. As a terrifying animal, the griffin was associated with demons and other hostile forces and with Nergal, the god of the afterlife. Sometimes, as an illustration of how these powers can be tamed and controlled, a god is shown enthroned above a griffin, riding one or in a chariot drawn by griffins. Similarly, the struggle between human and bestial forces, between good and evil, was represented by a human figure standing between two griffins; this was the Master – or sometimes the Mistress – of the Griffins. In one example of this motif two griffins, shown attending on the goddess Ishtar, may be acting symbolically as guardians of an essential crop, the date harvest. Sometimes griffins are depicted lying peacefully in repose; at others they are fighting a hero or some other animal, such as a lion, a serpent, a gazelle or a bull.

Impression from an Assyrian cylinder seal, *c.* 700 BC, showing two griffins flanking a winged and bearded figure. In ancient art, hybrid beasts such as the griffin (with a bird's head and wings, and the body of a lion) were often shown in pairs protecting some sacred object or, as here, with their master, a god or hero with the power to control these fierce creatures.

From Egypt and the Middle East griffins spread into Syria, Palestine and Anatolia (modern Turkey), and then to Cyprus. By about 1700 BC they had arrived on the island of Crete, where they continued to be shown clawing their prey or fighting with bulls or lions. A series of reclining guardian-griffins, with decorated manes but with coloured whorls instead of wings, lines the walls of the throne-room of King Minos in the palace of Cnossos.

Since the griffin was such a large, fierce creature, these early civilisations used it as a talisman, a warning to ward off evil, and as a guardian beast which protected sacred or symbolic objects by frightening off anybody who might try to steal or desecrate them. Indeed, for thousands of years from the ancient world up to more recent times, griffins have most commonly been shown in pairs flanking a tree (the Tree of Life), a candelabrum, a fountain, a ceremonial bowl, a funerary urn, an altar or a lyre (a symbol of Apollo). Griffin-hunters with sharp eyes may find them not only on ancient or medieval historic sites but also in neo-classical decorative designs of the eighteenth and nineteenth centuries, on the fronts of buildings and on friezes and cornices. Nowadays griffins have even become logos, such as those of a high-street bank, a make of car and a brewery. Over the main door of the headquarters of British Coal in London are two griffins, for griffins also used to dig up and guard the treasures of the earth.

The griffin must not be confused with the mere winged lion or the dragon. It is easily recognised because it has the head, hooked beak and wings of a predatory bird, the eagle, but with the addition of pointed ears.

The rest of it is like a lion, occasionally shown with its skin spotted like a leopard's. Strictly speaking, it is not a hybrid, half-eagle and half-lion, but a distinct species of flying quadruped, a bird. Even so, when the female griffin appears, she has a row of nipples.

There are two main types of griffin. In classical times it usually had all four legs like a lion's; this version is sometimes called the opinicus. Later it came to be shown with the two front legs and clawed feet of an eagle and the two hind legs of a lion, and this is the griffin of the more modern, post-classical tradition. Its name, 'griffin' – which is sometimes spelt 'gryphon', from one of the medieval Latin forms (*grypho, gryphonem*) – is thought to go back to an ancient Indo-European word meaning 'to grasp', and the Greek name (*gryps*) was connected with the word *grypos*, meaning 'hooked' or 'curved', like its beak. Another theory is that the word comes from the Middle Eastern *kerub*, which, like the griffin, was a winged guardian protecting the Tree of Life and which in the Bible gave its name to the cherub, a type of angel. Certainly, throughout the ages, the griffin has been an ambiguous creature. On the one hand, since it resembled partly the eagle, the king of birds, and partly the lion, the king of beasts, it could be taken as a symbol of royal and noble power; on the other, it was a large, hook-beaked bird which gripped and tore up its prey or greedily dug up treasures with its claws.

During the eighth century BC the Greeks adopted the griffin, and it began to appear in designs for a wide variety of objects: earthenware, ceramics, mosaics, ivories, seals, gems, gold items, coins and sculptured reliefs. As in earlier times, one of the main tasks of griffins was to act as watchful guardians, and the Greeks began to carve them on tombs, so that griffins also became protectors of the dead.

In addition to their decorative role and their function as guardians, Greek griffins, like their ancestors, were shown fighting against other animals, against men or, occasionally, against women – the Amazons. The explanation of the battle between griffins and men is provided in one of the earliest written references to griffins by the Greek writer Herodotus, who lived in the fifth century BC and has become known as the 'Father of History'. According to him, there was more gold in the north of Europe than anywhere else, but the men there, a race of one-eyed people called Arimaspians, could obtain it only by stealing it from griffins. Herodotus himself did not believe this story. It was not, however, the mention of griffins which worried him but the description of the Arimaspians. He could not accept that there existed men who were 'in all else like other men, yet having but one eye'.

Herodotus also tells how he picked up the story of the griffins and the one-eyed men who stole their gold. On his travels he had learnt about a certain Aristeas from Proconnesus (an island in the Sea of Marmara):

ABOVE Griffins drawing a chariot. Griffins were believed to draw the chariots of various gods, and the motif also appeared sometimes on funerary objects, illustrating the function of griffins as guides and protectors of the soul. Pottery bowl from Enkomi, Cyprus, Mycenaean, *c.* 1300–1200 BC.

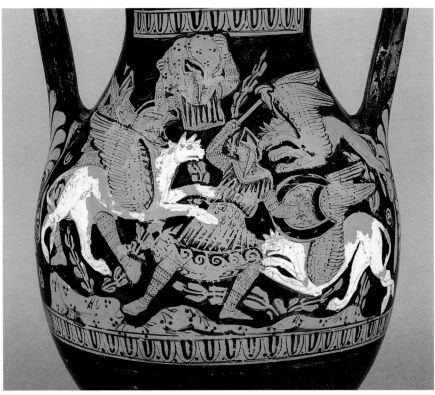

This Aristeas, being then possessed by Phoebus [the god Apollo], visited the Issedones; beyond these (he said) dwell the one-eyed Arimaspians, beyond whom are the griffins that guard gold, and beyond these again the Hyperboreans, whose territory reaches the sea. [. . .] It is from the Issedones that the tale comes of the one-eyed men and the griffins that guard gold; this is told by the Scythians, who have heard it from them; and we again have taken it for true from the Scythians, and call these people by the Scythian name, Arimaspians; for in the Scythian tongue *arima* is one, and *spou* is the eye.

So the Father of History records his information about griffins third-hand, as news taken from the Scythians (people living in an area roughly corresponding to modern Moldova and the southern Ukraine) who learnt it from their northern neighbours, the Issedonians; and he mentions an ancient traveller, Aristeas of Proconnesus, who visited these Issedonians and found out about the Arimaspians and the gold-guarding griffins living even further to the north.

So who was this Aristeas, the first man to report the existence of griffins? All that is known about him is the following story relayed by Herodotus. One day Aristeas entered a fuller's shop where all of a sudden he fell down dead. The fuller went off to inform the relatives, but as the news spread a traveller reported that he had just seen Aristeas on the road leading out of town, and when the relatives went to the shop to collect the body, they found no Aristeas there, dead or alive. In the seventh year after this disappearance he turned up again on Proconnesus, where he wrote a poem called the *Arimaspea* before disappearing for a second time.

Herodotus' story continues: 240 years – or, in other versions, 340 years – after this second disappearance, Aristeas appeared to the people of Metapontum (a town in the 'instep' of Italy), telling them that he had been there once before in the shape of a crow and accompanying Apollo. He instructed them to build an altar to Apollo and a statue of himself nearby, and these, Herodotus testifies, still stand in the market-place there, surrounded by laurel trees. From all this it is clear that Aristeas must be dated to at least two and a half centuries before Herodotus himself, perhaps therefore to around 680 BC. For hundreds of years writers cited Aristeas as the earliest authority on griffins, but apart from a few lines quoted centuries later and probably invented, his poem about the Arimaspians has since been lost – if it or its author ever existed.

In this way the griffin entered into history. It entered literature too, not only with Aristeas' lost work but also, a little before Herodotus' time, in *Prometheus Bound*, a tragedy by Aeschylus. In this Prometheus warns Io to 'beware the sharp-beaked hounds of Zeus that bark not, the griffins, and the one-eyed Arimaspian folk, mounted on horses, who dwell about the flood of Pluto's stream that flows with gold'. Pluto here is probably to be linked with Ploutos, the god of wealth, whilst the griffins are the hounds of Zeus himself, the king of the gods. Aeschylus too, therefore, had heard of the dangerous, beaked griffins which lived where there was gold and a fierce race of one-eyed men who rode horses.

The Greeks and, after them, the Romans took the griffin as an attribute or symbol of various other gods and goddesses too. According to the later historian Pausanias, the great statue of Athena in the Parthenon in Athens had a helmet adorned with bronze reliefs: an image of the sphinx in the middle, flanked by griffins on either side. He too quotes Aristeas and gives an accurate description of griffins:

> These griffins, Aristeas of Proconnesus says in his poem, fight for the gold with the Arimaspi beyond the Issedones. The gold which the griffins guard, he says, comes out of the earth; the Arimaspi are men all born with one eye; griffins are beasts like lions, but with the beak and wings of an eagle.

Perhaps a bit sceptical, Pausanias breaks off at this point with the words, 'I will say no more about griffins'.

The griffin was also connected with the god Dionysus (Bacchus), with the goddess Artemis (Diana), who thus inherited the ancient role of Mistress of the Griffins, and in a special way with Nemesis. According

A griffin on a Roman sepulchral chest of the 2nd century AD. In Greek and Roman art, one of the functions of griffins was to guard the dead and to act as the bearers of the souls of the blessed.

The griffin of the goddess Nemesis (Justice), represented by the wheel beneath its paw. Nemesis travelled round the world in a chariot drawn by griffins, protecting the good and punishing the proud with her avenging wheel. The Roman Empire adopted this symbolism to express its own role in the administration of universal justice. Coin of Antoninus Pius, Roman emperor (AD 138–61).

to the poet Nonnos, Nemesis was the goddess of justice who flew round the world in a chariot drawn by vengeful griffins; her task was to protect the good but also to punish the proud, rolling them down from on high to the ground with her avenging wheel. Hence the griffin is sometimes shown with a paw resting on a wheel, standing for Nemesis herself and later for the Roman Empire which took on her duty to administer justice throughout the whole world; in the famous words of the poet Virgil, 'to spare the vanquished and cast down the proud'.

The most interesting detail in Herodotus' story about the mysterious disappearing and reappearing Aristeas is that he was a companion and servant of Phoebus or Apollo, the god of the sun. Indeed, his apparent sudden death and first disappearance have been interpreted as his seizure by the god who put him into a trance and sent him on his travels. The Egyptians had sometimes shown griffins with their sun-god Malakbel, and from about the sixth century BC the Greeks too took up the theme. For centuries, right down to the end of the Roman Empire, griffins were Apollo's birds, which, according to a poem by Sidonius Apollinaris, with beating wings drew his chariot over land and sea in the sun's great daily journey from east to west; together with the tripod and the lyre, they became the symbols of Apollo and his cult. A flying griffin shown on the breastplate of a statue of the first Roman emperor, Augustus, celebrates his debt to Apollo in defeating Mark Antony, and this motif was adopted on public statues of later emperors too, in recognition of their divine power and status. Later still, as oriental religions were absorbed into Roman culture, the griffin, like the phoenix, became an important symbol in the worship of the *Sol invictus*, the 'unconquered Sun', and in the grades of initiation into the mysteries of Mithras, the god of light. In pagan religion, therefore, from Apollo to Mithras, griffins were above all the birds of the sun.

In addition to this, Roman religious art sometimes gave the griffin another important function by showing it carrying a cloaked figure on its back. This illustrated the griffin's role as a 'psychopomp', that is, as the guide of the soul of a dead person to the afterlife, its protector from dangers and demons on its way to the world of the Blessed, and, in the case of a deceased emperor or empress, the bearer of the soul upwards to apotheosis or glorification in the world above. On the temple of Antoninus Pius and his wife Faustina in the Roman Forum, there is a marble frieze of paired griffins guarding candelabra, showing them as protectors of the eternal light to which the souls of the imperial couple have travelled.

For the Greeks and Romans griffins lived not only in Scythia in the north but also, as Apollo's steeds, in the east, in India, where likewise they were said to be venerated as sacred to the sun. There too they guarded gold, which they dug up with their powerful beaks; and they were said to be so strong that they could overcome elephants and dragons. By about

AD 200 one writer, Aelian, had accumulated quite a lot of information about the Indian griffin: it is a quadruped like a lion, with claws of enormous strength; it has black feathers along its back, whilst those on its front are red, its wings are white, and its neck is variegated with feathers of a dark blue; its head and beak are like an eagle's; and its eyes are like fire. It builds its lair among the mountains, and it is impossible for men to capture the full-grown animal, though they can take the young. Griffins fight with other animals but not, says Aelian, with lions or elephants. They dig up gold and build their nests with it, and the Indians can come along and collect any of the gold that the griffins have dropped on the way. The griffins fight with the Indians too, though not for the gold, since they have no need of it, but in order to protect their young. Great teams of Indians go out into the wilderness with spades and sacks on expeditions lasting three or four years. Approaching by night, they have a better chance of escaping death from the invincible griffins and so of returning home alive and with immense wealth in gold.

Knowledge about griffins was transmitted to later generations mainly in Latin by three Roman writers: Pliny, Solinus and Virgil. The natural historian Pliny, who died while observing the eruption of Vesuvius in AD 79, took up the 'evidence' of Herodotus and Aristeas of Proconnesus and told how, near the land of the Scythians, live the one-eyed Arimaspians who constantly fight for metals with griffins – flying creatures which dig up gold and guard it with extraordinary greed. Another first-century writer, the geographer Pomponius Mela, similarly reported that in a sun-baked but uninhabitable region there are griffins, 'a fierce and tenacious species of beast', which dig up gold and lovingly guard it, attacking any men who approach, namely the Scythians and the one-eyed Arimaspians.

From these sources, in about AD 200, Gaius Iulius Solinus compiled a collection of facts about the world, its different regions and its wonders. He too says that in Asiatic Scythia there is an abundance of gold and jewels, but that the country is uninhabitable because griffins block access to the rich mines and fight with the Arimaspians for the precious stones. Griffins are large and very ferocious winged creatures, 'cruel beyond all the bounds of fury', and they will tear a man up on sight. In fact, Solinus thought they were so dangerous and fearsome that it was as if the very purpose of their existence was to punish men so greedy and rash as to try to steal the treasures. This account was very influential on later writers who included the griffin in their books of beasts, presenting it as a fierce and invincible guardian of treasure and a warning against human greed.

Probably because the Arimaspians rode on horseback to fight with them, griffins were also said to be particularly hostile to horses. This enmity became widely known in a pastoral poem by Virgil which refers to the amazing and unsuitable marriage of the shepherd Mopsus to Nisa: 'Nisa

A griffin lying at the feet of Apollo. In Greek and Roman religion, griffins drew Apollo's chariot, the sun, in its great daily journey across the sky. During the Roman Empire they became important symbols in the cult of Apollo and other solar deities. Detail from the silver Corbridge Lanx (tray), Romano-British, 4th century AD.

has been married to Mopsus. What may the rest of us lovers not hope for, then? [In other words, if Mopsus can find a wife, there is hope for everyone.] Griffins must already be mating with horses, and any time now timid does will be going to drink at the water-holes alongside dogs.' Commentaries on the poem explained that, since griffins always attack horses, it would be entirely against the natures of the two species to mate. It would be just as unexpected as if natural enemies like deer and hounds were to be found drinking together peacefully side by side. So what Virgil meant was that Mopsus' marriage is a marvel in an age of marvels where the impossible has become true. When griffins are mating with their favourite prey, an age of miracles has dawned.

The Middle Ages

A section of the Bayeux Tapestry showing a pair of griffins in the centre of the lower margin. In the Middle Ages, griffins were portrayed not only as guardian beasts but also in a decorative role, illustrating the rich and exotic variety of the wonderful animal world created by God. Norman embroidery, late 11th century.

The pagan tradition of griffins as sun-birds and Apollo's steeds died out in western Latin Christendom after about the fifth century AD, although it did survive in the east, in the Byzantine Empire and in the countries later occupied by the Slavonic nations. The Greek *Physiologus*, a book about beasts and birds and their symbolism, tells how in the morning a griffin catches on its wings the rays of the rising sun, and with another griffin it carries them across the sky. At the same time, the archangel St Michael and the Madonna pray for Christians. The religious lesson, typical of the medieval books of beasts, is that Christians should praise and thank God as the source of their being.

Even to the Greeks of the Middle Ages, however, griffins might be

edifying symbols whilst still being a very frightening reality. *The Suda*, a tenth-century lexicon, reported that the Avars, an eastern tribe, had been forced to migrate westwards by a great sea-fog and by the appearance of many griffins which, it was rumoured, would not stop until they had devoured the whole human race.

Greek culture was not generally known in the west before the Renaissance, and in the Middle Ages people learned about griffins mainly from surviving classical sculptures, from Latin writers such as Pliny and Solinus, and from the two brief mentions of the griffin in the Bible. In this last respect, what had happened was that the Hebrew word *peres* had been translated in the Greek Bible as *grypa* and then into Latin as *gryphem*, 'griffin'. The references occur in the two accounts of Moses' instructions to the Israelites concerning unclean animals and birds: 'These are the birds which you must not eat but which you must avoid: the eagle and the griffin and the osprey and the kite and the vulture [. . .]', and many more (Leviticus, 11: 13–14); 'Eat all clean birds, but do not eat the unclean birds, namely, the eagle and the griffin and the osprey [. . .]', and so on (Deuteronomy, 14: 11–12). Since the Bible, God's word, mentioned the griffin, it must certainly exist.

In medieval times the griffin was thought of as an exotic northern or oriental bird, huge, wild and frightening, one of the marvels of the amazing world created by God. So artists would sometimes include it in lively, decorative designs of animals and birds in mosaics, on tiles and floors, and in the work of weavers, such as in the margin of the Bayeux Tapestry and on the richly embroidered vestments of an emperor of Constantinople and of Pope Boniface VIII around 1300.

The griffin, combining the powers of the king of birds and the king of beasts, could be considered as therefore doubly royal and strong. Like the eagle and the lion, it was adopted as an emblem by some cities, such as Schweidnitz (now Swidnica in Poland), Perugia in Italy, and a region of Rome called Parione, thought to mean 'part-lion', because a griffin had arrived from the east and had been taken there. The crest of the Livery Company of Barbers in London bears the type of griffin known as the opinicus, and some knights and noble families emblazoned griffins on their shields and coats of arms, or used one as an armorial supporter. The basic message of the heraldic griffin was: 'Beware of me; I am like a griffin, protected by the griffin's power, and if you oppose me, I shall unleash that power on you.' As a heraldic emblem, the griffin also became an inn sign, though presumably not so as to frighten the customers away – unless perhaps they were troublemakers or dared to complain about the ale. However, in spite of its occasional adoption as a family symbol, there was no connection between the beast and the emergence of the family name Griffin, which was first a forename (appearing in the Domesday Book)

A she-griffin suckling two children, who represent *condottieri* (captains of mercenary armies). The griffin's collar is marked 'Perugia', and the scene links the city and its military heroes with the she-wolf which nursed Romulus and Remus, the founders of ancient Rome. Medal by Antonio Pisanello, Italian, 15th century.

Drawing by the English artist and critic, John Ruskin (1819–1900), showing griffins supporting the portico of the medieval cathedral of Verona in northern Italy. Because of their great strength and ferocity, griffins were most frequently shown as protectors of sacred places and objects, warning any sacrilegious robbers to beware. The wheels carved on these griffins' flanks recall the ancient motif of the griffins of Nemesis.

and later a surname. This was a pet-form of the Old Welsh *Gruffudd*, originating in Wales and the Celtic south-west of England and, in the eastern counties, with Bretons who arrived with William the Conqueror.

Just as in ancient times, the griffin in the Middle Ages was above all a guardian creature, strong, fierce, invincible. Griffins can be found as gargoyles on cathedral roofs, standing guard by the porticoes of churches, on doors, book covers and so on. As of old, the griffin may sometimes be a

A typical medieval image of a griffin, a wild and fierce flying quadruped, thought to live in remote parts of northern Europe or India. Whereas in classical art the griffin is usually shown with all four legs like those of a lion, in the Middle Ages it has front legs which are clawed like an eagle's. Pavement tile from Chertsey Abbey, Surrey, second half of the 13th century.

talisman to ward off evil, but its basic meaning is usually just 'Beware!'. It is a frightening sentinel, reminding the profane or sacrilegious of the terrible punishments they will incur if they try to desecrate or steal the sacred, precious treasure which it guards. The medieval griffin could also be the protector of the dead: in St Mary's Church in Warwick, by the tomb of Richard Beauchamp, Earl of Warwick, who died in 1439, together with other animals (including the bear, the family emblem), there stands a griffin which both reminds the visitor of the late Earl's fearsome power

BELOW Two griffins flanking a rosette design, in a medieval version of the ancient motif of griffins as guardians of sacred objects and the Tree of Life. Ivory plaque, part of a casket said to have been found in the ruins of Old Sarum, Wiltshire, 12th century.

and stands guard over his mortal remains. Sometimes another ancient theme crops up in religious art, showing griffins protecting the Tree of Life in the Garden of Eden. Here too the griffin's message is a warning to Christians to beware of repeating the sin of Adam and Eve who disobeyed God by picking and eating the fruit of the forbidden tree, with fatal consequences for their descendants.

Not only did artists of the Christian Middle Ages inherit the ancient griffin, but writers too continued to pass on information about it. Particularly influential here was St Isidore of Seville, who in the seventh century AD wrote a massive encyclopaedia of knowledge taken from the classics, early Christian writers and commentators on the Bible. In this griffins are said to guard gold and emeralds in Scythia, whilst in India too there are 'the Golden Mountains which it is impossible to approach because of the dragons and griffins and enormous, monstrous men'. St Isidore also gives the following summary of griffin lore which the medieval books on beasts repeated again and again:

> The Griffin is a winged animal and a quadruped. This species of wild beast is born in the Hyperborean Mountains [that is, in the far north of Europe]. They are lions in every part of their bodies and resemble eagles in their faces and wings, and they are violently hostile to horses. They also tear men up on sight.

A wild and fearsome griffin clutching a horse in its talons. The caption beneath this illumination in a late 12th-century bestiary gives the most common description of griffins, taken from the *Etymologies* of St Isidore of Seville, who wrote that they are particularly hostile to horses and that they also 'tear men up on sight'.

Other writers varied this last phrase slightly: according to Hugh of St Victor, the griffin 'tears men up alive and carries them off whole to its nest'. Griffins were thought to be peaceable enough among themselves, but they were so ferocious and lethal to humans that their natural habitat could only be in the wildest and most inaccessible places. Even so, there is one story, told by a writer on geography known as 'Aethicus', which describes how certain 'clever' hunters had found a rather cruel way of trapping and killing griffins. First, they set up long iron lances like tridents or three-pronged forks. Over these they built a platform of woven reeds beneath which were concealed large torches and some men ready for action:

> On the platform they put fresh, fattened joints of calves' and sheeps' meat along the dark routes by which the beasts normally fly at speed to hunt their prey. When the griffins return in the evening to the cave and their young, they spy the fresh, fat joints of meat and think of them as food for their cubs. Settling on the trap, they rejoice and flap their wings, calling to their companions to come and eat the meat. The men lying in ambush beneath set fire to the torches which quickly burst into flame, setting the pile of reeds alight with amazing force, and they crackle and are burnt up. The griffins fall down, plunging on to the red-hot lances, and are killed.

During the Middle Ages news about these fierce griffins living in distant lands began to arrive in Europe, together with actual relics of the beast. Several places found themselves the proud possessors of a griffin's egg or a claw, from which it was also said that drinking-horns could be made. Since griffins lived in such wild places and were extremely strong and dangerous, only an exceptionally brave or holy man could have acquired these specimens, and so they were believed to have spiritual or magical powers and were mounted in elaborate jewelled reliquaries. Robert the Pious, King of France (996–1031), enclosed a griffin's egg in a silver case and ordered his lesser nobles and the peasants to swear oaths upon it. No doubt this 'pious fraud', as his biographer calls it, was designed to instil in them fear of the terrible consequences of perjury. The griffin was becoming a bogeyman.

Griffins began to feature in sailors' and other travellers' tales. A huge bird called a 'griffa' attacked St Brendan and his companions on their voyage across the Atlantic. A twelfth-century Jewish traveller, Benjamin of Tudela, brought back the story that sailors in peril at sea would wrap themselves in ox-skins and then jump overboard; griffins would swoop down and carry the fake carcasses away to the desert to eat them, but once on dry land the men could kill the griffins and escape. A similar story was told of Duke Ernest of Bavaria and his friend Wetzel who escaped death from hunger and disease at sea by disguising themselves as corpses in skins;

A griffin's claw from the shrine of St Cuthbert in Durham. Since griffins were so fierce, only saints or great heroes could obtain relics of them, which were consequently highly prized for their magical or medicinal powers. This one, recorded in an inventory drawn up in 1383, is really the horn of an ibex, and the griffins' eggs, which belonged to the same treasure, were those of ostriches.

griffins carried them away as food for their young, and when the parent birds left the nest, the two men were able to climb down from the tree and travel on to the land of Arimaspia. The twelfth-century letter said to have been sent to the Greek Emperor Manuel by Prester John, a king in 'India' (that is, the Far East), described how in his kingdom there was a valley full of jewels. Men used to throw sheeps' carcasses down, and the jewels became embedded in them. Griffins would then swoop down into the valley and, as they carried the carcasses away as food, the jewels would fall out. All the jewel merchants had to do then was to pick them up from the ground.

This last story shows that the griffin is closely related to another famous bird, the rūkh (or roc), which appears several times in the *Arabian Nights*, where it is said to be so strong that it can even carry off a rhinoceros with an elephant skewered on its horn. The rūkh, a relative of the Persian simurgh, plays a leading role in the story of Sindbad the Sailor who tells how one day he found himself next to an enormous white object resembling a dome:

> I could not believe my eyes until I recalled that travellers and sailors had told me in my youth that there existed, in a far island, a bird of terrifying size called the rūkh, a bird which could lift an elephant. I concluded then that this must be a rūkh and that the white dome, at whose foot I found myself, was none other than one of its eggs.

When the great bird comes to sit on the egg, Sindbad ties himself to one of its claws with his turban. Next morning it flies off, carrying him to a valley full of jewels and snakes. As he looks round, a great joint of mutton suddenly lands with a loud slap on the rocks beside him, and he remembers a story he has heard from merchant-adventurers and explorers who had visited the diamond mountains:

> It seemed that men, who wished to take diamonds from this inaccessible valley, followed the curious practice of cutting sheep into quarters and throwing them from the top of the mountain, so that the diamonds on which they fell pierced them and became fixed in them. Soon rūkhs and mighty eagles would swoop upon this provision and carry it from the valley in their claws, to their nests in the high hills. Then the jewellers would throw themselves upon the birds, with great cries and beatings of their arms, so that they were obliged to let fall their prizes and fly away. After that the men had only to explore the quarters of meat and pick out the diamonds.

Sindbad fills his pockets and clothes with jewels, ties himself to the rūkh again, and is carried off to its nest. Just as the bird is about to devour him, a merchant arrives making a great noise; the rūkh flies away; and of course Sindbad rewards his saviour with some of the finest jewels.

Although the pagan theme of Apollo's chariot-drawing griffins had died out during the centuries of Christianity, it had survived in a different form in one of the best-known stories of medieval Europe, the Alexander romance. This was a collection of tales and legends of conquests, exploration and adventures which had grown up around the heroic figure of Alexander the Great, who had conquered half the known world in the fourth century BC.

According to these tales Alexander travelled to India, where his army was attacked and some of his men were killed by fierce flying griffins. Alexander then conceived the brilliant idea of using griffins to explore the sky. One story tells how he wrote a letter home to his mother, describing how he went up to a high mountain:

> I thought carefully about how I might build a machine so that I could go up into the sky and see if it is the very same sky which we can see.

Early 14th-century manuscript illumination showing Alexander the Great in his cage-like flying-machine, borne through the air by four griffins. The scene illustrates one of Alexander's adventures in the east when he captured some griffins and, by putting meat on poles above them, lured them into carrying him on a great flight through the sky.

Alexander flying through the sky between two griffins. The motif may derive ultimately from the ancient illustrations of the master of the griffins and of Apollo and the chariot of the sun. In the Middle Ages, Alexander's flight became an example of heroic daring but also, sometimes, of rash and presumptuous pride. Carved wooden misericord from Wells Cathedral, 1330s.

I built a machine to sit in, and I caught some griffins and tied them with chains. Then I put poles in front of them, and on the poles I put their food, and they began to fly up into the sky.

The story grew and developed, telling how the griffins, stretching up to their food, flew so high that 'the world appeared to Alexander like a little plot of baked earth on which grain is threshed; and the sea seemed to be winding all around the world like a dragon'. After this adventure, the ingenious Alexander went on to explore the depths of the sea in a glass diving-bell.

The most common illustrations of griffins in medieval manuscripts and church decorations show Alexander seated in his flying-machine between two or four griffins straining up to the food on the poles and carrying him through the air. Below him may sometimes be seen the little plot of earth surrounded by water. This is the dry land of the northern hemisphere, which in those days was the whole known world inhabited by the human race and was thought to be encircled by a great uncrossable sea, Oceanus. Because scribes sometimes mistook similar words in the manuscripts they were copying, Alexander's flying-machine is sometimes shown as a chariot, and it may have iron bars for safety; at other times, it is an iron cage or even a leather room. Although some of the details may differ, however, the main point of the story is always the same: Alexander, hero and inventor, organised an amazing exploration of the sky and cleverly managed to lure some griffins to take him up there. In this way the image of an all-conquering Pharaoh, emperor and ruler of the world absorbed several ancient motifs, and Alexander the Great took on the role of Apollo, the sun-god and Master of the Griffins.

The griffins which were tricked into carrying Alexander through the sky are not usually given any symbolic meaning in the story. In order to descend, Alexander merely points the bait downwards, and the griffins follow it back down to earth. Sometimes, however, in describing how Alexander came down again, the storytellers found a useful moral for their listeners and readers. They told how the griffins were overcome by 'a divine power' or blinded by a mist or cloud because they had flown too high; or how, as in the myth of Icarus, the sun began to burn the griffins' feathers or the 'leather' of Alexander's machine. There was even a poem which was thought to be the epitaph carved on Alexander's tomb. In this the flight is presented as a message from Alexander himself beyond the grave: the great king and world-conqueror tried to fly up with griffins to the heights of the sky; now he is down in the depths of the Underworld. The message is that pride comes before a fall, and so does greed:

> O, mankind, who will die, why do you desire to be lifted on high? Why, the more you gain, the more do you desire to possess? Everything passes away, and the flower of life also comes to an end. The higher you climb, the greater your fall from the heights to the depths.

Alexander was forced to come back down to earth because he had been too proud and presumptuous in trying to overstep the limits set upon human powers, in greedily wanting to know too much, and the griffins were the heavenly means by which his ambitious pride was limited and punished. Of course, the griffins themselves did not know what they were doing, and in the story they remain the wild, instinctive birds everyone knew them to be. Indeed, although Alexander did manage to tame them, it was not for long, for when they landed they perversely deposited him miles away, and it took him days to walk all the way back to his army.

Writers were fascinated by the tales of these fierce birds which lived in the wilderness, and some even wondered how they could fly if they were so big and heavy. By the twelfth century, the learned German nun and mystic, St Hildegard of Bingen, had collected quite a lot of 'scientific' information about the griffin. The reason why it can fly is that, though huge, it is also very swift. Partly a bird and partly a beast, it is very cunning, and although it eats people, its own meat is quite unfit for human consumption. St Hildegard had also found out some details about the griffin's egg-laying habits:

> When the time is near for it to lay its eggs, it seeks out a cave which is spacious inside but outside at the entrance is so narrow and constricted

that it can hardly get in. Inside the cave it guards its eggs carefully because it is afraid of the lion. The lion can smell them from a distance, and if it can get to them, it tramples on them and smashes them to pieces. So the griffin always watches out for the lion; it cannot stand its presence and is very wary of its strength. However, it does not mind the bear because it is weaker than the lion. It lays its eggs in a place where neither the sun's light nor the blowing of the wind can touch them.

St Hildegard concludes that the griffin is bad in both its natures, as bird and as beast, and neither its meat nor its eggs have any medicinal value at all.

Other writers reported that griffins are powerful enough to carry off a horse together with its rider, a yoke of oxen or two goats, and that they are 'strong and terrible animals', which can 'run along the ground like lions and fly through the air like birds'. The *Travels* of the so-called Sir John Mandeville describes griffins as like eagles in front, and behind as like lions, but they are stronger than eight lions and a hundred eagles. Their claws are as big as ox-horns and can be used as drinking cups, and men can make strong bows and arrows from their feathers. The English translation of the *Mirror of the World* printed by William Caxton sums up the subject. In India there are:

> grete montaynes of gold and of precyous stones and of other richesses plente. But noman dar approche it for the dragons and for the gryffons wylde which have bodyes of lyouns fleyng, whiche easily bere a man away armed and syttyng upon his hors, whan he may sease hym with his clawes and ungles [talons].

The griffin's eyes are particularly fierce and frightening, as Chaucer's Knight tells in his description of the mighty King of Thrace, whose eyes, glowing with a colour between yellow and red, have a griffin's stare.

Symbolism in the Middle Ages

The medieval griffin was a real creature of the animal world, living in far-away Scythia or India. Typically, however, some writers also looked for any symbolism it might have, trying to see if there might be some useful moral or message in its nature and behaviour. John Scotus, a ninth-century Irish writer, thought the griffin was a model of chastity in that the male would remain celibate after the death of his mate. Apart from this, however, the meanings medieval writers found were extremely negative. Basically, the griffin was thought of as greedy and cruel.

Pliny had described how griffins were greedy guardians of gold, and Solinus how they punished men driven by avarice to such a rash act as to try to wrest the gold or jewels from them. By about 1200, in England at least, some people had begun to compare the greedy aristocracy with griffins. Alexander Neckam argued against the analogy, but he was by no means defending the aristocrats. His point was that since griffins are animals, they cannot deliberately commit sins; their delight in their yellow gold is purely natural and instinctive. The nobility, on the other hand, are consciously greedy:

> Griffins dig up gold and gloat over its shining brilliance; their eyes delight in the yellow metal. If you think they are like the nobles, you are wrong: the nobles are spurred on by their greedy hunger for gold, whilst the griffins have no nagging desire for lucre but naturally rejoice in the quiet pursuit of looking.

If griffins seem to be greedy, it is not their fault for they are only animals. The truly greedy are the men who, like the Arimaspians, try to steal their gold.

A short fable by Nicolaus Pergamenus has the same message. Once there lived a tyrannical griffin who ruled a province. He banned all trade and forbade any foreigners to enter, or any of his subjects to leave, his country, while he himself lived in great comfort and luxury. When famine struck, however, the people appealed to him, and he sent ambassadors to neighbouring countries, asking for help. Because he had been so uncooperative with them, they refused. The moral of the story is: 'Beware of greed'.

From another point of view, griffins were such fierce guardians that their treasures were virtually impossible to steal. They even appeared as a warning in a sermon preached in Florence in 1305 by Brother Giordano of Pisa. In the east, said the preacher, are griffins which guard mountains of gold, and they are very strong and immeasurably fierce. 'So go there,' he told the congregation, 'go and fight with them.' The point of the sermon was that it would be useless for anyone to try to steal the griffins' gold; he would just get himself killed. From this it is clear that God, who created these invincible guardians, does not want people to seek gold but better things – that is, the spiritual treasures of Christianity.

In the Latin Bible, Moses had included the griffin in his long list of unclean birds which it is forbidden to eat. This had puzzled Origen, an early Christian writer, who had been quite unable to understand why Moses had banned eating some extremely inedible creatures, particularly since no one had ever seen or caught a griffin, let alone tried to eat one. He concluded that the Scriptures here were not to be taken literally but that the griffin and all the other unclean creatures were to be interpreted purely as symbols. So the list of unclean birds came to stand for all sorts of greedy people, thieves and robbers, gluttons and drunkards, and so on; and the griffin was the grasping ruler, the cruel tyrant, the persecutor

A powerful griffin standing on a bale of cloth, in a 14th/15th-century series of manuscripts containing the emblems of the guilds of the city of Perugia. Traditionally, griffins were frightening guardians of treasures; the griffin was also the heraldic emblem of Perugia. The message was therefore that your goods and your money are doubly safe if you trade with Perugians.

In nomine sãc in-
diuiduc trinitatis
pris et filij i sps

sãt añi. anno dñi oyillio qua
tricentesimo tertio. Indictione
vndecima tp: dñi Bonifacij.

especially of those who wanted to follow a holy life of Christian contemplation. A Bible in verse explains that the griffin, living in the far north – that is, away from the sun of charity and kindness – rejoices in killing people and so it represents 'the cruel criminality of the powerful who ferociously drink up human deaths'. The thirteenth-century theologian, St Thomas Aquinas, concluded that with the eagle, which flies up on high, Moses was forbidding the sin of pride and with the griffin, which is hostile to horses and men, he was condemning the cruelty of those in power. According to another preacher, greedy seekers after high office in the Church or in government were like grasping griffins living in the mountains.

The ancient story of the griffins' fight with the Arimaspians had survived well into the Middle Ages. As well as gold, griffins also liked jewels, particularly emeralds, which they stole away and kept safely in their nests. Visitors to Hereford Cathedral can still see the *Mappamundi*, or World Map, painted by Richard of Haldingham some time around 1300, and on it, in an area showing various savage Scythian tribes, there is the scene of a griffin facing two armed men, with the caption: 'The Arimaspians fight with griffins for emeralds'. In this story, some medieval writers saw symbolised the struggle between Christians and the devil.

The medieval lapidaries – books about the powers of precious stones – reported that the emerald, the greenest of all green things, is produced in the east from one of the rivers flowing from the Garden of Eden. It has excellent mirroring qualities and many miraculous powers, including those of improving the eyesight, protecting people from various illnesses, calming storms, wars and lustful passions, and even giving the power of prophecy. As one of the jewels of Aaron in the Old Testament and one of the foundations of the Heavenly Jerusalem in the Book of Revelation, it was interpreted as a symbol of the Christian faith. The one-eyed Arimaspians with their emeralds came to represent good Christians possessing the jewel of faith, whilst the griffins were the devils who tried to steal it from them.

A well-known book of beasts attributed to Hugh of St Victor explained the moral. Griffins are faithless, cold and lacking in charity and goodness. They stand for 'the devils who envy men the precious jewel of faith and who want to possess it and take it away from them', not because the emerald is of any use to them, but out of sheer envy. The one-eyed men symbolise those who direct their undivided attention towards God and who 'defend the grace of faith which the griffins – that is, the devils – want to take away from them'. Similarly, a dictionary and reference book written in the 1280s interpreted the name 'Arimaspians' as deriving from two words meaning 'virtue' and 'see', and so they are men who see virtuously and acutely – that is, good Christians. The emerald, which is found in the desert, symbolises Christ living in the hearts of the saints. The griffins are wicked spirits who come along and try to steal Christ away from them, but the good men, the Arimaspians, fight back. A related story also makes the griffin into a symbol of the devil who carries the soul of a sinner away to the desert of hell to feed the griffin chicks, the other devils.

Centuries later Milton took up the same theme in *Paradise Lost* when he compared the devil to a griffin in hot pursuit of his stolen gold:

> As when a gryphon through the wilderness
> With winged course o'er hill or moory dale,
> Pursues the Arimaspians, who by stealth
> Had from his wakeful custody purloined
> The guarded gold [. . .]

In the Middle Ages, therefore, when it stood for anything at all, the griffin stood for very negative things indeed: avarice, cruelty, tyranny and the devil. There is, however, one good symbolic griffin which appears in the *Divine Comedy* by the Italian poet, Dante (1265–1321). In this poem Dante describes his journey through the three realms of the afterlife, Hell (the *Inferno*), Purgatory and Paradise. The griffin appears when Dante has reached the top of the enormously high mountain of Purgatory and has entered into the Garden of Eden, a forest of blossoming trees and flowers. Across a clear, flowing stream he sees coming towards him a great procession led by seven lit candlesticks, followed by twenty-four elders and then by the four animals from the prophecy of Ezekiel and the Book of Revelation; in the space between these comes a two-wheeled chariot drawn along yoked to the neck of a griffin.

Dante's griffin is a truly spectacular creature. Its eagle parts are gold, with wings which stretch high up out of sight; the rest is white mixed with red. The procession comes to a halt, and everyone turns towards the chariot in which, amid a host of angels casting flowers around, Beatrice appears. Dante immediately feels the power of his love for this Florentine lady who had died ten years earlier and who has now come down from heaven to meet him. So the griffin, which had once drawn the chariot of the sun, now draws that of Beatrice in the triumphal procession of Love. Later, looking into the 'emeralds' of Beatrice's eyes, Dante miraculously sees the griffin's two forms of eagle and lion reflected in them. Then the procession moves to a tall, bare tree – the tree of Adam – and the griffin is praised for not having tried to steal its fruit, as Adam and Eve did. Speaking the words, 'So is preserved the seed of justice', the griffin ties the chariot to the tree which immediately puts forth leaves and blossoms of a colour between purple and red. Beautiful music lulls Dante into an ecstatic sleep, and when he awakes, the griffin and most of the other processioners have gone, ascending up to heaven.

Dante's griffin has for centuries been seen as a symbol of Christ, with the

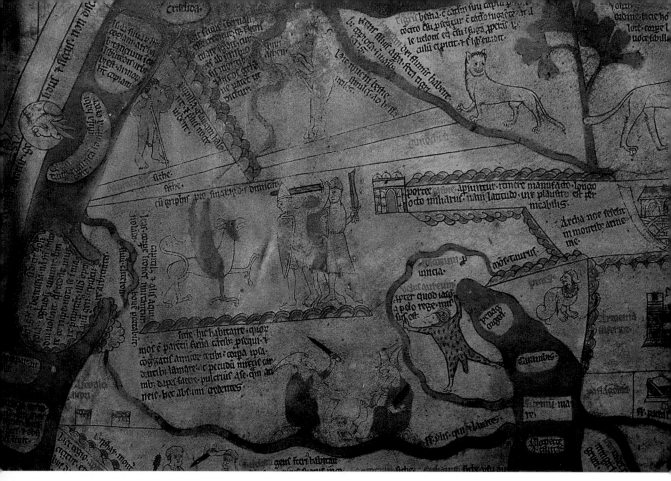

golden eagle's parts representing his divinity, the rest his flesh-and-blood humanity. For many reasons, however, this interpretation is not very convincing, and this griffin may well stand for something which for Dante was similarly a mixture of the divine and the human – the Roman Empire, which had been revived in the west first with Charlemagne's coronation in AD 800 and which still existed in Dante's day under the German emperors. Between 1310 and 1313, when the Emperor Henry VII was in Italy, Dante was filled with the hope that he would re-establish Roman peace, justice and law in the war-torn Italy of the time. The military symbol of the Roman Empire had been, and still was, the eagle; the emblem of the medieval Roman Republic was the lion. So, joining together these two symbolic creatures, Dante's griffin – potentially violent but here shown peacefully harnessed in the service of love and justice – comes to have a political rather than a theological meaning. It represents the poet's image of ideal earthly government, the perfect union of the power of the emperor (the eagle) with the power of the people (the lion). In this way, Dante's griffin has a parallel in developments taking place in England at around the same time, with the meeting of the first Parliaments, which were to lead to the present British constitution in which supreme power lies with the monarch acting in union with the representatives of the people, the Crown in Parliament.

Detail from the Hereford Cathedral *Mappamundi* (World Map), painted by Richard of Haldingham *c.* 1300, showing the fight between griffins and Arimaspians for emeralds. For some medieval writers, this ancient story symbolized the struggle between devils and Christians for the jewel of the true faith. In the upper right there is another mythical beast, the manticora, with a deceitfully honest human face and the body of a lion (see p. 175).

94

The end of the griffin?

In spite of the general belief in griffins and of the various symbolic stories which grew up around them, for centuries there had been some who doubted whether they really existed. Strabo had dubbed Aristeas, Herodotus' shadowy source, 'a charlatan, if ever there was one', and Pliny had stated outright that he thought griffins were fables. Arrian, too, one of the writers on Alexander's travels, was sceptical. He thought that the stories of the strange animals in India, including the griffins which guard gold there, had been made up for amusement rather than as a description of reality. After all, one could tell all sorts of ridiculous lies about such a distant country, and no one would be any the wiser. Whilst Alexander and his fellow-soldiers did prove some of the stories to be false, they also invented others. Origen, who had been puzzled by the mention of griffins in the Bible, had also wondered how anyone could regard Christ's miracles, described by his disciples, as pure fiction while continuing to believe in such a patently invented fable as the story of Aristeas. The so-called Aethicus tried to find a rational explanation for griffins by suggesting that they mistakenly originated in statues set up in honour of a man called Grypho who had specialised in building ships with beaked prows, known in the Middle Ages as 'griffins'.

By the mid-thirteenth century, St Albert of Cologne, a learned theologian and inquisitive observer of the natural world, had realised that no one had ever discovered or described griffins from personal experience. They appeared only in the writings of 'historians' or 'storytellers' (the two words mean the same), the descendants of Herodotus, transmitters of second-hand knowledge through the ages: 'It is books of history rather than the experiments of thinkers or rational enquiry into the physical world which hand down the information that griffin-birds exist.' St Albert's doubts were soon shown to be well founded, for missionaries and merchants were already making the journey to and from the Far East and the court of the Great Khan of the Mongol Empire, so opening up the secrets of the Eurasian landmass. On their travels they looked for the races of monstrous men and the strange beasts recorded by writers and 'historians'; they met up with foreign merchants and asked them; but no one had ever seen any of these marvels. They could not be found anywhere.

In his description of the world which he dictated in gaol to a fellow prisoner after his return to Italy, the most famous of the merchants, Marco Polo, included some information he had heard about Madagascar:

> Some merchants who have been there have told me that there are griffin-birds, which appear at certain times of the year. However, they do not have the form that people here say they have, that is, half bird and half lion, but they are like eagles and are big, as I shall now tell

you. They can pick up an elephant and carry it high up in the air, and then they drop it, and it is completely smashed to pieces, and then they feed on it. [. . .] The inhabitants of that island call this bird the rūkh, but because of its great size I believe it is the griffin-bird.

So the griffin started to become identified with its relative, Sindbad's rūkh, and to be thought of as no longer partly a lion but as an extremely large bird of prey.

For more than four thousand years the griffin had roamed the world in the art of Egypt and the Middle East, of Greece and Rome, of medieval cathedrals and manuscripts. It had been described and discussed by writers from Herodotus' highly suspect Aristeas down to the rather sceptical St Albert. As soon as Europeans began to explore the world by land, the griffin began to be consigned for ever to the history not of the world but of the imagination. It was exploration and observation by merchants, friars, crusaders, pilgrims and other travellers which led to the discarding of the medieval image of the world, with all the strange monsters and races of men created by God, and it was because of them that one of those marvels, the griffin, a creature which had never existed, was doomed to extinction.

For a century or two after them, the griffin was perhaps in something of the same position as the yeti, the abominable snowman, today. The yeti has never been proved to exist, but some people are convinced that it does and occasionally launch expeditions to find it. Similarly, the griffin, although it remained undiscovered, continued to feature in romances, adventure stories, legends of the fabulous east and travellers' tales, like those of the impostor, Mandeville. As late as 1564, at Michelangelo's funeral in Florence, the decorations illustrated the grief of the world at the artist's death by showing symbols of each of the continents. Asia was represented by the River Ganges and a griffin with a garland of jewels.

By this time, however, an educated person could afford to smile at the whole idea of griffins. The Italian poet Ariosto, writing earlier in the sixteenth century, certainly did not believe in their existence. In his poem about the great paladin Orlando, who goes mad when his beloved Angelica marries the young Medoro, Ariosto invented a creature called the hippo-griff, a rare animal from the far north, sired by a griffin and born of a mare. Ariosto is having a bit of fun here, for he was well aware that most of his readers would know their Virgil, according to whom griffins would mate with horses only in an age of miracles. Like Alexander's griffins, the hippogriff can be tamed and ridden only by a hero, and it carries the Saracen knight Ruggiero on numerous adventures round the world. Another knight Astolfo even flies it up to the earthly Paradise on his way to the moon where, among many other things lost on earth, he finds a

An episode in *Orlando Furioso*, in which the Saracen knight Ruggiero, mounted on the hippogriff, rescues the beautiful Angelica from the sea-monster. In this ironic chivalric poem by Ludovico Ariosto (1474–1533) the hippogriff is a powerful flying beast from the northern parts of Europe, sired by a griffin and born of a mare. Illustration by Gustave Doré (1832–83).

bottle labelled 'Orlando's wits', which he brings back so that he can cure the lovesick madman.

The griffin is mentioned in Shakespeare's *Henry IV, Part 1* where Hotspur complains about Glendower's superstitions:

> [. . .] sometimes he angers me
> With telling me of the moldwarp and the ant,
> Of the dreamer Merlin and his prophecies,
> And of a dragon, and a finless fish,
> A clip-wing'd griffin, and a moulten raven,
> A couching lion, and a ramping cat,
> And such a deal of skimble-skamble stuff
> As puts me from my faith.

97

However, the point here may not be so much that griffins are legendary but that someone, incredibly, has managed to clip the wings of such a rare and powerful beast. Anyone who believes in this unlikely occurrence will believe anything, however 'skimble-skamble'.

The beginning of the end for the griffin may perhaps be dated more exactly to 1518, when a Polish writer, Maciej of Miechów (known in Latin as Mathias Michovius), published a description of the northerly regions of Europe and Asia. There are no mines of gold or silver or any other metal there, he says, and so it is a pure fable that griffins and great birds guard the gold and prevent it being dug up: 'So because of this, and in contradiction of the ancient authors, I state that griffins do not exist in reality in that northern region nor in any other part of the world.' For Michovius, belief in griffins had been the result of a mix-up with the great eagles found in those countries. He also denies that there are any monstrous men there, such as those with one eye.

During the Renaissance early natural historians began to produce the first books which attempted to describe the animal world, including the many strange hybrids, from a more objective and empirical standpoint. In Ulisse Aldrovandi's *Ornithology* (1599), the griffin heads the list in the chapter on fabulous birds in which Aldrovandi gives a survey of griffins in Egyptian hieroglyphics, Apollo's griffins and writers on griffins from Herodotus to Sir John Mandeville (whom he calls a great exaggerator and liar) and Michovius. He agrees with Pliny and St Albert that griffins are merely a legend transmitted by 'historians'. They are the same as the rūkh, and Origen had no need to worry because the griffin in the Bible is nothing more than a mistranslation of the Hebrew word for a very large eagle. The so-called griffin's claws kept as relics are really the horns of an ox or buffalo. Later, in 1642, Aldrovandi's pupils published his *Monstrorum Historia* ('History of Marvellous Creatures') which puts the hybrid monsters – the griffin, the chimaera, the harpy and so on – into a chapter on images ('Simulacra'). From drawings of three Egyptian griffins, all different, it is shown that they are fabulous and that in antiquity griffins had been nothing more than symbols of Apollo, the griffin-god.

In England in 1646, Sir Thomas Browne published his book on *Popular Errors*, which included a chapter entitled 'Of Griffins':

That there are Griffins in Nature, that is a mixt and dubious Animal, in the fore-part resembling an Eagle, and behind the shape of a Lion, with erected ears, four feet and a long tail, many affirm, and most, I perceive, deny not. The same is averred by Aelian, Solinus, Mela, and Herodotus, countenanced by the Name sometimes found in Scripture, and was an Hieroglyphick of the Egyptians.

Notwithstanding we find most diligent enquirers to be of a contrary assertion. For beside that Albertus and Pliny have disallowed it, the learned Aldrovandus hath in a large discourse rejected it; Mathias Michovius who writ of those Northern parts wherein men place these Griffins, hath positively concluded against it; and if examined by the Doctrine of Animals, the invention is Monstrous, nor much inferiour unto the figment of Sphynx, Chimaera, and Harpies.

Like seventeenth-century scholars of the Old Testament, Browne goes on to interpret Moses' griffin as a mistranslation for the ossifrage, the 'breaker of bones', not the fabulous griffin but merely a very large eagle. He continues:

As for the testimonies of ancient Writers, they are but derivative, and terminate all in one Aristeus, a Poet of Proconesus; who affirmed that near the Arimaspi, or one-eyed Nation, Griffins defended the Mines of Gold. But this, as Herodotus delivereth, he wrote by hear-say; and Michovius who hath expresly written of those parts, plainly affirmeth, there is neither Gold nor Griffins in that Country, nor any such Animal extant.

Two decorative griffins on a pair of candlesticks. The ancient Greek and Roman artistic motif of griffins, usually shown in pairs, reappeared in various forms and adaptations in the neoclassical art of the late 18th and 19th centuries. English jasperware (Staffordshire), late 18th century (after a design by Sir William Chambers published in 1792).

Browne concludes that the griffin originated in Egyptian hieroglyphics and is a pure fantasy. It symbolised a guardian, its ears showing attention, its wings swiftness, its lion-like shape courage and audacity, its hooked bill hoarding and tenacity. As a combination of the two noblest animals, it stood also for bravery and so was used in heraldry. From the Egyptians, who linked it with the sun, the Greeks turned it into the bird which drew the chariot of Apollo.

Not everyone agreed. Only five years later, Alexander Ross attacked Browne and defended the ancient writers in a chapter entitled, 'What the Ancients have written of Griffins may be true'. It is not necessarily a fable that griffins hide gold in the earth, for Ross himself has seen a magpie which stole some money and hid it in a hole. In any case, he agrees with Aelian that it is not for the gold that the griffins fight but to protect their young. Maybe the Bible was referring to the ossifrage, but this could still be the griffin which is strong and fierce enough to be a breaker of bones:

> Hence then it appears, that the negative testimony of *Michovius* is not sufficient to overthrow the received opinion of the ancients concerning Griffins, especially seeing there is a possibility in Nature for such a compounded animal. For the *Gyraffe* or *Camelopardalis* is of a stranger composition, being made of the Libbard [leopard], Bufft [buffalo], Hart, and Camell. Besides, though some fabulous narrations may be added to the story of the Griffins, as of the one-ey'd *Arimaspi* with whom they fight, yet it follows not that therefore there are no Griffins. If any man say, that now such animals are not to be seen; I answer, it may be so, and yet [they have] not perished: for they may be removed to places of more remotenesse and security, and inaccessible to men: for many such places there are in the great and vast countries of Scythia and Tartaria, or Cathaia, whither our Europeans durst never, nor could venture.

Sir Thomas Browne had, however, already won the argument. Ross's suggestion that griffins (like today's yetis) might still live in some remote wilderness not yet explored by Europeans had no serious support. The griffin was doomed. A century later, Sir Richard Steele was able to make fun of the whole debate, when he wrote that he was preparing to publish two discourses: the first would be 'a learned Controversie about the Existence of Griffins', which Aldrovandi and Michovius have clearly argued out of Creation; the second was to be a treatise on sneezing.

A recent theory has suggested that the ancient belief in griffins originated with the discovery of dinosaur remains and eggs in the region of the Gobi Desert, alleged to be the part of the world once inhabited by Herodotus' Issedonians. Hence the griffin was originally the beaked Protoceratops, the clawed Mononykus or one of the early Velociraptors, the links between the dinosaurs and birds, and was extinct millions of years before it was born again in Egyptian and Mesopotamian art thousands of miles away. Certainly by the nineteenth century not only explorers but zoologists and students of fossils had clearly argued the griffin out of existence and into the realm of human fantasy. The fierce predator became reduced to a creature of fables, fairy tales and children's stories, no longer frightening but quaint and even at times rather kindly. The most famous griffin of all turns up in Lewis Carroll's *Alice's Adventures in Wonderland*, where Alice and the Queen of Hearts come across a Gryphon lying fast asleep in the sun. It takes Alice to the Mock Turtle who, after a long silence interrupted by the occasional exclamation of 'Hjckrrh!' from the Gryphon, tells the sorrowful story of his studies at school. After this, the two show Alice how to dance the Lobster Quadrille, and the Gryphon takes Alice off to the trial of the Knave of Hearts. At the end of the story, as Alice slowly wakes up, she knows that, if she opens her eyes, 'all would change to dull reality' and that 'the sneeze of the baby, the shriek of the Gryphon, and all the other queer noises would change (she knew) to the confused clamour of the busy farmyard – while the lowing of the cattle in the distance would take the place of the Mock Turtle's heavy sobs'.

Other Victorian griffins include one who guards treasure and smokes a pipe, together with his wife, the griffiness, in a fable which Bulwer Lytton tells in *The Pilgrims of the Rhine*. In Jerome K. Jerome's *Three Men on the Bummel* the friends are cycling in Germany where dog-breeders are trying to produce the strangest hybrids. At the suggestion that they might be aiming to breed a griffin, the narrator comments:

The most famous of all griffins (or 'gryphons'): 'They very soon came upon a Gryphon, lying fast asleep in the sun. (If you don't know what a Gryphon is, look at the picture.) "Up, lazy thing!" said the Queen, "and take this young lady to see the Mock Turtle."' From John Tenniel's illustrations to Lewis Carroll's *Alice's Adventures in Wonderland*, first published in 1865.

The German is extremely practical, and I fail to see the object of a griffin. If mere quaintness of design be desired, is there not already the Dachshund? What more is needed? Besides, about a house, a griffin would be so inconvenient: people would be continually treading on its tail.

That would have been the least of the inconveniences of having a griffin as a pet.

In the nineteenth century the griffin also crossed the Atlantic. In *The Great Show in Kobol-Land* by the American writer, Frank R. Stockton, there is a griffin which is expert at growing chrysanthemums and has even named one after a Miss Sophia Hypogrif, clearly his beloved (and a descendant of Ariosto's hippogriff). This is a vengeful griffin, however, who punishes the young Prince Atto by taking him on a great and terrifying flight through the air, thrilling the assembled crowd. It was Stockton too who, in *The Griffin and the Minor Canon*, inspired by a visit to Chester Cathedral, told of the sad death of the last griffin left alive. From his home in the wilderness the griffin flies to a town to see a great stone statue of himself carved hundreds of years before and put up over the church door. This griffin eats only at the equinoxes, and when he is angry or excited, his barbed tail glows red hot and needs to be cooled in a stream. He is befriended by the Minor Canon, but as the autumn equinox and the griffin's mealtime approach, the frightened townsfolk persuade the Minor Canon to leave, in the hope that the griffin too will go away. The griffin takes over his friend's class of the most unruly schoolchildren and achieves excellent results, but when he learns what has happened, he tears down the stone griffin and carries it off to his cave. He finds the Minor Canon and returns him to town. Then he goes back into the wilderness, where, refusing his equinoctial meal and looking at his statue, he pines away and dies. Of this story, with its selfish and cowardly townsfolk, the appropriately named Martin I. J. Griffin, Stockton's biographer, remarks that it is 'as thoroughgoing an indictment of herd-fear and herd-malice as we have in American literature'.

In Vachel Lindsay's poem 'Yet gentle will the griffin be (*What Grandpa Told the Children*)', the griffin has become a fantasy creature of the sky, entirely harmless. Tomorrow night, when it hatches out from its egg, the moon, the little boys and girls will see it walk up to lap the Milky Way, like a cat.

So the griffin has become a creature of fables and stories for children – and all because it had the misfortune never to have existed. It was a cruel and humiliating fate for this once mighty and terrifying beast. But is it really extinct? Might it not still exist in exactly the same place where it was born five thousand years ago? In fact, all that has happened to the griffin is that it has left Herodotus and the 'historians', the elusive Aristeas and the poets, and has joined the history of the human imagination, to be replaced today by science fiction monsters, by all those strange creatures and beings which inhabit distant planets, stars and galaxies and come into contact with today's Alexanders, the astronaut explorers. These too are as alive as the griffin once was, in what is both an imaginary universe and a believable image of the real universe. Moreover, as in the Middle Ages, writers today often project social or moral problems and values upon them. Occasionally, extraterrestrial beings provide positive images of innocence, peace or friendship, but more commonly they are hostile, destructive forces, tyrants, space invaders, against whom the heroes must fight for the precious gold and jewels of, say, freedom or democracy or one-eyed Arimaspian capitalism. As once the griffin, so too today is the creature from outer space both a credible myth of the unknown and a symbol representing one side – the other side – in the never-ending conflict between 'good' and evil.

Sphinxes

The sphinx, a creature with a human head and a lion's body, is one of the unmistakable symbols (with obelisks, pyramids and the ubiquitous lotus plant) of ancient Egypt. Though there is equally early evidence for the monster in Asia Minor, dating to the end of the third millennium BC, Egypt is perceived to be its true birthplace. Once established in a form which was male, magnificent, threatening, representative of pharaonic power and prestige, the sphinx changed very little, except in detail, throughout the dynastic period, probably because of the essentially unchanging nature of Egyptian civilisation during which fixed forms in art were upheld, the view being that having created something so pleasing in the first place, it was impossible to improve it by much. Even when the human head was replaced by that of an animal or a bird, such as the ram sacred to the god Amun (a criosphinx) or the falcon sacred to Horus (a hierocosphinx), the general impression remained very much the same.

The Great Sphinx

The Great Sphinx at Giza is not only the earliest complete sphinx (except for a small limestone example found at Abu Rawash nearby) but the largest and best known. It also diverged from the canon of proportions so strictly established and afterwards adhered to by Egyptian artists and craftsmen as early as the Old Kingdom (2575–2134 BC) in that its head is far smaller in relation to the length of its body and its front paws are more extended. This may be because it was a prototype and the form had not yet been perfected, but it may also be because geological constraints – a large fissure in the sandstone from which it was carved – forced an extension of the back of the beast. At the time it was carved, however, in its place in the pyramid complex, it would have been viewed from the front beyond

The Great Sphinx at Giza in about 1880, mostly buried in sand, which was cleared during 1885–6. Tuthmosis IV (1400–1390 BC) was the first to record restoration of the Sphinx, and others followed including two emperors as far apart as Nero (54–68) and Napoleon, who rediscovered the Sphinx in 1798. The first proper scientific investigation began in 1926 under Emile Baraize, whose findings have never been published and are now apparently lost.

the Sphinx Temple and to the right of the causeway leading to the pyramid of Khephren, so its abnormally long body would have been mostly obscured. The Great Sphinx is 240ft (73.8m) long and its face is over 13ft (4m) wide. It may have been sculpted during the reign of Radjedef (2528–2520 BC), the successor to Khufu, builder of the Great Pyramid, or slightly later during the reign of Radjedef's successor, Khephren (2520–2494 BC). People have seen a facial resemblance between the Great Sphinx and Khephren, but such judgments are obviously subjective.

There are no Old Kingdom texts which mention the Sphinx and its exact significance remains unclear. The temple that lay directly in front of it was robbed of its facing stones during antiquity and these might have had texts carved upon them with perhaps some explanation of the Sphinx. Presumably the original idea of the composite monster was to ally the superior intelligence of a man to the superior power of an animal, thus creating a hybrid that was invincible, being both wise and strong. There is a further element in that specific facial features could be modelled for the beast, thus making it a recognisable individual, invariably a king or god. Then to the tensed power of a lion ready to spring was added the awesome aura of a specific king or deity. The Great Sphinx at Giza, if it represented Khephren, doubtless induced his own particular dread into the hearts of onlookers. Whatever the message of royal propaganda the Great Sphinx conveyed, it was certainly emphasised by its colossal size.

The egyptologist Alan Gardiner believed there were four possible ways in which an Egyptian sphinx could be interpreted: 1) as the king in the image of a lion; 2) as a god in the image of a lion; 3) as a victorious king manifesting himself in the leonine form of a god; and 4) as a powerful god revealed in the dreaded person of the king. It is of course possible that more than one of these categories could apply to each and every Egyptian sphinx and the ancient Egyptians themselves may have changed their opinions about individual sphinxes at different times.

Strangely enough, Herodotus, one of the earliest travellers to Egypt (c. 450 BC) does not mention the Sphinx, though he provides a certain amount of information about the kings who built the three great pyramids at Giza. Pliny (AD 77) mentioned both: 'In front of these pyramids is the Sphinx, a still more wondrous object of art, but one upon which silence has been observed, as it is looked upon as a divinity by the people of the neighbourhood.' The colossal statue, like the pyramids, still stands, albeit a little damaged, but still magnificent in size and concept. It is couchant, its front legs extended and parallel, and its back legs folded underneath its powerful body. On its head it wears the *nemes*-headcloth with the *uraeus* (serpent symbol) at the front. It has a false beard, most of which is missing. Its tail is not visible, though it would doubtless be wound round its haunch. The expression is fixed and the overall impression is one of stillness, tension and power.

After the end of the Old Kingdom, at some time during the First Intermediate Period, the area of Giza and the Sphinx itself were abandoned, and it was not until the start of the Eighteenth Dynasty (1550–1307 BC) that the Sphinx once more came to life. Amenophis II (1427–1401 BC) built a temple dedicated to the Sphinx and his son, Tuthmosis IV, left a stela between the front paws of the beast to commemorate the works of restoration and sand clearance he had done. There are too a number of stelae of private individuals attesting to a cult of the Sphinx. It was at this time that it began to be worshipped as a manifestation of the god Horus, Horemakhet, or Horus-in-the-Horizon, and this cult lasted until as late as Roman times.

Egypt and beyond

The Middle Kingdom (2040–1640 BC), separated from the Old Kingdom by a period of disunity called the First Intermediate Period, brought in a span of stability, prosperity and high civilisation. There are plenty of sphinxes dating to this period, mainly couchant as Old Kingdom sphinxes are, but some now have front feet with claws or even human hands so that they can clutch offerings, sometimes in the form of a rounded bowl. The wig has become very stylised, falling first to the shoulder and then on to the chest between the front paws to the baseline. There is also evidence for female attributes, without going as far as a true female sphinx: some wigs descend to the chest with large looped curls with emphasised terminals, suggesting nipples. From Tanis come strange sphinxes with human faces, but with lion ears and a realistic mane. For the first time, sphinxes acquire identifiable expressions on their faces. Since Middle Kingdom kings had to show their might, those expressions are grim and intimidating, kings portrayed as ruthless overlords. The diorite sphinx of Senwosret III (1878–1841 BC), now in the Metropolitan Museum in New York, is one of the finest examples of this.

Across the Mediterranean to the north and west, sphinxes did not often appear either in monumental contexts or colossal manifestations, but more often on cylinder seals and amulets. In Syria, sphinxes were less popular than griffins or lions. Their form was not fixed at any time, and tended to alter without any significance which can be easily interpreted. In the second millennium, their iconography was oriental: they wear headdresses, are winged (wings being the attributes of monsters), and are usually passant, with one paw raised, moving either to right or left in a somewhat menacing fashion, in contrast to a true Egyptian sphinx which was menacing from a static, crouching position. They can also be seated and either bearded or beardless. In the Twelfth Dynasty in Egypt, contacts with north Syria increased. Ita, the daughter of Amenemhet II (1929–1892 BC), sent from Egypt and dedicated to a local goddess at Qatna a pair of true Egyptian sphinxes, and Amenemhet III (1844–1797 BC) sent another pair to guard the entrance to the temple of Baal at Ras Shamra (Ugarit). As a result of closer links, sphinxes now became more familiar, and thus egyptianising motifs more evident. Though sphinxes continued to be winged, passant or even rampant, they were now sometimes couchant, with proper Egyptian wigs, winged sun-disks and Egyptian-style crowns, (e.g. *atef*-crowns with plumes), and their tails were often correctly wound over their haunches instead of describing a big loop in mid-air. In turn, the influence of Syrian-type winged sphinxes spread back to Egypt.

A Syrian female sphinx type was evident from the late second millennium, characterised by two curling spiral locks. This feature may also have

travelled back to Egypt (where female sphinxes remained uncommon) but
certainly travelled eastwards, to Hittite stone sculpture, and is frequently
seen on ivories of Syrian and Phoenician origin found at such sites as
Carchemish and Nimrud, when this type of female sphinx often wears a
ceremonial necklace.

Foreign influences and natural progression both played a part in the
innovations of wings to sphinxes and the portrayal of queens as sphinxes
which developed during the Egyptian New Kingdom (1550–1070 BC).
Egyptian winged sphinxes always look distinctly Egyptian: they are usually couchant, wear an orthodox red, white or (occasionally) blue crown,
and the wing is usually folded along the side of the beast so as not to alter
the integrity of the shape, though it could be raised. There is a fine example
of a standing sphinx with folded wing on the inner panel of a chariot
found in the tomb of Tuthmosis IV by Howard Carter in 1903. This is a
good example too of how New Kingdom Egyptian sphinxes were less
muscle-bound, and look rather more feline and supple. This was also the
period at which sphinxes were used to flank the great processional avenues
of the temples of Luxor and Karnak.

Statues of queens as sphinxes remained rare. Tuthmosis III had his wife
portrayed as a beardless sphinx, and queen Tiy, the wife of Amenophis
III, was portrayed in a warlike scene of enemies being trampled beneath
the feet of a beardless sphinx. It may not be a coincidence that these
instances occur at a time when Egyptian kings were allying themselves
with notable women: Amenophis III, for instance, married two – Tiy, as

Drawing (by Howard
Carter) of a panel from a
chariot of Tuthmosis IV
(1400–1390 BC) showing
a rampant winged
sphinx trampling hirsuit
enemies depicted in the
symbolic grovelling
pose and alien apparel of
captives from the Near
East. The sphinx wears
the *atef*-crown with two
pendant *uraei* to either
side, the *nemes*-
headcloth with ram's
horns curled round the
ears, false beard and a
garment with lappets
over the front legs. The
one visible wing is
folded along the flank.

mentioned above, and a Mitanni princess, Gilu-Hepa. His son Amenophis IV (Akhenaten) married Nefertiti. That they were beardless was doubtless a reference to their femininity and role as consorts. Earlier in the same dynasty, Queen Hatshepsut (1473–1458 BC), given to having herself portrayed in full male royal regalia, had herself sculpted as a male sphinx in red granite, complete with false beard. Nonetheless the face has a certain sweetness of expression, and the cheeks are softly rounded.

Queen as male sphinx. Fragments of this red granite sphinx of Queen Hatshepsut (1473–1458 BC) were found at the site of her funerary complex at Deir el-Bahri. It was one of probably six that formed an avenue which was destroyed during the reign of her successor, Tuthmosis III (1479–1425 BC). Despite the beard, the male sphinx has an unmistakably feminine face with a broad forehead, a narrow chin and a finely chiselled nose.

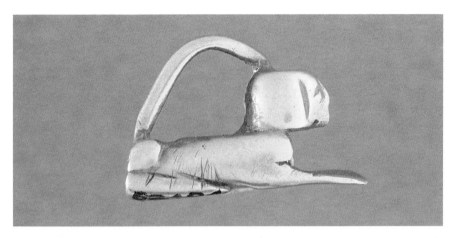

Funerary amulet in the shape of a sphinx. Its owner doubtless hoped that it would be imbued with the power and authority of the king himself, and therefore by association provide its wearer with royal protection in the afterlife. From el-Mustagidda in Middle Egypt, First Intermediate Period (2134–2040 BC).

It would be wrong to think of Egyptian sphinxes only in monumental contexts. They were a popular decorative motif at all periods and appear on small objects, such as beads, amulets and small bronzes. The earliest sphinx amulet is probably from the First Intermediate Period, and is made of gold. It is couchant, with its back legs folded beneath its body. Its tail is curved over its back to join the top of its wig in order to form the loop from which it was hung. Other small objects of this type found in Egypt are undoubtedly Syrian in origin: for example, a black haematite cylinder seal dating to roughly 2000–1500 BC found at the ancient capital of Nubia, Napata, in 1914. It shows clear egyptianising influence with a sun-disk and rampant winged sphinx. One paw is raised as if in salute, while the other rests on the level of its back haunches. Its tail describes an S-shape. It is both wigged and bearded. From the Second Intermediate Period (1640–1532 BC) comes a small ivory sphinx holding between its front paws a human victim. The sphinx probably represents a Hyksos king with his Egyptian captive. Though found at Abydos in Egypt, this ivory is undoubtedly also Syrian in style and probably manufacture.

A fine example of a Syrian egyptianising sphinx found at Damascus in the ancient kingdom of Aram dates to the ninth to tenth centuries BC. The basalt slab on which it was carved was re-used in the north enclosure wall of the later Hellenistic sanctuary and thus its original placing is not known. It is possible that it once faced another identical sphinx and they may have fulfilled roles as guardians and protective figures. This sphinx is passant and faces left. He is unique in that his striding muscular legs reveal his sex quite clearly. Both his wings are raised and visible; a line marked parallel to the outer edge divides muscle from feathers, though the latter are not defined. His tail curves upwards and away from his body in an S-shape. The egyptianising features are remarkable: the sphinx wears the double crown of Upper and Lower Egypt, albeit somewhat flattened for spatial reasons, and his wig, profile and false beard all look truly Egyptian. He

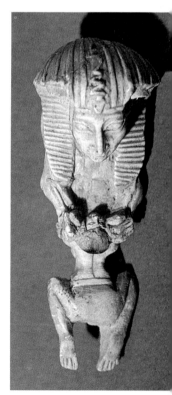

Powerful striding winged sphinx probably from the Adad temple at Damascus built by King Hazael (*c.* 842–798 BC). Hazael had established powerful trading links with Tyre, and ivories found at his palace site at Arslan Tash (ancient Khadatu) in northern Syria are similar in style. The kilt depicted between the front legs, the long false beard with curved point and the flattened egyptianised crowns are characteristic of Phoenician workmanship in the 9th–8th centuries BC and similar to examples on the gold cups found at Mount Ida in Crete (see illustration p. 117).

LEFT Perhaps once the handle to a box, this small ivory object shows the head and front paws of a sphinx, between which struggles his prisoner – a rare example of a sphinx in action, unlike most Egyptian sphinxes who adopt a static pose. The style and workmanship indicate a Syrian origin. From Abydos in Middle Egypt, Second Intermediate Period (1640–1532 BC).

even wears a schematic form of kilt, defined by a line on his back and by an apron shape falling to his feet at the front. A much cruder and perhaps earlier example, probably dating to about 1000 BC, can be seen at the Syrian site of 'Ain Dara, some 40 miles (70km) north-west of Aleppo, a site at which excavations have only recently been resumed and which may reveal much more of interest. The entrance to a large temple there was guarded in antiquity by a pair of colossal winged sphinxes, in profile, but with their massive heads facing forwards so as to make eye contact with anyone crossing the courtyard towards the entrance they guarded. The sphinx to the right is better preserved and shows a wig ending in Hathor locks, an elaborate breastplate and raised muscled and feathered wing. The facade of the temple was also decorated with lions and sphinxes. The execution of the colossal sphinx is powerful though rather naive, reminiscent of those found in central Turkey.

A somewhat later and most unusual example of a bronze weight in sphinx shape dating to the mid-eighth century BC came from the Syrian kingdom of Hamath which lay north of Aram, traversing the Orontes. Hamath is described in the Book of Amos as 'the great', but it was overrun by Sargon II in 720 BC and has disappeared. The exact provenance of the sphinx is unknown. It is couchant with its back legs folded beneath its body in Egyptian fashion. Its tail is unusual: it curves over and lies flat against its back, exactly between its two haunches. Its head faces forward and it wears a flat cap from which falls hair from a centre parting, dividing into six heavy dreadlocks descending to the shoulder. The edge of a garment is just discernible on the chest. Underneath it bears a short inscription in Aramaean: '2 sicles of Hamath' (about ½oz/15g).

The sphinx was certainly also known in Palestine. The First Book of Kings states that Solomon called upon Hiram, the King of Tyre, to send his servants to work upon his Temple at Jerusalem: 'And the king commanded, and they brought great stones, costly stones, and hewed stones, to lay the foundation of the house. And Solomon's builders and Hiram's builders did hew them, and the stonesquarers: so they prepared timber and stones to build the house' (1 Kings 5: 17–18). Tyre was a major craft centre and had long been familiar with and inspired by the work of Egyptian craftsmen. From the descriptions of the Temple's decorations, it seems that egyptianising themes were used, in particular a monster known to the Hebrews as the *kerub*, or cherub. Twin cherubim decorated the mercy-seat in the Tabernacle with outspread touching wings (1 Kings 6:27). In the house of Pharaoh's daughter there were pillars, designed personally by Hiram who 'came to king Solomon, and wrought all his work', on which there was 'lily work' and borders of 'lions, oxen and cherubim'. It sounds like an Egyptian design, appropriate to its owner (1 Kings 7). The prophet Ezekiel, banished into captivity where he doubtless encountered Syrian sphinxes, had a vision of the Temple Restored, with different sorts of cherubim, some familiar from the Egyptian repertoire: 'And every one had four faces: the first face was the face of a cherub, and the second face was the face of a man, and the third the face of a lion, and the fourth the face of an eagle' (Ezekiel 10:14).

Western Asia and the Mediterranean

Further east, in Mesopotamia, sphinxes are known from the first half of the third millennium from cylinder seals. Later on, they are seen on ivories, and in the first millennium there are giant human-headed winged lions (and bulls) which flanked the entrances to kings' palaces. These standing monsters, with five legs visible so that their massive power is constant whether they are seen from the front or from the side, do of course conform to the definition of a sphinx as a human-headed lion, but it is an idiosyncratic Assyrian interpretation of the form, and since its nearest relation is the human-headed winged bull, which does not conform, they are together classified as lamassu in the Glossary at the end of this volume. There are some bronze, couchant, human-headed, winged lions which have more recognisably egyptianising features. They usually have their front legs folded beneath their chests, face sideways, are bearded and wear not only crowns but also girdles round their flanks and sometimes have an elaborate pattern, suggesting armour or heavy embroidery, over their chests and extending down their folded front legs.

The Assyrian word for these human-headed winged lions in the palace of Sennacherib (704–681 BC) at Nineveh was *apsasātu*, a feminine plural of the word *apsasû*, which the Chicago Assyrian Dictionary defines as 1) an exotic bovine or 2) a stone or copper colossus in animal shape. It concludes that the various references to *apsasātu* in the palaces of Sennacherib and his son, Esarhaddon, '. . . probably describe a mythological animal, perhaps a sphinx'. The use of the feminine gender is interesting. The word was used only during the reigns of Sennacherib and Esarhaddon. Before that, human-headed winged lions appeared to be male. It may be

Winged human-headed lion found in the south-west palace at Nimrud by Austen Henry Layard. One of a pair which framed the entrance to a chamber, the couchant beardless monster, with raised wings, carved from an alabaster block about 5 ft (1.5m) square, collapsed into fragments shortly after discovery. Luckily an accurate drawing had already been made. Note the ornamental flat crown, with horns.

that these female colossi were inspired by examples in palaces at Sakcegözü and Zincirli in northern Syria, a region in which both they (and earlier) Assyrian kings were interested.

On cylinder seals, there is a fine example of a bearded standing sphinx on a serpentine cylinder seal dating to before 2000 BC, now in the collection of the British Museum. Other early examples are from the Dynasty of Akkad (2334–2154 BC) and the Third Dynasty of Ur (2112–2095 BC). These sphinxes are also passant, and face right. From the First Dynasty of Babylon (1894–1595 BC) there is a tablet dating from year 9 of Ammi-saduqa (1646–1626 BC) depicting a winged sphinx. The famous fresco in the palace of Zimri-Lim of Mari (1779–1747 BC) showed a multi-coloured winged sphinx (one wing is raised), bearded and wearing a feathered tiara, in the company of a griffin and a bull. Marching majestically forward, it does not look Egyptian. Two seals which were probably from a workshop at Byblos, and which were more or less contemporary (c. 1800–1750 BC) do show Egyptian influence, unsurprising perhaps in view of that city's trading connections with Egypt since earliest antiquity. But as Mesopotamia had always had its own gods, demons and traditions, it had little incentive to adopt motifs from elsewhere, however appealing. Examples of sphinxes from Mesopotamia generally are not plentiful at any period.

At the site of Tell Nimrud (Kalhu, biblical Calah), the first-millennium capital city of Ashurnasirpal II (883–859 BC), many thousands of pieces of carved ivory have been found, particularly in the excavations made by W. K. Loftus in the south-east palace and by A. H. Layard in the north-west palace during the last century, and by M. E. L. Mallowan in the 1950s. Most of the pieces had come to Nimrud in the royal collection or as booty gathered on victorious campaigns to the east. Though some were earlier, most date to the first millennium and were mainly plaques used to decorate furniture, chariots and ceremonial harness. A great many show unmistakable Egyptian influence, and quite a few depict sphinxes, as a miniature and purely decorative device.

From the finds in the south-east palace there emerged several representations of female sphinxes, winged lionesses with the heads of women. Their hair was in a spiral lock, in one case neatly held by a band or fillet and, in two others, capped with a hat with a drooping point to which was attached a band, perhaps leather, tied in a bow above that point. There is also an example of a passant ram-headed sphinx with wings outstretched, bearing no resemblance to anything found in Egypt, though its derivation must be a true Egyptian criosphinx dedicated to the god Amun. (Similar examples of this type were found at the site of Arslan Tash in Anatolia.)

In the Layard group of finds from the north-west palace there are several fine representations of sphinxes, one beardless winged variety with true Egyptian iconography including pectoral and crown, and a unique rep-

Drawing from an impression of the cylinder seal of king Saushtatar of Mitanni (*c.* 1450 BC) showing an upright female sphinx with forepaws and feathered wings outstretched to either side. She holds two lions suspended. The sphinx wears a characteristic flat helmet with spiral lock emerging at the back, and has an attenuated neck and a short plaited tail, which may be the twisted edge of some tasselled garment worn over the upper part of the body.

resentation of a facially full-frontal sphinx. Its round and placid visage gazes straight forward at the spectator, above outstretched wings under which crouch two vultures devouring a goat upon which the front feet of the sphinx rest. The feet look curiously like birds' claws, as does its pouting chest, which has been carved to look as though covered in feathers.

There are only a very few examples of sphinxes from the Kassite Dynasty. Their impact is therefore limited, though, in the examples we have, these sphinxes reflect the attributes of figures on seals, specifically conical bonnets and beards. Their significance is apparently not great, the sphinx being interchangeable with other animals as a companion of human figures.

Ivories found at Megiddo in what is now northern Israel are clearly Egyptian in influence and produce many familiar motifs, such as winged sun-disks, lotus flowers and of course sphinxes, and have some accurate and specific detail of *nemes*-headcloths and *atef*-crowns.

The second half of the second millennium saw the rise and fall of empires to the east. Cultural influences were exchanged with such readiness that few conventions were static in the depiction of sphinxes. From Mitanni, the second-millennium Hurrian kingdom lying north of the Euphrates, there are winged and non-winged sphinxes and they are couchant or seated. These sphinxes look generally oriental as they wear turbans or flat skull-caps, and more particularly they seem Mitannian: they resemble the people who are depicted on Mitannian seals, with their long pointed noses, full lips and receding chins. The sphinxes have a characteristic short tail, suggesting that of a dog. Their claws are well defined. They are not aesthetically pleasing. The seal of Saushtatar of Mitanni (*c.*1450 BC) depicts a rampant female sphinx, human-headed and winged, with two reversed lions suspended from her outstretched wings.

The Middle Minoan period in Crete was one of high civilisation which had a wide network of contacts to the east. There is evidence that both Egyptian and Syrian types of sphinx were known there. The former show familiar egyptianising motifs, *atef*-crowns and the red crown of Lower Egypt, and the second orientalising type is perhaps best illustrated on a green jasper signet seal found by Arthur Evans. The wingless sphinx is couchant, has an upwardly curving beard and tresses that stream out behind its head. It has one large eye in the middle of its cheek. Another remarkable prismatic stone from Siteia shows a standing non-winged sphinx with all four feet visible. It has two horns protruding from its flowing hair which descends to its shoulder. It has one peculiar feature: it is poking out its tongue. The influence for this is hard to trace. The horns are ram's horns but they are not egyptianising as found on criosphinxes. On the other hand, the poked-out tongue may be a confusion with an Egyptian false beard. Later on, in the Middle Minoan III period, sphinxes acquire special Cretan characteristics – wings decorated with an 'adder mark', and bordered with spirals on the upper part, spirals on the chest, a plumed diadem – and are occasionally found galloping forward. But sphinxes were never as popular as griffins, and it is not clear what significance they had. Bronze fragments of a goblet found in a grotto on Mount Ida depict sphinxes with unmistakable Egyptian characteristics, though it probably came from a Phoenician site and probably dates to the seventh century, parallel to the Twenty-sixth Dynasty in Egypt. Both sphinxes wear the double crown and are winged, one with both wings raised behind its head, the other with one raised either side of its head. The former has an S-shaped tail and false beard, the latter a tail looped over its haunches and no beard. The fragments also depict papyrus plants, scarabs and winged falcons.

From Cyprus, examples of sphinxes are even more rare. There is a cylinder seal depicting a sphinx facing left before a seated goddess. Its wing is represented by a few oblique strokes. It wears a skullcap from which a single curled lock emerges at the back. Its tail is raised. It is oriental rather than Egyptian. From the site of Enkomi in eastern Cyprus there is a gold diadem and pectoral, both embossed with orientalising winged sphinxes. The diadem has an embossed repeated motif of sixteen seated sphinxes wearing elaborate headdresses. The pectoral shows two standing winged sphinxes on either side of a sacred tree. A remarkable ivory plaque (originally placed between the arms and seat of a royal throne) found at the nearby site of Salamis and dating to the end of the eighth century BC,

ABOVE Impression of a clay nodule found in a Mycenaean house at Kato Zakro in East Crete, dating to *c.* 1800–1600 BC. Of the 500 or so found, about eighty could be classified as monsters, with several sphinxes. Some have egyptianising tendencies (though all are winged), but this one suggests later Greek sphinxes. Facing front, but with head turned to the left, this sphinx wears a cap with a diadem familiar from other Cretan contexts, and has feline feet, rounded breasts and large frilled wings. The strands of hair emerging from the cap are reminiscent of another sphinx depicted on a seal found at Knossos dating to the same period.

RIGHT Rims of two complete bowls found in a grotto at Mount Ida in Crete, bearing distinct resemblances to egyptianising ivories from Nimrud and Arslan Tash. They undoubtedly originated in a Phoenician workshop and date to the 9th–8th centuries BC. The upper sphinx stands with both feathered wings raised behind, wears the double crown of Upper and Lower Egypt, and has a false beard. The lower sphinx, also standing, has a feathered wing raised to each side of the head, is beardless and wears an eccentric version of the white crown of Upper Egypt. Both sphinxes are surrounded by egyptianising motifs.

shows a true egyptianising sphinx of a type very familiar from ivories found at Nimrud, and is almost certainly of Phoenician workmanship. The sphinx wears the double crown of Upper and Lower Egypt, and is surrounded by lotus buds. It is standing, with raised wing, and wears the *nemes*-headcloth and schematic Egyptian kilt, falling between its front paws in an apron shape.

Squat Hittite sphinxes are splendid creatures; in concept if not manufacture they are worthy of the best sort of monumental Egyptian sphinx. Though for the most part their execution is clumsy, they have a primitive, solid charm, with docile expressions. Fine examples have been discovered at Bogazköy in middle Anatolia and from the site of Alaca Hüyük where they acted as colossal guardians on the main city gates. Despite relations, at different times friendly and hostile, with Egypt, the Egyptian influence is minimal. The horned helmets worn by these sphinxes are Mesopotamian, and their role as guardians is more akin to that of winged bulls and lions guarding temples and ziggurats along the banks of the Tigris and the Euphrates than the Nile.

Greece

Probably through cultural influences from the east, Syria and Phoenicia, the orientalising sphinx arrived in Greece about the eighth century BC, though there is some evidence on gemstones for an earlier version of the monster from Bronze Age Crete. Sphinxes began to appear in funerary contexts and as votive offerings within a temple complex; in both cases they were winged and were usually female, though a few were male. As grave markers, they acted as guardians and protectors of the dead. They often stood on top of stelae, facing the spectator – that is, with the face turned fully sideways. They were seated, and at first had a solid, somewhat lifeless look with the front part of the hind legs firmly attached to the baseline, but later in the sixth century such strict stylisation gave way to a more natural pose with the hind legs partly lifted. They were found in conjunction with graves primarily in Attica, though the practice spread to Corinth and later on to Sicily. Votive sphinxes looked forward and were usually placed on top of columns. Sphinx-topped column monuments were erected in several locations. Both types of sphinxes were at their most popular during the Archaic period, the seventh and sixth centuries BC. The best-known examples after this are the Nereid Monument from Xanthos (now in the British Museum) which has a winged sphinx between two springing lions and dates from the early fourth century BC, and the Naxian Sphinx at Delphi which stood atop an Ionic capital, and may once have been 33ft (10m) high, dating to about 560 BC. There was also the colossal statue of Athena Parthenos (c. 440 BC) whose helmet was adorned with sphinxes, though this was purely for decorative reasons.

Sphinxes were popular as a decorative motif on vases also, particularly during the middle proto-Corinthian period (690–650 BC). They appeared in a variety of guises: Corinthian sphinxes often wore the *polos* (head-dress), while Ionian sphinxes were invariably bare-headed and were usually shown seated. They could be either male or female. They frequently had a somewhat sinister significance: early reliefs from Mycenae show sphinxes carrying off fallen warriors from the field of battle, and there are scenes of sphinxes pouncing on humans. Orientalising human-headed lions were only one of several Greek monsters and demons popular in legend and hearsay, several of whom were female. They did not seem to have had an identifying name until the legend of Oedipus was first recorded (c. 700 BC) when the vengeful female creature described was specifically named the 'sphinx'. The word sphinx then became inseparable from the object, though it came to apply to sphinxes of either sex. The origin of the word is not known, though it is proposed that the etymology comes from the Egyptian *šsp'nh* ('living image'), which, when followed by a determinative depicting a sphinx, is usually translated as such. At the end of the sixth century, to people growing more sophisticated, stories concerning monsters became generally less interesting than those about human conflicts, and the sphinx began to lose its appeal as a decorative motif also.

Hesiod, in the eighth century BC, was the first poet to write about a sphinx, and to provide a genealogical history. It was the incestuous offspring of Echidna, half-woman, half-serpent and mother to Orthos by whom she bore the Sphinx, who was sent by Hera as a punishment for the homosexual rape of Chrysippus by Laius, King of Thebes. This Sphinx was the famous setter of riddles who wreaked terrible vengeance on those who failed to solve her puzzles, and her victims included Haemon, son of Creon, who was carried away and eaten. Eventually, of course, Oedipus solved the riddle of what animal walked on four legs in the morning, two at noon and three in the evening. (Answer: man, who walked on his hands and feet when young, in the noon of his life on two legs and, in the evening of his days, supporting himself upon a staff.) The Sphinx dashed her head against a rock and immediately expired, or alternatively was killed by Oedipus. According to later accounts by Sophocles (c. 496–406 BC) and Euripides (c. 485–406 BC), the Sphinx was sent by Apollo, whose shrine at Delphi was decorated with votive sphinxes. At the same time as the Sphinx's legend grew in literature, her image changed from straightforward man-eating marauding monster to something more subtle. In the sixth century she became riddle-setting and wise, and in the fifth she assumed the form so familiar from Renaissance times: full-breasted with ringlets cascading from a knot on the top of her head, a still and enigmatic figure with a beautiful face who fulfilled Euripides' description of a wise virgin who sang her riddle.

The Roman Empire

The great dynastic era of Egypt ended in 332 BC when the country was overrun by Alexander the Great. His own presence there was short-lived (though he did have himself sculpted as a sphinx); it fell to his successor, Ptolemy I Soter I, into whose hands Egypt passed in the division of the empire in 323, to realise Alexander's grand scheme for a major seaport on the Mediterranean. Alexandria soon became not only a thriving polyglot community of Egyptians, Greeks and Jews but also a centre of learning, with its famous library, and of the religious cult of the goddess Isis and her consort/brother Serapis (the hellenistic successor to the Egyptian god Osiris). This cult spread quickly to other populated centres of the time: to Cyprus, Sicily, the coast of Asia Minor, the Greek islands and to mainland Greece itself. The cult was already known in Rome, but when Egypt became a province of that imperial power after 30 BC, it became paramount. Partly because of association with the cult, and also because they

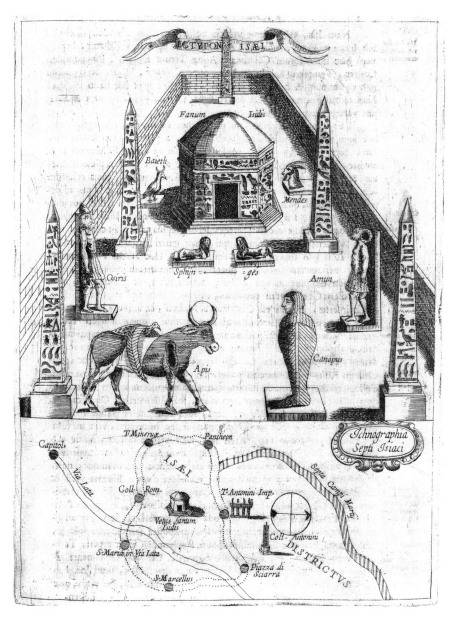

Imaginary reconstruction by Athanasius Kircher (from *Obelisi Aegyptiaca*, 1666) of the Iseum Campense in Rome as it was in the first century AD. It shows the entrance to the Isis Temple itself, flanked by two guardian sphinxes, though they look rather small and ineffectual in the context. The original building contained an Eighteenth Dynasty, green stone sphinx for which an exact mate was sculpted in Rome.

showed how subservient now was that ancient and mighty land of Egypt, Egyptian objects became highly popular in Rome. Augustus erected the first obelisk from Egypt in the Circus Maximus in 10 BC. Shrines to Isis, which were common, were enlarged and the foundations for a great Iseum, the Iseum Campense, laid. Caligula extended it in 37–41, and it was constantly being enhanced by his successors. The building was surrounded by walls and its inner arrangements copied Egyptian patterns. It had a dromos running through a courtyard leading to the entrance to the Isis temple itself, and this was bordered with sphinxes, lions and small obelisks. Such arrangements were imitated at Pompeii and Beneventum. The Iseum Campense contained at least one sphinx from Egypt, an Eighteenth-Dynasty green stone sphinx carved with the cartouche of Hatshepsut. An exact copy was manufactured in Rome, and may have been the work of Egyptian craftsmen. Both female sphinxes wore the Hathor wig and vulture crown and were found together in 1856 behind the church of Santa Maria Sopra Minerva.

The emperor Hadrian (AD 117–138) actually went to Egypt, visiting Alexandria, a place called Canopus which was alleged to be in the neighbourhood of Alexandria and to contain a temple dedicated to Isis and Serapis, and Sais. On his return, he built at Tivoli the celebrated Villa Adriana which was full of statues in the Egyptian style, many of his lover Antinoüs, who had drowned in the Nile (some said, while admiring his own beautiful reflection), and of the goddess Isis, and also included obelisks and sphinxes. These were probably the last direct link with Egypt herself. After this, obelisks, pyramids and particularly sphinxes represented an egyptianising trend in the Roman empire, conforming to Roman tastes. Roman sphinxes were intended to be decorative; to ideals of Roman beauty were added Egyptian characteristics. Stones, especially white marble, which were not traditional in Egypt were used. These Roman sphinxes presented an idiosyncratic interpretation of true Egyptian ones which went more or less unchallenged until the seventeenth century. An exception to this were the Etruscans who during the sixth century depicted sphinxes of a sportive, provincial and somewhat barbaric local style, suggestive of Greek sphinxes.

A century and a half after Hadrian, Diocletian (284–305) had sphinxes put in his palace at Split. At the city of Beneventum on the Appian Way,

Wall painting from a temple dedicated to Bacchus at Pompeii showing a small temple with curved pediment and guarded '. . . in the Egyptian manner, by sphinges'. Their role is more decorative than threatening. From *Pompeiana: The Topography, Edifices and Ornaments of Pompeii* by Sir William Gell and John Gandy, Architect (London, 1852).

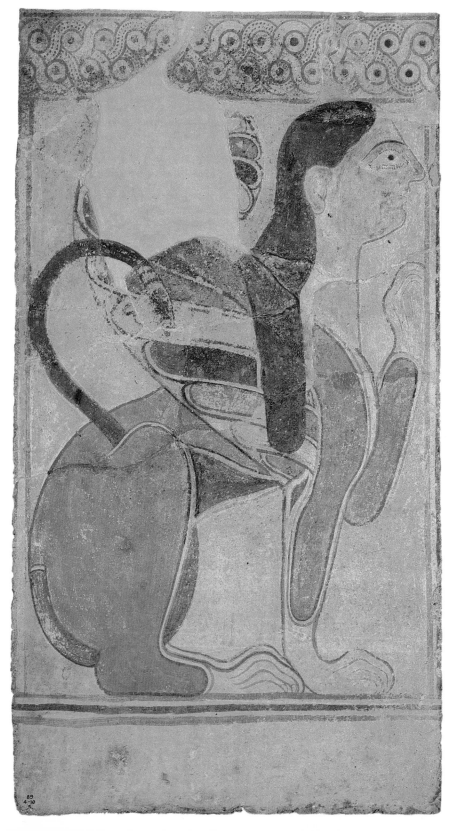

One of a pair of
Etruscan sphinxes from
Cerveteri, 7th century
BC. The two sphinxes
(which are not identical)
probably flanked the
interior of a doorway,
and the subject was
taken from Greek
mythology, reflecting
Corinthian vase-
painting.

he also built (or perhaps enlarged) an Iseum which contained not only a statue of himself in Egyptian dress, but also statues of sphinxes, falcons and lions. And at Praeneste (modern Palestrina) a little south-east of Rome, at the temple of Fortuna Primigenia, where Isis came to be identified, a fascinating mosaic has been found which depicts Egypt with all known Nilotic plants and animals, including a sphinx. At Pompeii a shrine was decorated with the same motifs, and in 1817 a temple dedicated to Bacchus was uncovered and found to contain paintings round its peribolus, including the depiction of an Egyptian temple with curved pediment, guarded in true Egyptian style by a pair of sphinxes.

The Middle Ages

Egypt seemed then to have faded somewhat into the background as the cults of Isis and Serapis dwindled and Christianity swam into focus, though the Iseum in Rome was probably not completely destroyed until 1084. In 642 Egypt herself was conquered by the Muslims and knowledge about her antique past was rapidly forgotten. Then during the thirteenth century the discovery of classical texts suddenly revived interest in Egypt again, and some new Roman sphinxes appeared. These were the product of the Cosmati group of marble-cutters, so called after the original family of craftsmen named Cosmas. The generic is a term given to coloured marble and other stone inlay work. There were later several families in the Cosmati group, including the Vassalletus and Laurentius families who were responsible for a pair of sphinxes in the cloisters of the San Giovanni in Lateran in Rome and for a sphinx at Viterbo (originally in the church of Santa Maria in Gradi). The sphinxes in San Giovanni in Lateran were made about 1222–4 and their design was certainly based on Egyptian originals, though influenced by Roman copies. They look neither purely Egyptian, nor like egyptianising copies, and as a mixed pair they start a new trend. One appears to be female, and is smiling, with eyes slightly creased in amusement. Her mate, with closely curled beard round his chin, has a more serious expression. The sphinx found at Viterbo has an Egyptian-looking body, apart from his furry front paws, but on his head, which is turned to the left, he wears a skullcap. All three sphinxes look rather unsophisticated and squat, partly no doubt because they were used to support columns.

The Renaissance

Interest in ancient Egypt was reinforced during the Renaissance by the ability to bring to a wider audience printed publications of translations of various original works and original treatises by scholars, to whom ancient

Egypt presented an irresistible enigma. The first of these publications was the discovery by Cristofero de Buondelmonte in 1419 of the transcript of a fifth-century Greek text on hieroglyphs by Horapollo, an erudite Egyptian, which was published in an Italian translation in 1471. The original Greek text was published in 1505. Lorenzo Valla (1407–57) published a Latin translation of Herodotus's *Histories* and Poggio Bracciolini translated parts of a manuscript of Ammianus Marcellinus and the works of Diodorus Siculus. All these gave rise to gravely misleading and fanciful interpretations of Egyptian so-called mysteries and magic. In 1450, Flavio Biondo published his *Italia Illustrata* which described the Villa Adriana at Tivoli; this was probably the first mention of that building during the Renaissance. It may have been this that alerted Pope Pius II (1458–64) to its glories. He erected two telamones from the villa at the bishop's residence at Tivoli, from where they were later removed to the Vatican Museum. They were extremely popular and widely copied by Renaissance artists who included Egyptian motifs such as obelisks and pyramids in their designs. Pope Sixtus IV (1471–84) exhibited Egyptian objects including sphinxes at the Capitoline Museum during the 1470s. Throughout the latter part of the fifteenth century in Italy, Egyptian motifs taken from such printed sources were introduced into designs for buildings and interiors. This of course meant they looked less Egyptian than egyptianised: that is, they were not based on original objects but on printed reproductions.

Bernardo Pinturicchio decorated the Borgia apartments in the Vatican in the Egyptian style for Rodrigo Borgia, Pope Alexander VI (1492–1503), mainly because that colourful family wished to trace its ancestry back to Osiris. Etruscan sphinxes were conveniently excavated in the quest for such authentication. In one room, The Lives of the Saints, the legend of Isis and Osiris was depicted, and included a winged sphinx. Pinturicchio and his pupils also worked in Siena where they decorated the Libreria Piccolomini in the cathedral with brightly coloured frescoes which depicted several sphinxes between the panels. There was also in the same cathedral a figure of Hermes Trismegistus with winged sphinxes. The Palazzo Saracini had a courtyard with a painted ceiling on which were depicted telamones and sphinxes atop plinths. The painter Andrea Mantegna (1431–1506) was influenced by Egyptian taste in his *Triumph of Caesar* (now at Hampton Court) which included somewhat bogus hieroglyphs, as was the illustrator of the beautiful *Hypnerotomachia Poliphili*, published in Venice in 1499. The sketchbook of Pirro Ligorio (*c.*1500–1583), the Neapolitan architect, painter and antiquarian, who designed the Villa d'Este, showed several Egyptian motifs, and this and the *Codex Ursinianus* (*c.*1560) probably inspired such artists as Mercati, *De Gli Obelischi di Roma* (1587), and J. G. Herwart von Hohenburg, *Thesaurus Hieroglyphicorum* (1608).

The sixteenth century in Italy produced one of the landmarks of egypto-logical sources, the Mensa Isiaca, a large bronze tablet, inlaid with silver, measuring more than a 3ft (1m) in length. It was also known as the Tabula Bembi, Cardinal Pietro Bembo having apparently rescued it after the sack of Rome in 1527 and taken it into his possession. A copy of it was first published by Enea Vico de Parma in 1559 and an engraving made in 1600. In 1605, the Italian Laurentio Pignorio, a friend of Galileo, published a treatise on the tablet which aroused great interest in scholarly circles, and as the fame of the tablet spread, so did its influence as an instruction manual for any divinity or object in the egyptological repertoire.

The tablet did in fact belong to the past, though not to antiquity. It was likely to have been made during the first century AD, and to have been associated with the cult of Isis, whose figure, in a naos-shrine surmounted by sun-disks, is the central feature. On three registers, surrounding the goddess, are gods from the Egyptian pantheon, and it is clear from the correct iconography that attends them that the artist was familiar with Egyptian theology and pharaonic art. The border of the tablet contains Egyptian motifs, including bearded sphinxes with curved-back wings. In the second half of the seventeenth century the tablet found its way into the collection of the Dukes of Savoy, and since 1832 has been in the Egyptian Museum in Turin.

A Dutchman, Maarten van Heemskerck, lived in Rome between 1532 and 1535 and drew most of her antiquities, including a square sarcophagus resting on two egyptianised couchant sphinxes which was to influence the design of several prominent tombs. The Colonna Missal (c.1520), a Renaissance catalogue of all Egyptian motifs so far, depicted sphinxes with cavorting naked cherubs brandishing tasselled ropes astride their backs, between an authentic-looking representation of a telamon from Tivoli on one side and a fanciful motif from the Tabula Bembi on the other. The Colonna family, like the Borgias, were intent on tracing their ancestry back to earliest antiquity. In about 1550 a tomb sculpted by Vincenzo de Rossi for Angelo Cesi incorporated two front-facing sphinxes, complete with wigs and breastplates but with hair from a centre parting quite visible, and elaborate knotted necklaces of overlapping leaves. Guillaume du Bellay's tomb of 1557, in Le Mans Cathedral, shows a Roman warrior reclining on an elaborate stone slab which is supported by benign-looking sphinxes. There may have been cross-influences between Heemskerck, de Rossi and the probable sculptor of this tomb, Pierre Bontemps, but it is perhaps more likely that the design was inspired by du Bellay's friend, Pierre Belon, who had gone to Egypt, the Middle East and India as an ambassador of François I and published his life story, entitled *Observations*, in 1553. His book contained a description of a sphinx. The tomb at Château d'Anet of Diane de Poitiers, mistress of Henri II of France, shows a boat-shaped sarcophagus resting on four full-breasted sphinxes, two of which have suns as the centres of their wigs and the other two crescent moons, no doubt a playful allusion to that other Diana, whose symbol it was.

Throughout the sixteenth century, sphinxes were often to be found in funerary contexts, as supports for and embellishments of tombs, thus looking back to Greek sphinxes which were found in similar contexts, linked to the solemn and mysterious rites of death. But they also found themselves in more cheerful surroundings. In France King François I employed Italian artists including Giovanni Fiorentino, Francesco Primaticcio and Benvenuto Cellini. At Fontainebleau, sphinxes bounded around the Galérie François Ier and the Galérie d'Ulysse, and the Chambre de la Reine had a sphinx-decorated chimneypiece. There were also four stone sphinxes in the garden facing a fountain, their large rounded breasts suggestive of the sphinxes supporting the tomb of Diane de Poitiers. The work of these Italian artists went on to inspire native Frenchmen, such as Ambroise Le Noble who included sphinx motifs on the richly painted ceiling of the Château de Bourdeilles in the Dordogne and a painted sphinx over the chimneypiece in the Chambre de César de Vendôme at the Château de Chenonceaux. French female sphinxes had an emphatically feminine presence enhanced by the invention by François Rabelais (c.1494–1553) of the French female form of the word, *la sphinge*.

In the mid-seventeenth century, Athanasius Kircher published several books about Egyptian philosophy, antiquities and hieroglyphs, including one entitled *Sphinx Mystagoga*. Though they amount to little more than learned sophistry, Kircher was an influential figure in his day. He founded the Museo Kircheriano in Rome where a collection of Egyptian objects, presumably containing some sphinxes, was housed. The museum – probably the first collection of original objects from ancient Egypt – no longer exists and its collection has been scattered, though some pieces can be seen in the Vatican. Meanwhile other collectors had been busy in the same field, notably Farnese in Rome, the Duke of Tuscany, and van Werle in Amsterdam.

Fashionable settings

Then began the age of the traveller to the Near East. One of the earliest was Tito Livio Burattini, a physicist and orientalist, who visited Egypt between 1637 and 1640. He inspired the Italian engraver Stefano della Bella, who made a drawing of the Great Pyramid and Giza sphinx in the 1640s. While in Egypt, Burattini met the Englishman, John Greaves, who was professor of geometry at Gresham College, London. Greaves published *Pyramidographia* in 1646. Between 1698 and 1701, a Benedictine monk, Bernard de Montfaucon (1655–1741) travelled in Italy and pub-

Plate entitled 'The Second Wonder of the World, the Pyramids of Egypt' (1737) in *Entwurff einer historischen Architeketur* by J.B. Fischer von Erlach. The 'surprising Head of a Sphynx' (marked D) 'cut out of one Single Stone, upon a Base proportion'd to this Gigantick Figure' looked quite authentic, especially with the body covered by sand. But the 'Roman Sphynx' (E), a female creature with pouting lips, large rounded breasts, huge swooping feathered wings and delicate drooping little front paws, looked unlike anything hitherto, Egyptian, Greek or indeed Roman.

lished a ten-volume work on what he had seen, entitled *Antiquité Expliquée*, between 1719 and 1724. Though Montfaucon never visited Egypt personally, he realised her significance and particularly the art of Egypt as a definitive style, while rejecting as speculative mumbo-jumbo much of the work of Kircher and other earlier writers on hieroglyphs. His comprehensive work contained many illustrations, including a strange blind falcon-headed sphinx, couchant and wingless, but with a headdress composed of a crescent moon and star. Johann Bernhard Fischer von Erlach (1656–1723) published in Vienna in 1721 his *Entwurff einer historischen Architektur*. Plate IV of this volume showed the Great Pyramid at Giza and the Great Sphinx, as well as two other smaller sphinxes in the background. The Great Sphinx looks Greek, though she wears an egyptianising wig, with large pendulous breasts and delicate drooping wrists. Fischer von Erlach was fascinated by the architectural achievements of the past and had done his research meticulously. At the bottom of each plate he listed his written sources, often going back to Herodotus and Diodorus Siculus. The book was published in England in 1730 with the title *A Plan of Civil and Historical Architecture*. The Dane F. L. Norden published his *Travels in Egypt and Nubia* in France in 1755 and in England in 1757. He had actually seen the antiquities he described. An Englishman there at the same time, Richard Pococke, had published his *Observations on Egypt* some ten years earlier.

Both these books were widely read and consulted, particularly Norden's, which contained much detailed illustration of Egyptian motifs, obelisks, pyramids and sphinxes, so that they became very familiar to eighteenth-century eyes.

Sphinxes now began to appear in every fashionable setting, particularly gardens, not only all over Europe but in England as well. Why gardens were considered such a suitable setting is not clear; it may just have been coincidental with the beginning of the taste for great garden landscapes and for orientalism, which demanded excursions into fantasy, especially classical antiquity. Greek sphinxes lent themselves perfectly to such fancies, half-woman, half-beast, ravishingly beautiful yet unknowable, mysterious. To them could be attached other capricious whims, fauns, or cherubs with puffed-out cheeks and impossibly dimpled legs. In France, Louis XIV's minister, Nicolas Fouquet, built a great house, Vaux-le-Vicomte, and employed Le Nôtre to design the gardens complete with sphinxes, some of which have cherubs astride their backs. After Fouquet was disgraced, the king removed Le Nôtre to Versailles where he was encouraged to eclipse his former glories. Versailles contained many egyptianising features, including more sphinxes. Some sphinxes were given the faces of the beauties of the day, Madame de Pompadour or Madame du Barry, and their necks were elegantly extended to ensure a large expanse of heaving stone (or lead) chest. Versailles in its turn inspired gardens all over western Europe. Fischer von Erlach put some full-breasted recumbent sphinxes in the courtyard of the Trautson Palace in Vienna, built in 1710. His contemporary and rival, Lukas von Hildebrandt, placed them *en filade* at the Belvedere, where they sit upright, rounded bosoms inclining towards heaven. At Veitshochheim in Wurzbürg, laid out between 1763 and 1775, there are examples of sphinxes which are about as far removed from ancient Egypt as it is possible to go. They are swathed in marble muslin drapery knotted on their bosoms and trailing round to their haunches with occasional tassels, adorned with ringlets, rosettes and lace cuffs, and their rounded rococo faces gaze serenely at passers-by. In a more sober vein, suitable to a Benedictine monastery remodelled by Josef Munggenast between 1730 and 1733, were the restrained sphinxes at the Stift Altenburg in Austria. At Chiswick House, just outside London, there are sphinxes on pedestals designed by William Kent, and some fine examples at Blickling in Norfolk. But despite the accurate sources described above which could have been consulted, it seemed to be much more fun to invent a sphinx rather than copy the genuine article. Female sphinxes were obviously far more appropriate to the romantic setting of a garden, and frilly draperies and winsome expressions far more conducive to flirtatious assignations, than a menacing black granite monster ready to pounce. The role of these graceful chimaeras was to provide a lighthearted, sportive, yet essentially exotic element.

Design for a chimneypiece in the Egyptian style by Piranesi (1769). Two couchant sphinxes with human arms touch fingertips. They wear a stylised form of the double crown of Upper and Lower Egypt, and the *nemes*-headcloth. Visible from their ears is a strap for the false beard, but they are beardless. Upon their barrel chests they wear a garment adorned with bogus hieroglyphs. They are set in an egyptianised scene: note the lotus flowers, apis bulls and winged scarab.

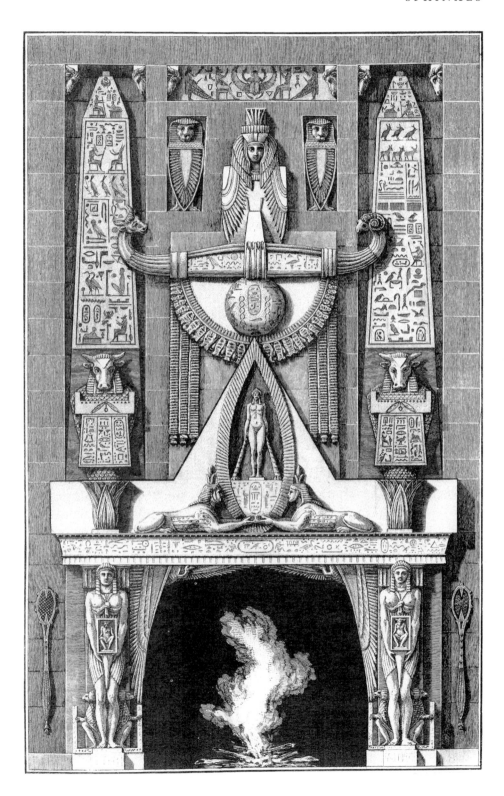

Rococo sphinx designed by Ferdinand Dietz for the Palace Gardens at Trier. Both she and her sister sphinx lie on barques with curved fronts upon which their powerful lion's forepaws with vicious claws rest. Everything else about them is fantastically feminine: the sweet faces with ecstatic smiles, the lace-edged, ruffled garments with tassels, the flower garlands upon their ringlets and tails, the jewelled wristbands, earrings and chokers. Their role is not only decorative, however: flanking the garden entrance to the palace, they act as guardian figures.

The exotic element was perhaps epitomised by Giovanni Battista Piranesi who produced the final flowering of rococo Egyptian style. Piranesi had studied ancient and modern printed sources, including the Mensa Isiaca and Fischer von Erlach, and he had used his eyes in and around Rome where he worked. Nothing escaped his sharp vision, brilliant draughtsmanship and vivid imagination. In 1769 he published *Diverse Maniere d'Adornare I Cammini*, much of which described the Egyptian style and used Egyptian motifs in contemporary interiors, one of the most famous of which was the Caffé degl'Inglesi in the Piazza di Spagna, where one wall depicted a pair of male sphinxes, back to back on top of a pediment. The book also contained several designs for fireplaces, some of which used sphinxes. One showed two winged sphinxes facing each other across a monstrous bearded face. The central face of the monster and the two outspread wings of the sphinxes made a perfect winged sun-disk in themselves. Piranesi's work had a widespread influence on his contemporaries in Italy, France and England, where Robert Adam (1721–92) used sphinxes on the entrance screen for Syon House, and John Nash put a sphinx on the top storey of Southgate Grove, Middlesex, in 1797. Wedgwood included sphinxes, lotus flowers, Cleopatra figures and hieroglyphs on red encaustic ware decorated in black at this time.

In 1752, however, a book by Anne-Claude-Philippe de Caylus entitled *Receuil d'antiquités égyptiennes, étrusques, grecques et romaines* had appeared, and this, together with another book published in England, Stuart and

Detail of a marble clock made by Wedgwood in 1799 and designed by Benjamin Vulliamy (1747–1811) for Anna Maria Borough. The jasperware plaque is decorated with couchant bronze sphinxes, whose drooping front paws suggest those of a pet dog. Wedgwood issued its first catalogue of egyptianising motifs in 1773.

Revett's *The Antiquities of Athens*, began a process which was to have a profound effect on the way in which people viewed the ancient world. They crested the tidal wave of classicism that was about to sweep the modern world, a wave which made for a realistic view of the ancient world based on personal discovery and excavation, on properly measured proportions and accurate calculations, casting aside frivolous imagination. Now Egypt's great monuments were seen as massive and severe, not to be prettified and belittled by fashion. They became suitable inspiration for tombs and buildings connected with death. Jean-Louis Desprez made designs for four such imaginary ones in Rome after he went there in 1777, massive, weighty prototypes with forbidding couchant sphinxes wearing authentic-looking wigs but sporting aquiline Roman noses in profile. Etienne-Louis Boullée (1728–99) wrote a treatise on architectural styles in the 1780s in which he praised the Egyptians for their grand ideas and images. His contemporary, Antoine-Chrysostome Quartremère de Quincy, compared the architecture of Egypt with that of Greece, and though he found the former lacking, he admired its solidarity and reassuring monotony. Claude-Nicolas Ledoux (1735–1806) published *Architecture* in 1804, commending the geometric simplicity of the pyramid. In England, the architect Charles Tatham (1772–1842) designed a large number of Egyptian-inspired buildings, including a pyramid mausoleum with pavilions at the corners guarded by sphinxes.

At the same time, Egyptian rites and motifs began to be used by the growing fraternity of Freemasons. Their links with ancient Egypt of course went back to earliest antiquity. The mason's craft originated in Egypt and it was believed the Israelites learned their craft of masonry in Egypt also. The first name to be associated with this trend is that of Carl Friedrich Koppen who published in 1778 *Crata Repoa, oder Einveihung der ägyptischen Priester* which concerned the initiation of Egyptian priests. Then Count Cagliostro, who turned out to be a fraud, but who had travelled in the east, set up a lodge in Paris with a temple dedicated to Isis attached to it where Egyptian rituals were practised. Soon thereafter Egyptian rituals became normal practice in other lodges. Ignatz von Born established a lodge in Vienna in 1781 and in 1784 began publishing a journal for masons entitled *Journal für Freimaurer*, the first number of which contained a long article on Egyptian mysteries. Mozart was once an apprentice in this lodge, then joined another one also in Vienna, at which time he wrote *The Magic Flute* (1791) with all its references to ancient Egyptian rituals and to Isis and Osiris. The title page to the original score showed several Egyptian motifs, including fairly authentic hieroglyphs, but no recognisable sphinx.

From Napoleon to Tutankhamun

This was the state of Egyptian revival and therefore the standing of the sphinx in popular imagination at the time of the great watershed, Napoleon's expedition to the Nile in 1795, the reports of which, when published some quarter of a century later, were to change forever people's views about ancient Egypt and the potent images she produced. Two publications were responsible for this. The first was Dominique Vivant Denon's *Voyage dans La Basse et La Haute Egypte* in 1802. An English version appeared in 1803, and an abridged version in New York in the same year. The second was and remains the definitive source for ancient Egypt and all her monuments in the precise state in which they were at the end of the eighteenth century, *La Description de l'Egypte* which was published between 1809 and 1828 in 20 volumes, eleven of which were volumes of plates. Both books contained detailed and accurate descriptions and measurements, not only of monuments but also of objects such as sphinxes, carefully drawn. They were an inspiration.

In London, Thomas Hope, the architect and designer, decorated part of his house in Duchess Street in the Egyptian style. It was completed in 1804 when the public was admitted to view. His main sources were Piranesi and Denon, though he had also been to Egypt himself. In 1807 he published *Household Furniture and Interior Decoration* which contained designs for several items of furniture, including a fine stone seat with sphinxes at either end and the back decorated with stylised lotus flowers. Perhaps not surprisingly in view of Piranesi's fanciful influence, the sphinxes do not look very

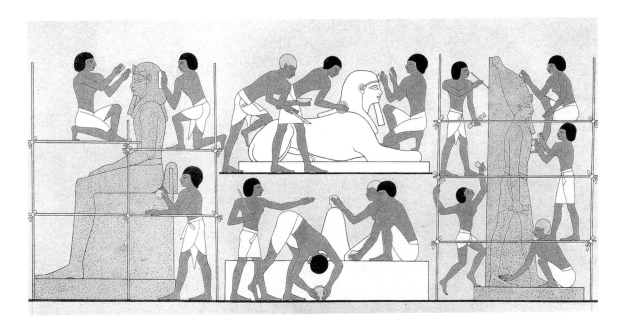

Illustration from *Histoire de l'art égyptien* . . . (1878) by A.C.T.E. Prisse d'Avennes. The original wall painting on which this was based is in the Theban tomb of Rekhmire, the chief vizier of Tuthmosis III (1479–1425 BC), and showed sculptors fashioning a sphinx (top centre), colossal statues and an altar.

Egyptian, in that they are seated, with prominent breasts and looping S-shaped tails ending in furry brushes. Denon's influence is visible in the wigs, which really do look authentic, and the facial expressions, which are severe. In 1812, the famous Egyptian Hall, designed by Peter Frederick Robinson, was opened in Piccadilly. It was based on the temple of Dendera, recorded so carefully by Denon, and its central motif was a naos crowned by a cavetto cornice which was supported by two sphinxes, tail to tail. This building was aped some twenty years later by a practically identical Egyptian House in Penzance, though a somewhat bizarre touch was added by the replacement of austere Egyptian figures at the sides of the building with distinctly buxom, rosy-cheeked, Cornish maidens. Unfortunately the sphinxes, too, were replaced, with unicorns. In Bristol, Isambard Kingdom Brunel's suspension bridge at Clifton was started in 1836, though it was not completed until 1864, by which time some of the intended egyptianising detail was omitted, regrettably the pairs of couchant sphinxes on top of the pylons. Thomas Sheraton the furniture-maker included designs in the Egyptian taste in *The Cabinet-Maker, Upholsterer and General Artist's Encyclopaedia* (1804–6) and in 1828 designed a set of state chairs with winged sphinxes for Prince Karl of Prussia. The Scottish architect W. H. Playfair designed the Royal Scottish Academy in Edinburgh with sphinxes over the pediment. It was built between 1823 and 1833, and in the 1840s at Biddulph Grange, in Staffordshire, an exotic Egyptian Court was made in the garden. Against a dramatic setting of dark green clipped yew, two extremely ugly and bulbous sphinxes on plinths gaze at each other across a path that leads to a stone pylon in

which there is a statue of the Egyptian god Bes. All these designs showed unmistakably that Denon and the *Description* had done their work.

The publication in 1846–9 of David Roberts's *Egypt and Nubia*, which contained beautiful watercolours of the romantic ruins of those lands, also kept interest in Egypt alive. Even Queen Victoria bought a copy.

In France the influence of Denon and the *Description* was if anything even greater. The Egyptian fountain flanked by four massive sphinxes in the Place du Châtelet, designed by J. M. N. Bralle, shows a familiarity with antiquity. On a more domestic scale, the designs for the Sèvres Egyptian dinner service originally made for the Empress Josephine between 1810 and 1812 and presented to the victorious Duke of Wellington in 1817 (and now displayed at his London residence, Apsley House) were actually overseen by Denon himself. Apart from the plates which depict several different scenes and objects, including sphinxes drawn in dark browns against a white background, all of which have royal blue rims with golden hieroglyphs, the dinner service had a centrepiece which consisted of two pylon gates fronted with a pair of colossal figures before each one, and with hypostyle halls and kiosks beyond, four obelisks, a central temple in the style of the one at Edfu, and two avenues of criosphinxes, all made of biscuit porcelain. The temptation not to do any eating must have been almost irresistible.

In Italy the magnificent whole of the Piazza del Popolo was designed

and completed between 1816 and 1820 by Giuseppe Valadier. This is an authentic Egyptian scene, complete with obelisks and true Egyptian sphinxes serenely gazing out from the vantage-point of the ramps on which they are placed. There were Egyptian bridges in Germany and Austria, and at the Berlin Opera House the 1815 production of *The Magic Flute* had stage designs made by the great Prussian architect Karl Friedrich Schinkel. Sarastro's garden in Act II contained an Egyptian sphinx set on a podium in a lake. Though brooding in romantic shadow, the details of its wig look authentically Egyptian and it is both colossal and couchant.

Now that ancient Egypt had been exposed, and published, and was available to anyone, designers, architects and artists had a fine choice on their hands. They could consult serious sources while maintaining the

RIGHT Detail of a late 19th-century necklace in the egyptian style with enamelled sphinx motifs. The central scarab decorated with lotus flowers and buds is flanked by two outward-facing half-sphinxes with blue enamelled wigs. Facing them across scarabs set on the hieroglyphic symbol for the word 'gold' are seated sphinxes on the same symbols. Both sphinxes have raised wings enamelled in red, green and blue, and have wigs and *uraei* but are beardless.

freedom to opt for fanciful interpretations. Nowhere was this more apparent than in the vogue for Egyptian funerary monuments that characterised the second half of the nineteenth century. Both obelisks and pyramids had a vast appeal for an age that was as obsessed with death in an ordered manner as the ancient Egyptians themselves, and there are some fine examples of egyptianising tombs, both in England (particularly at Kensal Green Cemetery, London, and in Bradford) and on the Continent. Occasionally sphinxes loom on to the forbidding scene but they are perhaps perceived as being too fierce, too frivolous and ultimately too heathen to be truly proper in a funerary context.

They were far more appropriate to the Thames Embankment where a red granite obelisk from Egypt was erected in 1878. Two vast bronze sphinxes were commissioned from G. Vulliamy to flank it, and in a bold gesture of solidarity benches were made to fit in with the whole Egyptian scene. These benches consist of planks of polished wood supported at either end by one-legged winged standing sphinxes. Their back leg(s) are not visible, having become the support for the back of the seat.

Commissioning sphinxes as guardians in monumental contexts became quite popular, particularly on the Continent, where many imposing art galleries, office blocks and even opera houses have their pet pair by the front door, functioning very much as they did in antiquity and looking large and forbidding. One particularly ugly pair was commissioned by the millionaire German industrialist family of Krupp for their villa near Essen, the Villa Hugel. These appear both male and female in that they have authentic-looking stern male faces with wigs, but no beards, and large pointed breasts. Their oddest feature is their stance: their front legs protrude from under their chests at a steeply sloping angle, as if they have just put on the brakes and skidded to a halt. The sculptor was Max Demert.

In the twentieth century the discovery of the tomb of Tutankhamun in 1922 caused a wave of near hysterical egyptomania whose most concrete manifestation was probably cinemas, the two crazes, for ancient Egypt and the movies, happening roughly at the same time and attracting the same sort of popularity. None of these cinemas had an avenue of sphinxes, or even a guardian pair, as far as can be ascertained. Sphinxes were confined to the interior decoration, some of which was extremely lavish and carefully researched. The effect of Tutankhamun was otherwise of a somewhat ephemeral nature: sweet peas, cigarettes and a rag-time melody. The find coincided with a new artistic craze, art deco, which was itself brought to prominence by the Exposition Internationale des Arts Décoratifs et Industriels Modernes which was held in Paris in 1925. The taste then engendered for brightly coloured, geometric decoration found a natural ally in the Egyptian style, specifically the block border. The more swooping, delicate and curvaceous style of art nouveau had already found new impetus in revived lines and colours, in particular in designs for jewellery. Sphinx heads were a popular motif, though they were perhaps a little too monumental for the fashionable flat chests of the period.

The appeal and role of the sphinx

What was the appeal of the sphinx over five millennia? Why was it so potent an image for so long, and why does it continue to be so? It is an image which, though alien, is instantly recognisable, as familiar as the cat lying curled up on the hearthrug. Yet it remains a puzzle, a beautiful object merely, self-possessed, reclusive, inscrutable indeed. No one ever believed it had once really existed and stalked the land as they did in the case of other mythical beasts. Even the meretricious sphinx of Greek legend was really a cipher.

The sphinx lives only in the imagination, beyond human experience and contact. It has no personality; it is neither happy nor sad. It does not dance or drink, sing or procreate. It is above all silent. In literature its strongest characteristic is its silence, in art its stillness. It is a symbol of the unknown and unknowable.

Context and history have created its different roles: at first a monster, placed at a gate with its pair to ward off unwelcome visitors, be they real or ghostly, then a protector of the dead, a more kindly role. Then it became deadly again, the seeker of human corpses, then female, subtle, riddle-setting and full of vengeance. It was sportive in an Etruscan landscape, went to Rome and became monumental again, then was mysterious and inscrutable throughout the Renaissance. It was a guardian of tombs, it was connected with death. Then suddenly it put on frills and went out into the garden where it enticed lovers into shady groves. It prowled around inside too, particularly around flames and fire: as a fireguard, on a chimneypiece, holding aloft sconces and candles. It was also a stern supporter of the correct time, it haughtily dispensed ink from marble inkwells. It glided around the frames of looking-glasses, glittered dangerously from cut-glass finger-bowls, and gazed unwinkingly from gilded china plates. Then the tide turned again and it was considered only suitable in the sober settings of tombs, bridges, fountains and opera houses. Then Tutankhamun turned everything Egyptian into a fashion accessory.

Whatever its context, the role of the sphinx has always been the same: to inject an authentic aura of antiquity into its surroundings. And whatever antiquity suggested at the time, the sphinx was endlessly adaptable: threatening, mystic, morbid, decorative, amusing, exotic, even erotic. Regardless of where it found itself, the sphinx retained its integrity, its dignity and its power; with its archaic charm, its formal elegance and ambiguous sexuality, it is the brooding enigma of the most remote and perennial past.

Half-Human Creatures

Many of the most popular and enduring creatures in the fabulous bestiary are represented in half-human, half-animal form. These include the sphinx, but the sea is also teeming with mermaids, and the skies swarm with sirens and harpies. What meanings have been attributed to these beasts, and why do they tend to be seen as female rather than as male?

Boundaries and definitions

All human cultures need to define those characteristics which they regard as essential to 'humanity'. They need to establish what counts as socially acceptable behaviour, particularly when they come into contact with other cultures with different social practices based on different sets of values. In a variety of cultures throughout history, one of the most common ways of defining what it is to be human is to draw comparisons with the animal kingdom, imposing on it characteristics diametrically opposed to those regarded as distinctive to the human condition. So, for example, where monogamous marriage has been elevated to the status of a defining human characteristic, 'the beasts' will be seen as promiscuous, perhaps with one or two species singled out as showing a sort of primitive monogamy, as exceptions to the rule. Where a diet of agricultural products and cooked meat defines humanity, the beasts must by definition eat wild foods and raw meat. Anyone in human shape whose behaviour is on the 'bestial' side risks ostracism – or worse.

But at the same time as the animal kingdom is 'other', it may also be recognised as being, in some respects, quite similar to our own. The world of the beasts can be graded into more and less 'bestial', from the jungle to

One of the human-headed, winged lions from the ninth-century BC palace of Ashurnasirpal II at Nimrud, which acted as guardians of entrances, to keep evil powers at bay.

the farmyard, from the wild and uncontrolled to the tame animals who are sufficiently 'human' even to live in our homes and share our lives. From the eighteenth century onwards, western cultures tended increasingly to classify 'humanity' on similar lines, from the most civilised forms to the most bestial.

Whether there is a simple opposition between 'the beasts' and 'us humans', or a chain extending from most bestial to most 'human', the creation of mixed beings who violate the boundaries by sharing in both natures acknowledges and explores the similarities between humans and beasts. Where are such beasts to be found? Like other marvellous beasts, hybrid creatures tend to live at the margins of the known world, encountered mainly by explorers and traders. Those who meet them may, like Odysseus and his sailors, find their own humanity threatened. Creatures who cross boundaries in their own bodies can often act as guardians of important places or of further boundaries. As will be seen, the four beasts considered in depth in this chapter, the centaur, the siren, the harpy and the mermaid, are all associated with boundaries – between the living and the dead, between the known and the unknown, between the permitted and the forbidden.

As for their origins, human/beast hybrids, whether fearsome or marvellous, may simply be seen as necessary parts of Creation; in western medieval thought, the marvellous was seen as an integral part of the world, proving the power of God to make such odd creatures, and reminding people that God remains in control. They may, however, be explained as the result of interbreeding between human and animal, thus graphically demonstrating the precarious nature of any separation of humans from beasts. Among such creatures is the Minotaur, a bull above the shoulders and a man below, born after the Athenian inventor Daedalus made a device shaped like a cow from within which the Queen of Crete, Pasiphae, was able to satisfy her lust for a bull. They may, finally, owe their origin to mating between gods and other beings, in which case they can themselves share divinity. In Greek myth, a whole line of monsters derives from the children of Earth and Sea. Some are unique, like the Chimaera and Echidna; others occur in groups, like the harpies and the gorgons. In all cases, human/animal hybrids allow us to explore the characteristics we share with the beasts, particularly our sexuality, seen as 'animal' because it is perceived as a dangerous and uncontrolled force. Myths of the defeat of such mixed beings by heroes reassure us that, in the last resort, human civilisation triumphs over the wild beasts, and reason triumphs over the body.

Connections with the prolific fertility and sheer power of the animal world can also be seen in a more positive light. Families and nations may attribute their origins to an animal. In classical antiquity both Herodotus and Diodorus Siculus traced the origin of the people of Scythia to a union between the god Zeus or the hero Hercules and a woman who was a snake below the waist, while Keith Thomas has found a number of families in eighteenth-century England who traced their descent from a bear or a bitch. Something similar applies to specific half-woman, half-animal creatures; long seen as embodying the dangerous attractions of women, they have recently been reclaimed by feminist writers as metaphors for female power.

Our earliest detailed evidence for the use of half-animal, half-human creatures in a culture's definition of itself comes from fifth-century BC Greece. Page duBois has shown how the most culturally significant 'monsters' here were those with a part-male human, part-beast nature: in particular, the man-horse centaurs and the man-goat satyrs. The Greeks were concerned with self-definition achieved by exploring the boundaries between 'self' and 'other', 'self' being the Greek male subject. He was not-barbarian, not-woman and not-beast. The three negatively valued terms of barbarian, woman and beast, all excluded from the ordered life of the city, were thought to share many features. Thus barbarians were seen as effeminate; according to the first-century BC writer Diodorus Siculus, Sardanapalus, the last King of the Assyrians, stayed indoors like a woman, spinning wool and wearing women's clothing. Women themselves were seen as bestial, particularly in their lack of control over their appetites. For the eighth-century BC poet Hesiod, whose work – like that of Homer – became something of a Bible for the ancient world, the first woman, Pandora, had 'the mind of a bitch' and greedily consumed all that man could provide for her, while in early Greek gynaecology the womb was sometimes seen as an uncontrolled animal, moving around the body to satisfy its craving for moisture. Amazons combine the female and the barbarian, but as female warriors they are also used to explore aspects of the male/female boundary. In one variant of the Amazon myth, given by Diodorus Siculus, they keep tame men to do the spinning and look after the children, but take the precaution of laming them to prevent escape. In another, given by the first-century BC geographer Strabo, the Amazons meet the men of a neighbouring tribe annually for reproductive purposes; like animals, these Amazons both keep to a mating season and copulate in the open air.

All three excluded categories could, and did, threaten the ordered harmony of the male city. Women, although outsiders, were necessary for its reproduction. Once taken into the city, however, they were liable to endanger its smooth running, being supposedly less rational and more open to possession by demonic forces. Barbarians could enter the city in war, as the Persian assault on Athens demonstrated in 480 BC. In classical Greek thought, even the Amazons came closer; once an exotic tribe living on the north-eastern fringes of the Greek world, it came to be believed that they had attacked Athens itself.

Centaurs

The threat from the beasts is illustrated in myth by the violent, often drunken actions of centaurs which threaten the ordered exchanges on which society is based: the exchange of women, and guest-friendship. The most famous centaur story is the one represented on the metopes of the Parthenon: the Lapith wedding, which the centaurs violated by trying to run off with the women at the feast. On the frieze inside the temple of Apollo the Helper at Bassae in Arcadia, which dates to the late fifth century BC, two battles of civilisation versus barbarism are depicted: centaurs versus Lapiths, and Greeks versus Amazons. In neither is there a victor; both are seen as never-ending struggles.

Paul Baur has argued that, in the Greek world, the visual image of the man-horse, perhaps derived from Hittite culture, historically preceded the

A metope (447–443 BC) from the Parthenon shows a Greek fighting one of the centaurs who disrupted the wedding feast when Pirithous, King of the Lapiths of Thessaly, married Hippodamia. The drunken centaurs tried to carry off not only the bride but all the human women present.

various Greek myths about these creatures. The earliest Greek images consist of a male human body with a horse's body and rear legs tacked on behind, rather than a male human torso on a horse's body. In the former case, there may even be two sets of genitalia – human in front, horse at the rear – thus further emphasising the creature's sexuality. Both types, those with human and those with equine forelegs, coexist in Greek art.

The only 'good' centaur in Greek myth is Chiron who, unlike the rest, is married, immortal and skilled in the fields of medicine and hunting. His parentage is totally different from that of the other centaurs. He is the son of Saturn and Philyra, while the others come either from a union between the intoxicated Ixion and Nephele – a cloud image of Hera – or from intercourse between Centauros, son of Ixion and Nephele, and the mares of Thessaly. Chiron is represented in art bearded, wearing a tunic and carrying a pine branch from which a number of captured hares are suspended; in the archaic period he always has human forelegs. In myth he acted as tutor to a number of heroes, among them the monster-killing Achilles and Hercules, and taught Asklepios the art of healing. It is as if the process of instruction by which an individual moves from the category of boy to that of man is best achieved by a creature which itself straddles otherwise separate categories. Napier has noted that the dancing, singing, cheerful and permanently sexually aroused satyrs, in common with wild half-human creatures in many other cultures, are associated with another

A *dinos*, a large serving-bowl for wine, showing a rather different type of centaur at a wedding feast: Chiron arriving as a guest at the wedding of Peleus. Chiron went on to become tutor to the child of the mortal Peleus and immortal Thetis: the hero Achilles. Athens, 580 BC.

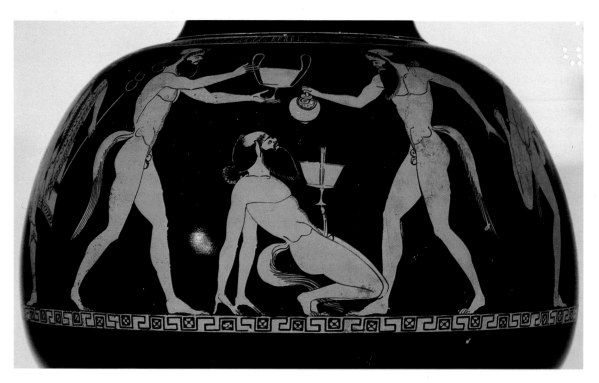

Painted by Douris, this *psykter*, part of a wine-cooling system of inner and outer containers, shows a satyr being encouraged by others to show off the power of his erection. His companions do not have erections; their foreskins may be tied with ribbons to prevent this. Athens, 500–490 BC.

type of boundary, the change between seasons, since they are connected with seasonal festivals.

The behaviour of half-human, half-animal creatures can thus throw into relief what it is to be human; by breaking boundaries, within their bodies as well as in their actions, they can show exactly where those boundaries should lie. Centaurs crash drunkenly across the division between civilised and uncivilised behaviour, but hybrid beings, their very bodies showing that the apparently opposed can coexist, can also mediate gentle change between social categories and seasons.

Sirens

The first literary description of the sirens occurs when Odysseus encounters two of them in Book 12 of Homer's *Odyssey*. Their beautiful and fatal song is given, but their parentage and appearance are not described. They may once have been human maidens; in some ancient myths they were the companions of Persephone, who grew wings in order to search for her over the sea after her abduction by Hades, Lord of the Underworld, or who were punished with bird-woman form for failing to prevent Hades from taking her. Although winged, they are sometimes presented as having arms as well so that they can play musical instruments to accompany their song. Servius, in his fourth-century AD commentary on Homer, described three sirens, claiming that one sang, one played the pipes and the third played the lyre. A fifth-century Athenian vase-painting shows a siren playing her pipes to Odysseus; another shows two sirens playing the lyre, while in Euripides' *Helen*, Helen addresses them as 'virgin daughters of Earth' and asks them to play their flutes and pipes in harmony with her lament. The poet Pindar suggested that the flute was the instrument most resembling the sound of the sirens' song. Later classical mythographers tried to create a genealogy for them which combined their musical talents with their traditional location on an island, off the coast near Sorrento, or between Italy and Sicily. Their mother was a Muse – usually either Terpsichore, the Muse of choral dance and song, who played the lyre, or Melpomene, Muse of tragedy – and their father the sea-god Phorcys or the river-god Achelous.

Although Homer does not say what they looked like, vase-paintings of Odysseus' encounter with the sirens show them as birds with women's heads; the earliest such vase-painting dates from the sixth century BC. They also appear in this form on Athenian tombs of the classical period. Before this time, however, clay perfume vases were sometimes produced in the form of birds with women's heads, perhaps linking the allure of the sirens' song with the seductive powers of scent. In Laurence Binyon's ode, *The Sirens* (1924), this connection is expressed by their location: they live 'on a far spice-island'.

Ovid's poetry, written at the beginning of the Roman Empire, continues the Greek tradition of the sirens as Persephone's companions who grew wings and now combine a virgin's face with wings and a human voice. In his 'Art of Love', however, they are called *monstra maris*, sea-monsters, who stop boats with their song. 'Sea-monsters' may suggest that their

Clay perfume containers showing a bird with a woman's head may link the seductive powers of scent with the sirens' song. This example was found in Corinth and dates from the 7th or 6th century BC.

A siren, her bird's feet and wings clearly visible but her body that of a mature woman, is moments away from intercourse with a sleeping shepherd. Does this marble relief, from the Hellenistic or Roman period, illustrate his dream or his nightmare? The presence of human arms as well as wings means that this figure may perhaps be a harpy; whatever her identity, she illustrates the sexual appetites of bird/woman creatures.

natural element is not the rocks off an island, but the ocean itself, and this reference may explain the later transformation of winged sirens into fish-tailed sirens, or mermaids.

Only two men in myth broke the power of the sirens' song, which, according to the Roman poet Martial, made death seem alluring: Orpheus and Odysseus. Orpheus drowned out the song with his own music; Odysseus blocked his crew's ears with beeswax and had himself tied to the mast of his ship, so that he could still hear the song. These were not, however, the sirens' first defeats. Hera once persuaded them to enter a musical contest against the Muses. The sirens lost, and the Muses – with the exception of whichever one was their mother – plucked their feathers and made them into crowns.

Early Christian writers added their own interpretations to classical myth. From the fifth century AD onwards, writers used the story of Odysseus and the sirens to warn that safety can only be found in the ship of the Church, by blocking your ears with the wax of lawful doctrine and tying yourself to the mast – the cross – with the rope of divine favour or the chains of virtue. Other Christian writers suggested that the wax was

philosophy, used to enable reason to conquer temptation; the story was also used to teach leaders to look after the welfare of their followers. It is interesting that, in Homer's story, neither the wax nor the rope was Odysseus' own idea; both were recommended to him by the sorceress Circe. This point, which would clearly diminish the effectiveness of the Odysseus/Christ allegory, is conveniently forgotten by Christian commentators.

In Christian symbolism the siren represents lechery or, more generally, the delights of this world. Medieval Christian imagery emphasises the dangerous femininity of the monstrous siren. For example, the eleventh-century Marbod of Rennes writes about women as the root of all evil, using the siren to warn men to 'beware the honied poisons, the sweet songs and the pull of the dark depths', while Eustathius, the twelfth-century commentator on Homer, suggested that the sirens were 'no more than some Greek seaman's recollection of a sailors' whorehouse'. The sexual appetites of the sirens can be traced back to the Hellenistic period; marble reliefs and lamps show a siren, with human arms and the wings and feet of a bird, about to have intercourse with a supine shepherd. In Tennyson's 'The Sea-Fairies', the sirens' song simply becomes one of sexual invitation:

Section of a Corinthian drinking cup from around 600 BC showing two part-human, part-animal creatures – a siren and a sphinx – facing a griffin.

A *stamnos*, or wine-jar, from Athens (*c.* 460 BC) showing Odysseus resisting the sirens' song; one defeated siren appears to be jumping to her death from her rocky home. Whether or not the sirens would ever kill themselves as a result of defeat is discussed in Giuseppe di Lampedusa's short story, *The Professor and the Siren* (see p. 164).

O hither, come hither, and be our lords,
For merry brides are we:
We will kiss sweet kisses, and speak sweet words,
O listen, listen, your eyes shall glisten
With pleasure and love and jubilee . . .

This is not simply a modern interpretation: in the tenth-century AD encyclopaedia known as *The Suda*, the sirens lure their prey 'with certain lewd songs'.

Like the first woman, Pandora, whose beautiful appearance contrived by the gods conceals the mind of a bitch, the siren comes to be used as an example of the contrast between the world of sensory perception and the underlying reality. Marbod of Rennes warns, 'Do not let the charm of contrived appearances seduce you.' The siren in the nineteenth canto of Dante's *Purgatory* stuttered, squinted and had deformed hands and feet; when Virgil looked at her she became fluent and beautiful, but Virgil was able to reveal the reality once more by tearing open her clothes, at which a terrible stench awakened him.

Another view of the sirens was taken by Cicero, who argued that it was not the song but its content which was most desirable: 'It was not the sweetness of their voices or the novelty and diversity of their songs, but their professions of knowledge which used to attract the passing voyagers; it was the passion for learning that kept men rooted to the Sirens' rocky shores . . . It is *knowledge* that the Sirens offer.' This too can be supported from Homer, who says that the sirens invited Odysseus to listen with the words, 'We *know* all that happens on the much-suffering earth'. In Binyon's *The Sirens*, the 'tormenting sweetness' of their song entices the hearer 'beyond the borders of knowledge' into matters in which man should not meddle. The sirens' knowledge can be seen simply as an ability to foretell the future; this features in Camoens' sixteenth-century epic of Portuguese exploration, *The Lusiads*, in the second canto of which Vasco da Gama's fleet is saved from attack off the coast of Africa by the intervention of Venus and the silver-tailed nereids: much of the tenth and final canto, in which the mariners feast with the nereids, consists of a siren singing prophecies of great heroes yet unborn. Hugh Lloyd-Jones suggests, however, that their boast of knowledge to Odysseus simply provides a further example of the sirens' seductive power. They know exactly which words will captivate each specific victim, and they are aware that what is most craved by Odysseus, with his deep curiosity, is knowledge.

Another tradition focuses on the music rather than its words. Plato, in the Myth of Er which closes his *Republic*, places a siren on each of the eight spheres; each sings one note of constant pitch, and the Fates sing to this music of past, present and future. The sirens' song thus becomes pure knowledge, the music of the spheres, an interpretation used later by Milton in his poem 'At a Solemn Music', in which he calls on 'Blest pair of Sirens, pledges of Heav'ns joy/Sphere-born harmonious sisters, Voice and Verse'. Francis Bacon, in *The Wisdom of the Ancients*, regards the strength of the song as lying in its musical complexity, combining a 'variety of melodious tunes'. The West Indian poet and dramatist Derek Walcott suggests in his recent stage version of the *Odyssey* that after the sirens' song 'any music is noise'.

Harpies

Pliny included the sirens in his section on fabulous beasts in the *Natural History*; although he denied their existence, he cited Dinon, whose son Clitarchus accompanied Alexander the Great on his travels, and who located them in India. According to Dinon, 'they charm people with their song and then when they are sunk in a heavy sleep tear them in pieces'. Here the siren seems indistinguishable from the harpy, although generally, as Lloyd-Jones writes, 'If one's hostess at a dinner-party asked if one would rather sit next to a harpy or a siren, one would choose the siren'.

A 17th-century representation of a harpy. At that time interest in monsters, both non-human creatures and those which could be born to human women, led to a plethora of illustrations in works of natural history and medicine, including new images of the traditional beasts of classical mythology.

Harpies, literally 'snatchers', look like women with arms as well as wings, whereas sirens generally look like birds with a woman's head. Their parentage is unclear: they are daughters of Thaumas, Poseidon or Typhon, and Electra. Like women in general in early Greek thought, they are characterised by insatiable appetites: they are indeed maddened by these appetites, and in Athenaeus, 'Many were the mocking dinners they seized with ravening jaw, in the first joy of their eager lips'.

Their principal victim in classical mythology was Phineus of Thrace. Blinded – in return for immortality, in punishment for using his prophetic powers to reveal the gods' secrets to men or as revenge for mistreating his first wife – Phineus was either carried away by the harpies to distant lands and strange peoples or prevented from eating by the harpies stealing his food. As Apollonius Rhodius' third-century BC poem, the *Argonautica*, put it, 'the harpies with their crooked beaks incessantly snatched the food away from his mouth and hands . . . and they poured forth over all a loathsome stench'. The smell they leave is said to be that of decay. Phineus was saved when he gave a banquet for the Argonauts, and the sons of Boreas finally drove the harpies away. They took refuge in the islands known as the Strophades, where Virgil tells how they attacked Aeneas and the Trojans when they were fleeing Troy. Virgil's harpies have clawed feet and talons at the end of their human arms, and attack the Trojans' meal as they did Phineus' food. They are filthy and noisy, with a foul stench and permanent diarrhoea. However, like the sirens, they have prophetic powers: they announce that the final destination of Aeneas will prove to be Italy.

In some respects sirens and harpies, despite their similar bird-woman form, are directly opposed: where the sirens produce a sweet song and may be linked with perfume, the harpies make a discordant noise – they swoop down 'with a sharp scream' – and are associated with a foul stench. In other respects they are very similar. As well as having knowledge of the future, both have links with the underworld; sirens are, in some versions, given this form because of their failure to keep Persephone safe from the lord of the underworld, and they are shown with Persephone on Greek vases. Harpies 'snatch' the soul to take it to Hades and, like sirens, often appear as figures on tombs. The most famous example of this is the early fifth-century BC Lycian funerary pillar known as the 'Harpy Tomb', showing four figures each with a woman's head, arms and breasts but a bird's legs, wings and tail. Each carries a small female human, possibly a soul; this suggestion is supported by the mourning woman seated beneath one of them. The bird-women hold their charges tenderly, almost as though breast-feeding, while the humans clutch at their carriers as if afraid to fall.

Images such as these have been used as evidence for a connection

Panel of the 'Harpy Tomb', a 5th-century BC Lycian funerary pillar, showing a bird-woman who is apparently carrying human souls to the underworld. This and another similar panel flank a central section where a young warrior offers his helmet to a hero or god.

between sirens and harpies and the soul-birds of Egyptian mythology; wall-paintings of the soul-bird (*bai*) date back to the thirteenth century BC. Human-headed birds occur in other cultures, where other meanings may come to the fore. In Islamic literature and art, there are the murgh-i-adami, two peacock-like birds with human faces who speak the truth in answer to questions. Eva Baer has found four different types of human-headed bird in medieval Islamic literature and folklore, all of which are believed to live in remote, inaccessible areas. In art of the period, however, all four are represented by one type, apparently based on the classical harpy,

introduced on Coptic textiles in the eighth century AD. The peak of popularity for such birds was the period from the eleventh to the thirteenth centuries AD, and they are often shown in court scenes, where they seem to symbolise royalty and happiness. The harpy as guardian of parts of the world not open to mankind features on a manuscript from the mid-seventh century, where a sailor lands on an island inhabited by four monkeys, a sphinx and a human-headed bird. In many versions of the Alexander Romance, Alexander the Great encounters two birds with human heads, who in the Armenian version tell him to turn back, because he has reached a country open only to the gods. In the Greek version, written in the third century AD, Alexander meets these birds in the Islands of the Blessed; everything his soldiers pick up in that land turns out to be gold or pearls. Alexander's cook drinks from a stream which, unknown to him, contains the water of immortality. Later on, Alexander's daughter Kale drinks some of the water brought back by the cook, and is exiled by the envious Alexander; she is then known as Neraida, because she was given immortality by the water. As will be seen, this connects her with the classical mermaids, the nereids.

Non-western cultures have sinister bird-women as well. In Maori myth, Kura ngaituku is as tall as a tree, has wings as well as arms, and spears birds with her nails. She catches a boy, Hatupatu, and takes him home with her; he steals the beautiful and valuable clothes which she owns and runs away. On his return he has grown from boy to man, suggesting that here we see a further example of the association of the hybrid human/animal with transitions between age categories.

Mermaids

In Isidore of Seville's seventh-century AD bestiary, the Latin 'siren' still denotes a creature which is part-woman, part-bird, with wings and claws, but by the tenth century AD 'sirens' can be women who have the form of fish below the navel. Manuscripts even exist in which the text describes a bird-woman, while the accompanying illustration shows a fish-woman. Some medieval bestiaries acknowledge the confusion, by saying that there are several kinds of siren – some bird-women, some fish-women and even some snake-women.

According to Edmond Faral, the fish-woman type of siren originates in the *Book of Monsters* dating perhaps to a late seventh- or early eighth-century work by one Aldhelm. It is possible that Aldhelm was trying to rationalise the appearance to fit Ovid's image of 'sea-monsters', and certainly Homer's silence taken with the sirens' parentage – fathered by a river- or sea-god – could support the idea that they were fish-women.

It is only in the late twelfth century, however, that the fish-woman siren becomes the norm in western civilisation. It may be argued that this is not entirely fortuitous. Most trade routes on the Atlantic and Mediterranean shores of Europe kept close to the coast, until the early modern era. In the Mediterranean there are many small islands and mountainous coastlines to act as landmarks to the sailor. It is possible that, while the sirens on their rocks were a suitable object of fear for pilots navigating their ships along the shore by watching for landmarks, the mermaids of the ocean are more appropriate when ships move further off the coast – even, from about 1500, across the North Atlantic Ocean – supported by more sophisticated equipment, including the compass, which was in use from about 1200.

Another relevant feature may be the incorporation into western culture of the association of women with water. For the Hippocratic medical writers and for Aristotle, women were physically wetter than men. Because their spongy flesh retained more fluid from their diet, menstruation was necessary to remove the excess. The sea is then, in a sense, the female element, and the tradition that the presence of women is unlucky on board ship can be seen as expressing this belief; if the sea is female, the ship which masters it should be crewed by men. When female figures are used as figureheads, they have at least one breast bared, because a naked

The skiff of Marie Antoinette (1755–93) with a mermaid as its figurehead; since mermaids are often believed to have the power to raise or to calm storms at will, claiming the protection of a mermaid before sailing is a wise policy.

woman is supposed to be able to calm a storm at sea; Marie Antoinette's skiff had as its figurehead a mermaid. The idea that female monsters are somehow more at home in the watery element may relate to this.

A further explanation of the transformation of bird sirens into fish sirens may lie in the classical myth which tells how the sirens challenged the Muses to a singing contest and, after losing, were plucked by the victors. In Spenser's *Faerie Queene*, first published in 1596, we find a variation which can perhaps be seen as the 'missing link'. In Canto 12 Sir Guyon has to 'overcome' the various pleasures he meets on his voyage. The sea monsters he encounters are not seen as evidence of the richness of God's creation; instead, they are 'dreadful portraits of deformity', far more terrifying than anything seen on the earth. Guyon then hears the pitiful weeping of a 'doleful maid' calling for help from an island; he is advised to ignore her, for she is deceitful and would only lead him to ruin. He obeys, and next comes to the rocky bay where five mermaids live. Spenser explains that these were once 'fair ladies' who foolishly challenged the Muses for mastery; defeated, they were

> . . . deprived
> Of their proud beauty, and th'one moiety
> Transform'd to fish, for their bold surquedry.

From then on, they continued to use their musical talents to lure and kill travellers. Where Spenser has women transformed to mermaids, the classical version has women transformed to bird-women, then plucked for their failure against the Muses; featherless, they seem to cease to be birds and gradually to take on the form of fish.

In medieval church art, avian sirens – including some male ones, shown with beards, and some warlike ones in armour – exist alongside marine sirens, who often wear a short skirt or belt to cover the join between the human and the fish parts of their bodies. Sirens and centaurs often appear together, the centaurs hunting the sirens with bows and arrows. Just as the story of Odysseus and the bird-sirens was taken up by Christian writers and invested with a moral, so the fish-sirens could be made the vehicles of allegory; thus, a siren holding a fish is supposed to represent the soul held by passion.

A particularly interesting text for the study of hybrid creatures is Andreas Alciatus' *Emblemata*, first published in 1531. This includes as emblem no. 116 a picture of the sirens playing their music to Odysseus. In his discussion of the image, Alciatus plays with the multiple identity of the siren, incorporating both the classical bird and the medieval mermaid: 'Featherless birds, legless maidens, finless fish – what can they be? Nature denies ever having united them.' The message he derives from the image is simple: 'Woman is a trap.' He mocks the sirens, saying that the Muses plucked them, and Odysseus made a laughing-stock of them, thus showing that nothing can be learned from harlots. Among the many documented sightings of mermaids, on only one occasion has a combined bird/fish/woman been seen; this was in 1812, when a Mr Toupin of Exmouth was reported to have seen a mermaid with 'short round broad feathers' who sang 'wild melodies'. However, the belief that mermaids should have some features of a bird may have persisted; in the 1730s a mermaid with wings, allegedly caught off Exeter, was displayed in London.

The harpy also underwent transformations in medieval bestiaries; it could even be a horse-man with the body of a lion, the wings of a serpent and a horse's tail. In medieval encyclopaedias it represents the sin of avarice. It is also seen as cruel – it kills the first man it meets, then goes to water, sees its reflection and realises it has killed a fellow creature; stricken by remorse, its grief is renewed each time it sees its reflection and, in some

In medieval church architecture, sirens and centaurs are used with the additional level of Christian allegorical interpretation superimposed over their classical meanings. Sirens represent passion and are often hunted down by centaurs using bows and arrows. This mid-12th-century example of a centaur hunting is from Serrabone, Pyrénées-Orientales, France.

versions, it commits suicide. In Dante's *Inferno* both centaurs and harpies appear in the seventh circle of the violent. The centaurs – including the usually benevolent Chiron – guard the souls of those guilty of violence against others, while the harpies watch the souls of those who have committed violence against themselves, including suicides.

In Greek and Roman literature and art, where a 'siren' was still indisputably a bird, sea-nymphs also existed but did not necessarily have fish tails. Ino of the fair ankles, who helps Odysseus in Homer's *Odyssey*, lives in the sea but cannot be a mermaid, by virtue of her distinguishing feature. Mermaids have their own distinctive attributes – long hair, comb and mirror – but also have features in common with sirens; a beautiful song or voice, foreknowledge, and an association with death. In Hellenistic and Roman funerary art, processions of nereids, or sea-nymphs, appear riding marine animals including sea-centaurs, representing the souls of the dead being carried to the Isles of the Blessed. However, the mermaid's foreknowledge of stormy conditions is accompanied by the ability to cause them. In nineteenth-century Greek folklore a half-fish, half-woman creature called Gorgona stops passing ships – particularly on Saturday nights in the Black Sea – and asks, 'Does Alexander live?' If the correct answer,

'He lives and rules the world', is not given, she raises a storm and kills all on board the ship. If the answer pleases her, she calms the sea, plays her lyre and sings. Like the sphinx, this particular half-woman creature traps men with riddles.

Like sirens and harpies, mermaids can bring death. In folk tales they often set conditions on their benevolence to mortals, and are ruthless if these are not observed. In a Scottish folk tale, a mermaid kills a baby in revenge for her favourite rock being broken. The story of Melusina, dating to the fourteenth century, concerns a mermaid or snake-woman who marries a mortal man and promises to make him rich, but asks to have every Saturday to herself. One day her husband breaks this taboo, only to find her in mermaid form in the bath, at which she flees.

Outside western culture, female creatures who live in the water may have attributes similar to those of mermaids, but without their specific half-fish form. In Hawaiian myth Hina is a woman who lives at the bottom of the sea, but leaves it to live with a human chief; her brothers can, however, take the shape of fish. In Indian legend the asparases are water-nymphs who follow the god Indra; human in form, they share the mermaids' features of beauty, musical skills and knowledge of the future. Another of their characteristics is promiscuity: they are 'heavenly courtesans'. The jalpari, a river-fairy of the Punjab, kills any man who refuses her sexual advances.

One feature of mermaids which is not shared by sirens and harpies is their wealth; their undersea kingdom holds treasure, in the form of the cargo from shipwrecks. This recalls the ancient guardianship function of the half-human, half-animal creature. Hybrid human-animal creatures were used to guard doors and gates from an early period; eagle-headed men, winged men and winged lions with human heads protect against the entrance of evil influences, as for example on the ninth-century BC palace of Ashurnasirpal II at Nimrud. Women, and more specifically virgins, are the best guardians for treasure; the Greeks used the Caryatides (daughters of Caryas) as pillars on the Erechtheum, where the Athenian treasury was located, while the Romans lodged wills and other important documents with the Vestal Virgins. A woman who guards her virginity can guard other things, too.

The mermaid's treasure may thus combine the image of the virgin with that of the hybrid beast. This would also explain why mermaids' relationships with mortal men are so often disastrous; the mermaid, whatever her attractions, is a virgin, not to be touched. The sirens, 'virgin daughters of Earth' but also whores, share this combination of aloofness and allure.

What of the male of the species? Are mermaids and sirens supposed to be unattainable only by mortal men, or by all male beings? Mermen,

Matsya, shown here in a statue of the 18th–19th centuries, is the fish incarnation of Vishnu, the Hindu god of stability and royal power, and is only one of many half-human, half-animal incarnations of this deity. Vishnu is able to combine otherwise unstable images through his divine power.

sometimes called tritons, exist in literature and art, but are far less common than mermaids, just as bearded male sirens are found on some early Greek vases and in medieval art but are not developed in literature. In each case the usual form is half-woman. The male could, however, be seen as the original version. The Babylonian 'sage' Oannes, Akkadian in origin and perhaps dating back to around 5000 BC, was a man-fish or goat-fish, although he is also represented as wholly man, merely wearing a fish-head as a cap and a fish-skin as a cloak. He was seen as a culture-bearer, coming out of the sea by day to teach humans the arts and sciences; sharing the features of beast and human, he echoes Chiron, the ideal teacher. The Syrian moon-goddess Atargartis and the Philistine moon-goddess Derceto were both half-woman and half-fish.

Made in Italy *c.* 1580, the 'Canning jewel' was named after Lord Canning who acquired it when Viceroy of India. The torso of the merman consists of a single blister pearl and is decorated with gold, precious stones and enamel. In the 16th century there was a fashion for jewellery representing mermaids, mermen, dragons and sea-serpents.

The merman returns during the Renaissance as part of a renewed interest in merpeople in general, combined with a trend towards rationalising myth; mermaids have to reproduce somehow, so men become necessary. In the sixteenth century elaborate jewels featuring both mermaids and mermen became fashionable; the most famous is probably the Canning jewel, in which the body of the merman is made from a single blister pearl, formed when organic material, encapsulated in the pearl, decomposes and inflates the pearl. Matthew Arnold's poem, 'The Forsaken Merman' (1849) inverts the usual pattern of a mortal man loving, but being deserted by, a mermaid: here, the mortal woman is 'cruel' and 'faithless', 'the sound of a far-off bell' calling her to leave her mer-husband and children in order to save her soul. Here cruelty is ascribed not to the mermaid alone, but to females in general. In a moving modern version of the theme of merman and mortal woman, Jane Yolen's short story, *The Lady and the Merman*,

has a plain woman fall in love with a merman, 'his beauty and his power
. . . all motion and light'. She finally jumps into the sea to be with him:
'The water cast her face in silver, and all the sea was reflected in her eyes.
She was beautiful for the first time. And for the last.'

Mermaids and mermen are not, however, restricted to art and literature.
One of the most obvious features of these creatures, which sets them apart
from other half-animal, half-human hybrids, is the number of sightings
which have been documented. Among the earliest and most influential are
those in Pliny's *Natural History*. Here Pliny, a former commander of the
Roman fleet, lists two sightings off the coast of Spain of a triton seen and
heard playing on a shell and a nereid who died singing a 'sad song', as
well as a large number of dead nereids reported to Augustus by the legate
of Gaul. A number of *equites* – the group in Roman society most engaged
in trade and business – also saw a 'marine man' in the Gulf of Cadiz and
reported that he climbed on to ships at night. This creature is described
as being completely human in appearance. Finally, in the reign of Tiberius,
Pliny states that a large number of marine monsters, including many nereids, were washed up on the coast by the ocean tide.

It is clear from Pliny's separation of them from the 'marine man' that
the nereids and triton have a part-fish appearance. Pliny explicitly states
that they conform to the traditional description, except that he can report
that the nereids are hairy even on the human part of their body. This
combination of support for the familiar images of art and literature with
a little scepticism in order to demonstrate the superiority of scientific,
eyewitness accounts over myth recurs many times in the history of mermaid sightings. In Pliny's work the sea is regarded as a highly fertile
but also threatening and unpredictable element, with seafaring a rash and
unnatural activity, but here he seems curious and interested rather than
fearful. This seems to be the dominant response to mermaids in the first
century AD, a period when the rebuilding of the navy under Augustus and
the conquest of Britain – and, in the process, of the 'Outer Ocean' (i.e.
the English Channel) – by Claudius led to a shift in people's attitude to
the sea. This should not be overstated; Caligula's troops mutinied rather
than cross the Outer Ocean to Britain.

Another sighting which was to prove highly influential occurred in the
late sixth century AD on the banks of the Nile. A pair of tritons were
seen, but accounts of their appearance vary. Conrad Lycosthenes' list of
prodigies, signs of God's power intended to convert the faithless, was
published in the mid-sixteenth century and included the Nile monsters
under the year 586. In the 1557 edition the same picture of a triton and a
'siren' is given to illustrate both Pliny's accounts and the Nile sighting.
More detailed versions with a more elaborate engraving of the same illustration are given in the natural historians and medical writers of the mid-

sixteenth century onwards: Conrad Gesner, Ulisse Aldrovandi and Ambroise Paré. The male has a serious expression, is bearded and has clearly articulated arms. The female has a gentle face, long hair and breasts. In Paré's *Book of Monsters* the female appears on the third day after the male was seen; in Aldrovandi's *History of Marvellous Creatures* they apparently appear together, and the illustration shows them together, the male embracing the female.

Many mermaid sightings occurred in the age of trade and exploration, particularly from the late sixteenth century onwards, with the first attempts to colonise the New World, the search for a north-west passage to Cathay and the circumnavigation of the globe. These were linked to the idea of the 'marvellous' – that, when men travel to the ends of the earth and discover new realms, things utterly strange will be encountered, and apparently incredible and exaggerated stories will turn out to be true.

Stephen Greenblatt has argued that encounters with the New World did not contradict classical accounts of prodigies and marvels, but gave them a new life. By evoking the marvellous, Columbus set his voyages in the tradition of the heroic voyages of antiquity, from Odysseus onwards. The importance of the classical tradition is such that the traveller simply must see mermaids and other fabulous creatures. The expected gold and spices may not have materialised, but Columbus can still tell of people born with tails, one-eyed men and dog-nosed men. He distinguished between the marvellous and the monstrous: the marvellous is normal but particularly beautiful, fertile or prolific, while the monstrous violates the norm. Off the coast of Haiti, he reported seeing three mermaids (*serenas*) 'who came quite high out of the water'. But, like Pliny, when he compared his sighting with the traditional image of the mermaid, he begged to differ,

The account of the AD 586 sighting of the 'Nile monsters' (here illustrated by Aldrovandi in the seventeenth century) reads as follows in *The Doome warning all men to the Judgmente* (1581): 'In the river Nilus, there were seene living creatures, both male and female, which as far as the flanckes hadde mans shape, and being adiured by God, they stayed to be seen from ye morning till nine of the clocke.'

writing in his diary that they 'were not as pretty as they are depicted, for somehow in the face they look like men'.

Further sightings were made by explorers of the seventeenth century. Sir Richard Whitburne saw one during his discovery of Newfoundland in 1610: unlike Columbus, he found her beautiful, with 'blue streaks resembling hair, but certainly it was no hair'. This mermaid put her hands on the side of the boat, like the marine man in Pliny. In 1614 the sea captain John Smith saw a mermaid off the West Indies; again, she was attractive, with 'long green hair'. Members of Henry Hudson's crew saw one near Nova Zembla and he described her in 1625 as 'looking earnestly on the men'. Her skin was white, and her hair long and black.

The connection of mermaids with trade and exploration has continued in the modern era, sightings still being made in the twentieth century. The writer and sailor Ernle Bradford heard mermaids sing off the Galli Islands in September 1943, while one of Eric de Bisschop's crew saw one with seaweed 'hair' on the deck of his ship on 3 January 1957. De Bisschop described it in his *Tahiti-Nui*; a few days before the sighting, the crew had been discussing sea creatures seen by sailors too long at sea. When approached, the mermaid began to glow, and then jumped into the sea, leaving behind her a strong fishy smell. At Selfridges the statue over the main entrance, installed in 1931, shows 'the Queen of Time' flanked by two sea-nymphs holding a waxing and a waning moon respectively. One of Gordon Selfridge's sayings was 'I am an adventurer', while a Selfridges advertisement on 17 March 1909 read, 'Already in the gathering of vast stocks of merchandise from every quarter of the world have been practised sound business principles that make for confidence.' The sea-nymphs here express the spirit of adventure, control of the seas (through the moon's control of the tides), a wealth of trade goods and 'sound business principles' – guarding treasure.

Mermaid sightings, however, cannot all be classified as sailors' yarns, based on the expectations aroused by classical myth. On many occasions the marvellous has come nearer home, as in Pliny's reports and the case of the Nile mermaid. In 1403 a mermaid is supposed to have floated through a broken dyke near Edam in Holland; she lived in captivity for fifteen years. She was taught to spin and to kneel in front of a crucifix; she never spoke and kept trying to escape to the sea. The story occurs in the *Speculum Mundi* of John Swan. Sailors told of seeing a merman in the Bristol Channel in 1678, the ship's master reporting 'the face and head very like a man's'. There have been many other British sightings, most notably on the Cornish, Welsh and Scottish coasts, often near islands. A miniature mermaid, the size of a three- or four-year-old child, but with 'an abnormally developed breast', was seen swimming off the Hebrides in about 1830. Her body was washed up a few days later, and she was

The 'Queen of Time' statue, which was installed over the entrance to Selfridges in 1931. The sea-nymphs on either side of the central figure could be interpreted as representing trade, 'sound business principles' and, through the waxing and waning moons they hold, control of the tides.

buried in a shroud and coffin. A mermaid described in a Boston newspaper in 1881 has some features which recall a harpy; her arms ended in 'claws closely resembling an eagle's talons instead of fingers with nails'.

Some mermaids were captured, although they rarely survived for long in captivity. The most famous is the mermaid of Amboina, caught off the coast of Borneo and described by a Dutch colonial chaplain, François Valentijn. The illustrations given in the 1754 edition of Louis Renard's book on fish show her with blue eyes and webbed fingers; the preface to this volume argues first that the rarity of sightings cannot be considered as evidence that mermaids do not really exist, and second that dead mermaids are not found, simply because their human appearance may mean that their flesh corrupts as rapidly as man's. The Amboina mermaid is supposed to have survived in a jar of water for four days and seven hours, occasionally uttering plaintive sounds like those of a mouse. She refused to eat the fish offered to her; her excrement was like that of a cat.

The pitiful cries of a captive mermaid, which sometimes lead her finders to throw her back into the sea, are a recurrent feature of these stories, one which I would argue derives from Pliny's description of the nereid washed up on the coast of Gaul. The first English translation of Pliny was available in 1601, although earlier summaries of his work include the references to mermaids. The translator, Philemon Holland, rendered Pliny's *cantum tristem*, 'sad song', as 'piteous moan'. Pliny's 'marine man' putting his hands on the side of the boat also recurs in sailors' accounts. Miniature mermaids, like the Hebridean one, only about 3ft (1m) in length, may derive from Paré's account of a 'marine monster' washed up near Rome on 3 November 1523, the size of a child of five or six years, human in appearance above the navel, except for its ears, and a fish beneath. The ears of merpeople are shown in sixteenth-century engravings as resembling those of a bear; they may have vestigial legs with webbed feet, in addition to a fish-tail.

The availability of visual images, which explicitly influenced literary descriptions from Pliny onwards, also encouraged displays of fake mermaids. Mermaids' skins were exhibited in the sixteenth century, but from the late eighteenth century whole bodies were regularly displayed. These were made from the stuffed skin of a monkey attached to the body and tail of a salmon. In a rather different display in the 1820s Robert S. Hawker, the Vicar of Morwenstow, sat on a rock off the coast at Bude for several nights, naked from the waist up, wearing a wig made from seaweed and concealing his legs in oilskins, and sang to appreciative, if gullible crowds. When he decided the joke had gone too far, he sang 'God Save the King' and dived into the sea.

Nineteenth-century popular songs continued to keep alive the theme of marriage to a mermaid: 'Oh! 'Twas in the broad Atlantic' tells of a young

Fake mermaids were made by stitching the upper torso of a monkey to the tail of a fish. This example was donated to the British Museum by HRH Princess Arthur of Connaught, whose husband had been given it by Seijiro Arisuye; it was supposedly caught off Japan in the 18th century.

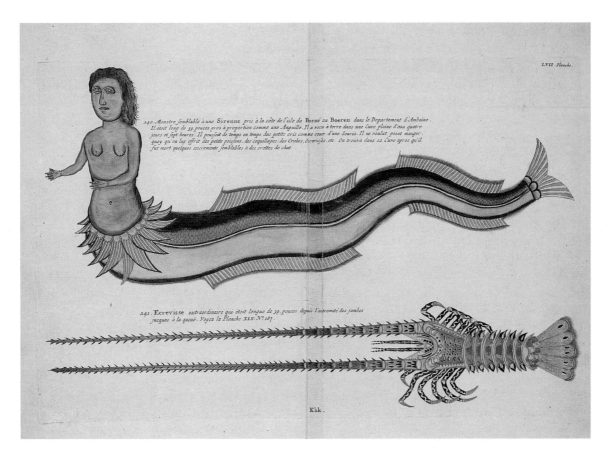

240. Monstre semblable à une Sirenne pris à la côte de l'isle de Borné ou Boeren dans le Departement d'Amboine. Il etoit long de 59.pouces avec a proportion comme une Anguille. Il a vecu à terre dans une Cuve pleine d'eau quatre jours et sept heures. Il poussoit de temps en temps des petits cris comme ceux d'une Souris. Il ne voulut point manger quoy qu'on lay offrit des petits poissons, des coquillages, des Crabes, Ecrevisses, etc. On trouva dans sa Cuve après qu'il fut mort quelques excrements semblables à des crottes de chat.

241. Ecrevisse extraordinaire qui étoit longue de 39.pouces depuis l'extremité des jambes jusques à la queue. Voyez la Planche XLV. N.º 187.

The 'mermaid of Amboina' (above), here illustrated with an 'extraordinary crayfish' (below) in a book of 1754, was captured in the early 18th century and reputedly drawn from life. This highly colourful mermaid could only be kept alive for four days, as she refused all food she was offered.

mariner who falls overboard in an Atlantic gale but lives on with a mermaid bride. The chorus runs:

> Singing, rule Britannia, Britannia rule the waves!
> Britons never, never, never shall be married to a mermaid
> At the bottom of the deep blue sea.

The most famous mermaid story today remains Hans Christian Andersen's *The Little Mermaid*. Here the merworld is explicitly a mirror-world; like our own, it has castles, parks and gardens, only instead of swallows flying in at open windows there are fish. For all her beauty and her singing talents, the little mermaid is atypical of her kind, in that she is fascinated by our world. After saving the life of a prince in a shipwreck, she falls in love with him, and eventually makes a bargain with the sea-witch, giving her tongue in exchange for a pair of human legs. At every step, the little mermaid feels the pain of walking on knives; her feet actually bleed. She is unable to win the love of her prince but, rejecting the chance to kill him, dies when he marries another. This has been seen as a castration story; she must lose her tail to marry the prince, but in so doing becomes

163

mute. The loss of her voice can be interpreted as an image of the silence imposed on women who accept the terms of the patriarchal system.

Twentieth-century fiction and art show the persistence of different sides of classical and later stories of the hybrid beast/woman, often locating fish-sirens as well as bird-sirens on islands off Sicily. E. M. Forster's *The Story of the Siren* uses the idea of the siren's song giving knowledge of the future, a knowledge which human beings cannot bear to possess. A Sicilian boatman tells how his older brother saw the siren when diving for money to entertain English visitors. He came up a lost man, 'unhappy because he knew everything. Every living thing made him unhappy because he knew it would die'. Here the siren has real power; Giuseppe's brother marries a woman who has had the same experience, but she is murdered by a priest because of fear that her unborn child will bring the siren up from under the sea, marry her and inaugurate a new world era.

Giuseppe di Lampedusa's *The Professor and the Siren*, written in 1957, returns to the image of the siren/mermaid as a sexually available but dangerous woman. The narrator, Paolo Corbera, meets a retired professor of Greek in a bar. The professor shows a hatred of women as diseased, squalid and foul, and longs for his favourite food, sea urchins, 'those images of female organs, tasting of salt and sea-weed'. Eventually Corbera goes to the professor's apartment, where the works of art on display include a vase showing 'Odysseus tied to the ship's mast, the Sirens crashing from a high precipice on to rocks in expiation for letting their prey escape' (see illustration p. 147). This is nonsense, the professor insists: nobody escapes the sirens and, even if they did, the sirens would certainly not kill themselves as a result. The professor then tells Corbera his story. At the age of twenty-four, he was in a rowing boat off Augusta in Sicily, when he felt the boat move. A girl with the face of a sixteen-year-old and a smile of 'almost divine delight in existence' climbed out of the water. Her name was Lighea and beneath her groin she had the body of a fish, with a forked tail. Her three charms were her smile, her smell – 'of sea, of youthful voluptuousness' – and her voice. In Greek, she offers herself to the professor: 'I like you; take me.' This is echoed in Alfred Bennett's description of the mermaid, written in 1953: 'She is the whisper which all men, consciously or unconsciously, wait to hear.' The professor accepts, and she stays with him for three weeks before leaving to return to the sea. The professor, unable to love any other woman, eventually returns to his Lighea – committing suicide by drowning.

In a modern, feminist version of the siren myth, Margaret Atwood portrays a siren who wants to get out of her bird suit:

> I don't enjoy it here
> squatting on this island

> looking picturesque and mythical
> with these two feathery maniacs.

Her song,

> . . . a boring song
> but it works every time,

recalls the words of the professor's Lighea; it is simply an invitation, found irresistible by any male listener, to come closer, to help her, as only he can. Mary Daly and Jane Caputi's feminist dictionary, *Webster's First New Intergalactic Wickedary*, gives a positive valuation to the sirens' song, guiding 'Wayfaring Wenches into the Realms of Deep Memory'. For them, it is the male sirens, redefined as pop singers, who are to be feared; these 'Little Sir Sirens of Siredom' are 'sweet-talking spookers who seduce women into the State of Sleeping Death' by persuading women to accept the restricting roles society imposes on them.

In modern art, Magritte's *Collective Invention* shows a sexually available mermaid, with the upper half of a fish and a woman's lower torso. This 'practical man's mermaid' avoids the otherwise difficult question of how, exactly, a man is supposed to have intercourse with a creature with a fish-tail. This critical question was rarely addressed explicitly until the twentieth century, although the double-tailed mermaids of medieval and later art may be interpreted as answering it in an indirect way. Alfred Bennett, writing in 1953, stated: 'Men may adore and worship mermaids with a passion that is fully three-quarters carnal; but they do not have sexual relations with them.' In the rare cases when they do, it is so 'difficult and embarrassing' that the men keep quiet about it. Herbert Draper's painting *Ulysses and the Sirens* (1909) offers another solution, portraying them as mermaids, whose fish-tails are transformed into human legs as they emerge from the water and climb aboard Odysseus' ship. In Derek Walcott's stage version of the *Odyssey*, Odysseus encounters two mermaids who propose three in a bed. Odysseus asks whether fishes present 'a technical problem', but the first mermaid simply says, 'There are ways.'

In recent years Patrick Woodroffe has created his own mythology of the freshwater mermaid, *Nympha pisciforma*, who can 'play dead' when captured; if she remains too long in this condition, real decay will begin, eventually consuming even the bones and leaving only apparently ordinary fish-scales. The males of the species live at sea; in an echo of the Amazon myth, they only meet the females once a year to mate. He also describes the 'sea-squitling' and the common mermaid, *Siren pulcella*, who flirts with passing sailors.

The siren/mermaid is thus alive and well in our consciousness. The creature which mixes beast and woman in its body is both powerful, knowing the future, and dangerous, leading men to death. To love such a beast is to leave behind one's life, either actually or figuratively; mermaids require total commitment, as their mortal husbands must live with them in the sea-world. The prospect of the beast-woman is both irresistible and terrifying; she combines enticing virgin and sexually insatiable whore. As Alfred Bennett's appreciation of mermaids puts it, she is 'the never-never girl' but also '(like all women) as cunning as a nest of Chinese boxes'. Her hybrid body has all that men most lust for, in the virgin face of the siren and the beautiful hair of the mermaid, combined with all that is most repulsive, the violence and the permanent diarrhoea of the harpy, and the fishy extremities of the mermaid. Where women, in western thought since Hesiod, are 'a beautiful evil', attractive on the outside but rotten inside, hybrid animal-women also carry their true nature on the outside, as a visible warning to men of what other women carry within. They inhabit the boundaries between sea and land – both bird-sirens and mermaids have an affinity with rocks – and cross the boundaries between what is known and unknown, between life and death. Like other creatures who combine two usually separate categories, they possess certain powers; but there is a sense in which beast-women reveal that women and beasts are not in fact separate but can have equally voracious appetites and a similar disregard for civilised behaviour.

An unusual solution to the technical difficulties of sex with mermaids: in Herbert Draper's *Ulysses and the Sirens* (1909), the tails of the mermaid-sirens become transformed into legs as they climb on board Odysseus' ship.

Glossary

Aigamuxa man-eating monsters of the south-west African dunes, with eyes, according to Hottentot mythology, on the insteps of their feet. In order to see, they must hold up one foot.

Amemait combination of lion, crocodile and hippopotamus, a symbol of retribution in medieval bestiaries.

Amphisbaena bird-serpent described by classical authors as having two heads, one at the end of its tail, which could see in both directions at once. If one head fell asleep, the other would remain awake.

Ananta 'the endless' divine thousand-headed world serpent of Hindu myth, upon whose infinite coils the god Vishnu reclines in the cosmic primeval ocean. Temporarily taking on human form as Balarama, half-brother of Krishna, it later spews forth venomous fire to destroy creation and is also used by the gods as a rope to churn the ocean for *amrita*, the elixir of immortality.

Ant-lion composite creature with the foreparts of a lion and the hindquarters of a large ant, which can eat neither plant nor flesh.

Anzu gigantic lion-headed Sumerian storm-bird (also called Imdugud) which steals from the gods the Tablet of Destiny. Pursued to its nest on an

Anzu pursued by Ninurta, from a Neo-Assyrian cylinder seal, 9th–7th century BC.

inaccessible mountain by the war-god Ninurta, the powerful bird is eventually slain by an arrow through the heart.

Aries fabulous ram with a golden fleece, fathered by the Greek sea-god Poseidon. Having been sacrificed to Zeus, its fleece is guarded by a dragon in a sacred grove at Kolchis, on the Black Sea, until the hero Jason, leader of the Argonauts, outwits the dragon and seizes the golden fleece. The ram later becomes the constellation Aries.

Audumla primeval cow which, in ·Germanic legend, licks the salty icy rocks from which the first man emerges.

Bai ma white Chinese horse with one horn, the tail of an ox and the cry of a tiger.

Baku powerful beast with an elephant's trunk, ox's tail and tiger's feet, which feeds on bad dreams and in Japan is considered a talisman against the plague.

Basilisk snake described in Pliny's *Natural History* as bearing a livid spot in the form of a crown on its forehead and later regarded by Christians as a symbol of the Antichrist. Appearing in medieval bestiaries as the king of snakes, with a serpent's tail and the head, feet and wings of a cock,

Basilisk with coat of arms of the city of Basel, printers' mark, woodcut, 1511.

it was thought to hatch from a cock's egg incubated by a toad or serpent and from the fourteenth century was called a cockatrice. Its glance is fatal but can be reflected back onto itself with a mirror or polished shield.

Bi-bi Chinese winged fox, whose cry is similar to that of a wild goose.

Bixie Chinese winged beast similar to the **Chimaera**, with one or two horns and the body and tail of a small lion.

Bo Chinese horse with one horn, tiger's teeth and claws, and a white body and black tail. Impervious to weapons, it makes a sound like that of a drum.

Boar various monstrous boars ravaged the Greek countryside until destroyed by heroes: the Calydonian boar, sent by the goddess Artemis in revenge for the neglect of her worship, is eventually killed by Meleager; Phaea, an enormous

Hercules offers the Erymanthian boar to a cowering Eurystheus, from an Athenian amphora, *c.* 530 BC.

sow, laid waste to Krommyon until slain by Theseus; and Hercules captures the Erymanthian boar as his fourth labour.

Bonnacon Asian beast with the body of a horse, the head of a bull and immense curved horns, which defends itself by excreting a fiery substance that burns anything it touches.

Bucentaur *see* **Bull-man**.

Bull-man guardian figure with human head and torso and taurine horns and lower body, also called Bucentaur (*see also* **Lamassu, Minotaur**).

Caladrius white bird attributed in medieval times with the power of divination: seeing a sick person who is destined to live, it can draw the illness to itself and fly away, but it will turn its head away from someone who is dying.

Callitrice Ethiopian creature, part human and part goat, with a beard and a broad tail.

Camazotz, from a Maya vase, 7th–9th century AD.

Camazotz killer bat, opponent of the Hero Twins in their descent to the underworld in the Maya epic the *Popol Vuh*.

Cancer giant crab sent by the Greek goddess Hera to prevent Hercules from killing the Lernaean **Hydra**. It duly attacks his heels with its great pincers, but is itself killed and becomes a constellation.

Capricorn originally a she-goat named Amalthaea, which suckled the infant Zeus while he was hidden from his father Kronos and is eventually rewarded by being turned into a constel-lation. Zeus also gave one of her horns to the nymphs who helped to rear him, and this became an emblem of fruitfulness and abundance known as the cornucopia or horn of plenty.

Catoblepas African animal, possibly based on the gnu, described in classical works on natural history. It holds its head close to the ground, and anyone who sees its eyes dies immediately.

Centaur half man, with the body of a horse from the waist down. Usually associated with lust and licentiousness, although the best-known classical example is Chiron, who was famous for his great wisdom and later became the constellation Sagittarius (the Archer). Centaurs also feature in Mesopotamia from the second millennium BC (*see also* chapter on Half-Human Creatures).

Cerberus many-headed dog which guards the gates of Hades, the Greek underworld. Offspring of **Echidna** and **Typhon**, he is first described as having fifty heads but later as a three-headed dog with a mane of snakes' heads and a serpent's tail. He is lulled to sleep by Orpheus with his lyre and is also dragged alive from Hades as Hercules' twelfth labour.

Chemosit half-man, half-bird demon of the Nandi of East Africa, with one leg and nine buttocks, which eats the flesh of human children.

Bellerophon chasing the Chimaera, terracotta plaque from Melos, *c.* 450 BC.

Chimaera fire-breathing monster with the head of a lion, the hindquarters of a dragon and the mid-section of a goat (also described as having three heads, one of each beast). Offspring of **Echidna** and **Typhon** and said to inhabit Lycia, it is eventually slain by the Greek hero Bellerophon on **Pegasus**, his winged mount (*see also* **Bixie**).

Cockatrice *see* **Basilisk**.

Criocamp *see* **Kriocamp**.

Criosphinx ram-headed lion (*see also* chapter on Sphinxes).

Da Aido Hwedo cosmic serpent, son of the dual creator-deity Mawu-Lisa of the Fon of Benin. Its 7000 coils support the earth from above and below. Seen in the rainbow, the male is the red and the female the blue.

Damballah Wedo powerful serpent-god of Voodoo mythology, manifested with his wife Ayida entwined as a rainbow in the sky above Haiti.

Delphyne female dragon, half woman and half serpent, responsible for rendering Zeus weak during the Olympian war of the gods by guarding his sinews and muscles. She is outwitted by Hermes and **Pan**, who restore his strength.

Dragon *see* chapter on Dragons.

Dzoavits huge ogre who, in the mythology of the Shoshoneans of Nevada and Utah, steals the two children of the Dove and is eventually outwitted by the Badger.

Echidna half snake, half woman with bright eyes and an appetite for raw flesh, who gives birth to **Cerberus**, the **Chimaera**, the Lernaean **Hydra** and other creatures, all fathered by **Typhon**.

Empusa shape-changing female spectre who lives in Hades, the Greek underworld, and feeds on human flesh. She appears most frequently to women and children, often assuming the shape of a young girl to attract her victims.

Erechtheus *see* **Erichthonius**.

Erichthonius half man, half serpent, offspring of Gaia (Earth) and the Greek god Hephaestus; sometimes called Erechtheus. Legendary fourth King of Athens, he introduced the Panathenaic festival and invented the four-horse chariot, and is later turned into the constellation Boötes.

Fafnir venomous dragon which, having stolen the treasure of the dwarves, is slain by the Norse hero Sigurd (Siegfried).

Faun horned beast, half human and half goat, identified with wild nature, fertility and the ancient Roman deity Faunus (*see also* **Pan**, **Satyr**).

Fei-yi Chinese snake described as having one head, two bodies, six feet and four wings.

Fênghuang *see* **Phoenix**.

Fenrir ravenous wolf, offspring of the Norse god Loki and an ogress. Bound with an invisible chain, Fenrir is destined to break free at the end of the world, swallowing the sun and biting the moon, before joining Loki on the final battlefield where he kills the god Odin and is himself slain (*see also* **Jormungandr**).

Ga-gaah wise crow, divine bird of the Iroquois of north-eastern North America, which flies from the kingdom of the sun carrying in its ear a grain of maize. Hahgwehdiyu, the benign creator-god, then plants the seed in the body of the earth-goddess, and this gift becomes the staple food of humans.

Gaja-simha composite Asian elephant-lion.

Garm in Scandinavian mythology, a dog guardian in the underworld.

Garuda vehicle of the Hindu god Vishnu. Referred to as the golden sun-bird, the bird of life and the enemy of all serpents, it has the beak and wings of a hawk and the body, arms and legs of a man. Cambodian temples are built as though resting on its back.

Hercules faces the triple-bodied Geryon, from an Athenian amphora, *c.* 540 BC.

Geryon a winged giant with three bodies joined at the waist, whose herd of red cattle, guarded by the two-headed snake-tailed dog Orthos (brother of **Cerberus**), is carried off by Hercules as his tenth labour.

Ghul in Arabic lore, a monster capable of changing its shape which dwells in lonely places and preys on travellers, who are lured away from their companions and then eaten.

Giants Hekatoncheires, three giants with a hundred arms and serpent legs, which in Greek myth aid the Olympian gods in their battle with the Titans and are later buried under Mount Aetna.

Glaistig half-female, half-goat creature of the Scottish Highlands, generally helpful to farmers but sometimes taking the form of an evil water-spirit (*see also* **Urisk**).

Gorgons winged, serpent-haired and sharp-clawed female monsters (named Stheno, Euryale and Medusa). Medusa alone was mortal and by

Gorgon's head on a Corinthian bowl, early 7th century BC.

far the ugliest, after the goddess Athena takes revenge on her for sleeping with the sea-god Poseidon and transforms her beautiful hair into a nest of serpents. The sight of Medusa turns the beholder to stone. The hero Perseus cuts off her head by looking only at her reflection in his highly polished shield (*See also* chapter on Half-Human Creatures).

Grendel monster of the seventh-century Anglo-Saxon epic poem *Beowulf*, 'grim and greedy, brutally cruel', the 'gruesome prowler of the border land, ranger of the moors, the fens and the fastness', eventually slain by the warrior-prince Beowulf.

Griffin *see* chapter on Griffins.

Hamsa Cambodian gander, the bird-vehicle of Brahma.

Harpies evil demons, part woman and part bird, 'robbers' which the Greeks believed were responsible for carrying off anyone who disappeared without trace. Originally personifications of the storm winds and represented as fair winged maidens, they were later described as ugly, noisy birds with the claws of a vulture and the head and breasts of a woman. Sent to spoil the tables of Phineus with their filth, they are eventually driven off by the hero Jason and his Argonauts (*see also* chapter on Half-Human Creatures).

Harpocrates half man, half crocodile, a Greek version of the ancient Egyptian god Horus depicted as a child.

Hemicynes humans with dogs' heads and voices, said by the Greeks to live on the shores of the Black Sea.

Hippocamp below a Phoenician galley, silver coin of Byblos, *c.* 430 BC.

Hippocamp sea-horse, half horse and half fish with a serpent's tail, depicted as the mount of the nereid Thetis (mother of the Greek hero Achilles) and drawing the chariot of the sea-god Poseidon. Similar images appear in Etruria and Gandhara in India (also called hydrippus).

Hippogriff half horse, half griffin (*see also* chapter on Griffins).

Holawaka mythical bird, carrier of a divine message to the Galla people of Ethiopia.

Hōō *see* **Phoenix**.

Hydra many-headed water-serpent (variously described as having seven, nine, fifty or a hundred heads), offspring of **Echidna** and **Typhon** and sacred to the Greek goddess Hera, which ravaged the Lernaean swamps of Argos. If one head were cut off, two new ones would grow in its place. Slain by Hercules as his second labour with the help of his nephew Iolaus who, after each head was cut off, seared the stump with a burning brand. Hercules then dipped his arrows in its poisonous blood. A similar image appears in Mesopotamia in the third millennium BC.

Hydrippus *see* **Hippocamp**.

Ichthyocentaur classical sea-centaur with a human torso, the chest and forelegs of a horse and the tail of a fish (*see also* **Centaur**).

Illuyankas dragon killed by the Hittite weather-god (*see also* chapter on Dragons).

Imdugud *see* **Anzu**.

Itherther primeval buffalo from whose semen all wild animals originate, according to the Kabyls of Algeria.

Jormungandr sea-serpent, offspring of the Norse god Loki and an ogress, which occupies the entire mid-portion of the earth and bites its own tail. At Ragnarok, the destruction of the gods, the enraged monster whips the seas into violence and blows clouds of poison over the earth and sky. Ultimately it is killed by the god Thor at the final battle with the gods (*see also* **Fenrir**).

Kalamakara combination of lion and crocodile (*see also* **Makara**).

Kaliya many-headed Hindu serpent-king who lives in the River Yamuna and is overcome by the boy Krishna.

Karkadann Islamic rhinoceros-unicorn (*See also* chapter on Unicorns).

Kappa fierce Japanese river-spirit which, although it eats human flesh, is also extremely

Seated Kappa, Japanese wooden netsuke, late 18th century.

polite and can be overcome by being induced to bow, since its power resides in the liquid contained in a saucer-shaped depression on the crown of its head. The resident spirit may also be placated by throwing cucumbers, a favourite food, into a river. *Kappa*, a novel by Ryūnosuke Akutagawa, tells the story of a human's adventures in Kappa-land.

Keres black winged female creatures with huge white teeth and pointed talons, who tear corpses apart and drink the blood of the wounded and the dead. In Homer's *Iliad* they are personifications of death, present at all scenes of battle and slaughter, who control the destinies of the heroes; in later times they were regarded as the vengeful spirits of the dead.

Keryneian Hind Arcadian stag with golden antlers and brazen feet, sacred to the Greek goddess Artemis, which is captured unharmed by Hercules as his third labour.

Kilin *see* **Qilin**.

Kimat faithful dog of the thunder-god Kadaklan, of the Tinguian people in the mountainous interior of Luzon, northernmost island of the Philippines. As lightning, the dog bites houses, trees or fields whenever its divine master wishes a special ceremony to be performed.

Kirin Japanese equivalent of the Chinese **Qilin**, and a powerful symbol of good luck (*see* illustration p. 2 and chapter on Unicorns).

Kitsune Japanese fox, which traditionally has the ability to change its shape in order to trick and mislead humans. In one fox legend, a beautiful

Kitsune (fox-priest), Japanese wooden netsuke, 18th century.

fox-woman is betrayed by the bushy tail poking out under her kimono. A more benign fox acts as the messenger of Inari, god of the rice harvest.

Kraken huge sea-monster with large tentacles, often mistaken by sailors for an island; described in Tennyson's poem 'The Kraken' as sleeping 'far, far beneath in the abysmal sea'.

Kriocamp half ram, half fish, and originally a symbol of the Mesopotamian water-god.

Kriosphinx *see* **Criosphinx**.

Kukulkan feathered serpent of the Maya, possibly related to the wind-god and to the Aztec plumed serpent-god Quetzalcoatl.

Ladon hundred-headed dragon, guardian of the golden apples of the Hesperides ('the daughters of evening' who lived near Mount Atlas, at the western extreme of the Mediterranean). The dragon is slain by Hercules as part of his eleventh labour, which was to carry off three of the golden apples.

Lamassu human-headed winged bulls and lions, commonly found as gateway guardians of Assyrian temples and palaces (*see also* **Bull-man**, and chapter on Sphinxes).

Lamia woman-headed, child-stealing snake, in classical myth a beauty loved by Zeus who becomes a monster, unable to sleep, after Hera kills her children as each is born. Zeus gives Lamia the power to remove and replace her eyes at will. She is the subject of a story by the Greek writer Philostratus, upon which John Keats based his poem 'Lamia', about a beautiful woman who is exposed by a philosopher as a destructive phantom creature. Lamiae (plural) later became voluptuous, blood-sucking women, the classical equivalent of the modern vampire (*see also* **Mormo**).

Leviathan literally, 'coiled'; huge and terrible sea-serpent, described in the Book of Job: 'He esteemeth iron as straw, and brass as rotten wood. . . . He maketh the deep to boil like a pot.' Considered by medieval Christians as the

'king over all the children of pride' and identified with hell, with a gigantic maw as the entrance.

Ling yu Chinese fish with a human face, arms and legs.

Long the dragon of Chinese folklore, regarded as a benevolent rain-bringer and lord of the waters of the clouds, rivers, marshes, lakes and seas. Described as having 'the horns of a stag, the head of a camel, the eyes of a demon, the neck of a snake, the scales of a fish, the claws of an eagle, the pads of a tiger, the ears of a bull and the long whiskers of a cat' (*see also* chapter on Dragons).

Lotan a monstrous primeval serpent or dragon slain by Baal, powerful young fertility-god of ancient Canaanite myth and protagonist of the mythological texts of Ugarit.

Makara South-East Asian water-beast, sometimes described as the mount of a water-goddess, with a curly lizard-like body and open crocodilian jaws (*see also* pp. 14–15 and **Kalamakara**).

Manticora, woodcut from Edward Topsell's *Historie of Foure-Footed Beastes*, 1607.

Manticora ferocious monster, first described by the Greek traveller Ctesias, with a lion's body, human face and ears, three rows of teeth in each jaw and poisoned spines in its tail, which it could shoot like arrows.

Mermaid half-human water-dweller, with the tail of a fish and the body of a beautiful woman from the waist up. The male version is the merman (*see also* chapter on Half-Human Creatures).

Theseus and the Minotaur, from an Athenian jar, *c.* 480 BC.

Minotaur bull-man, offspring of Pasiphae (sister of the enchantress Circe and wife of King Minos of Crete) and a magnificent white bull sacred to the sea-god Poseidon, which Minos had failed to sacrifice. In revenge the god inspires Pasiphae with an unnatural lust for the bull. Minos confines the Minotaur in the Labyrinth, an underground maze built by the master craftsman Daedalus, where each year it devours seven maidens and seven youths exacted by Minos as tribute from the Athenians. Eventually Theseus, son of the king of Athens, defeats and kills the Minotaur with the help of Minos' daughter Ariadne, who gives him a thread that enables him to find his way out of the maze (*see also* **Bull-man**, and chapter on Half-Human Creatures).

Mokele-Mbembe cave-dwelling beast the size of an elephant, with a long neck, single horn or tooth and a strong serpentine tail, reported by early European visitors to West Africa.

Mormo female monster invoked as a general bugbear to frighten children. She is said to bite the legs of naughty children and make them lame (*see also* **Lamia**).

Mušhuššu 'furious snake' or snake-dragon, one of the army of monsters created by the primeval dragon **Tiamat** and subdued by the Mesopotamian god Marduk (*see also* chapter on Dragons).

Mušmahhu seven-headed Mesopotamian snake-monster (*see also* **Hydra).**

Nāgas semi-divine, many-headed, Hindu water-serpents, with human faces and hooded heads on expanded necks like cobras, whose function is to guard treasure and esoteric knowledge. In temple architecture they stand guard at the portals of shrines. They inhabit underwater paradises, dwelling at the bottoms of rivers, lakes and seas in splendid, jewel-studded palaces full of song and dance (*see also* chapter on Dragons).

Nandi milk-white bull, guardian of four-legged creatures and the vehicle of the Hindu god Shiva.

Hercules wrestling with the Nemean Lion, silver coin of Heraclea, *c.* 330 BC.

Nemean Lion monstrous lion with a hard and impenetrable skin, offspring of **Echidna** and **Typhon**, killed by Hercules as the first of his twelve labours. Afterwards he skins the beast and wears its hide.

Nialyod rainbow-serpent and first mother of the Kunwinjku clan of Australian Aborigines. From her waterhole she swallows people and then regurgitates them as features of the landscape.

Nidhoggr Germanic dragon, 'dread biter', which in Norse mythology constantly gnaws at a mighty root of the cosmic ash tree Yggdrasil.

Killing the Nue, from a Japanese Kabuki theatre signboard, 1870s.

Nue monstrous Japanese beast with the body of a badger, the head of a monkey, tiger's feet and a serpent's tail, killed by the warrior Minamoto no Yorimasa when its howling and scratching disturb the sleep of the emperor.

Oni Japanese Shinto demons associated with disease, calamity and misfortune. Basically human in appearance, they can fly and have three eyes, a wide mouth, horns and three sharp talons on both hands and feet.

Oni, Japanese wooden mask, 19th century.

Opinicus griffin-like beast with the body and legs of a lion, the head, neck and wings of an eagle, and the tail of a camel, although sometimes depicted without wings.

Ouroboros *see* **Uroboros**.

Pan Greek god of flocks and shepherds, a son of Hermes, with pointed ears and the horns and legs of a goat. Associated with fecundity, he has some of the lascivious qualities of the **Centaur**. Inventor of the syrinx (Pan pipes, made of reeds), haunting caves and lonely rural places, he was said to inspire sudden groundless fear (panic) in both humans and animals (*see also* **Faun**, **Satyr**).

Pazuzu Assyrian demon, part human but with wings, horns, the claws of a bird and the paws of a lion; associated with storm winds and bringer of diseases.

Pegasus winged horse, said to have sprung from the blood of the **Gorgon** Medusa after her head was cut off by Perseus. The Greek hero Bellerophon tames him with a golden bridle and mounts

Pegasus, silver coin of Carthage, *c.* 265 BC.

Chinese Phoenixes, inlaid mother-of-pearl on a bronze mirror, Tang Dynasty, 8th–9th century AD.

Pegasus to fight the **Chimaera**. Bellerophon later tries to ride Pegasus up to heaven but is thrown off when Zeus sends a gadfly to sting the horse. The winged horse also appears in Mesopotamia, *c.* thirteenth century BC.

Phoenix a bird of ancient Egyptian myth which, in the classical world, became a symbol of immortality and resurrection; said to live for 500 years before incinerating itself upon a burning pyre of aromatic boughs and spices in the Arabian desert, whereupon it simultaneously gives birth to one offspring which arises from its ashes. The phoenix represents the eternal city of Rome on commemorative coins of the late Roman Empire, and in Western sources is described as being as large as an eagle, with brilliant gold plumage and a melodious cry. In China the phoenix (*fènghuáng*) is a creature whose rare appearance presages some great event. A common decorative motif, it has auspicious attributes as a symbol of peace and prosperity and is associated with the empress and the female yin principle. The Japanese word (*hōō*) combines two Chinese characters, *hō* (male) and *ō* (female),

suggesting bisexuality, and the bird is said to appear at times of peaceful and prosperous government, while in Tibet it may be depicted as a male–female pair holding a small peony, the national flower. In the wake of the Mongol invasion of the Islamic world in the thirteenth century the phoenix also became linked with the Persian **Simurgh**.

Python monster serpent, offspring of Gaia (Earth), which tries to attack Leto when she is pregnant by Zeus with the twins Apollo and Artemis. Killed in revenge by Apollo, who founds the Pythian Games and acquires the epithet Pythius in celebration.

Qilin Chinese unicorn (also spelled Kilin, Ch'i lin), a good and gentle creature associated with yin-yang, the two interacting forces that sustain the Chinese cosmos. According to legend, at the birth of Confucius in 551 BC a qilin appeared and spat out a piece of jade, on which it was written that the philosopher would be 'an uncrowned emperor' (*see also* **Kirin**, and chapters on Dragons and Unicorns).

Qingu leader of the army of monsters created by the primeval dragon **Tiamat** and subdued by the Mesopotamian god Marduk.

Rakhsh supernaturally strong horse, the faithful mount of the legendary Persian hero Rustam.

Rakhsh and Rustam fighting a dragon, from a persian *Shahnameh* manuscript, 18th century.

Rattlesnake dog belonging to Coyote, the trickster-god of Native American myth. The dog's bite brings sickness and death into the world for the first time.

Roc *see* **Rūkh**.

Rūkh in Arabic tradition, an enormous storm-bird strong enough to carry off elephants (also called Roc).

Salamander on a seal of Sir Thomas Smith, mid-16th century.

Salamander small, poisonous, lizard-like animal, considered to have the supernatural ability to survive in fire without being burnt because the temperature of its own body is so cold.

Sasabonsam hairy forest monster with large bloodshot eyes and feet pointing both ways; according to the Ashanti of West Africa, it sits in the high branches of trees and dangles its long legs to entangle unwary hunters.

Satyr part-human, part-goat spirit of the wild in Greek mythology, bestial in desires and behaviour and associated with Dionysus and wine, revelry and lechery. The satyr Marsyas competes with Apollo in a musical contest and is flayed as punishment when he loses (*see also* **Faun, Pan**, and chapter on Half-Human Creatures).

Scorpion-men human from the waist up with the lower body of a scorpion, they guard the gate to Mount Khumbaba in the Mesopotamian *Epic of Gilgamesh*.

Scylla six-headed sea-monster of Greek myth, with three rows of teeth and twelve feet, composed from the waist down of dogs which never stop barking. Transformed from a beautiful woman by the jealous enchantress Circe, she lives in a cave on the Italian shore of the Straits of Messina, opposite Charybdis, a violent whirlpool, from where she snatches unsuspecting sailors from their ships with her six mouths.

Senmurv *see* **Simurgh**.

Shan hui Chinese mountain dog with a human face.

Shang yang a bird with only one leg which, according to Chinese legend, takes water into its beak from rivers and expels it in the form of rain.

Shokuin man-faced dragon with a red scaly body over 200 miles long and a wide red mouth, horns, a horse's tail, and hooves on its hindfeet and claws on its forefeet. In Japanese mythology, night comes when it sleeps and its waking begins the day, while its inhalation brings summer and its exhalation causes winter.

Simurgh Persian composite of a huge bird with a dog or lion (also called Senmurv), sometimes associated with the **Phoenix**.

Simurgh on a late Sasanian silver-gilt plate, 7th–8th century AD.

Siren women, bird-women or **Mermaids** who sing or sometimes play beautiful music to lure sailors to their deaths on the rocks surrounding their island. The Greek hero Odysseus escapes them by plugging the ears of his crew with wax while he is lashed to the mast of his ship. Eventually bested by the music of Orpheus as he sails past with the Argonauts, they throw themselves into the sea and are transformed into rocks (*see also* chapter on Half-Human Creatures).

Sleipnir eight-legged horse of the Norse god Odin.

Sphinx *see* chapter on Sphinxes.

Stymphalian Birds monstrous birds with brazen claws, wings and beaks, which use their

Hercules aims his slingshot at the Stymphalian Birds, from an Athenian amphora, *c.* 530 BC.

own feathers as arrows and eat human flesh. They are despatched by the Greek hero Hercules as his sixth labour.

Taotie Chinese decorative motif comprising a face (the earliest designs consisting simply of eyes) with features such as horns and claws, resembling but never quite capturing the likeness of any one animal, real or imagined.

Taotie mask, from a Chinese ritual bronze vessel found in a late Shang Dynasty tomb, *c.* 1250 BC.

Teelget enormous four-footed man-eating beast with the horns of a deer, defeated by Nayenezgani, a hero of the Navajo of Arizona.

Tengu pursuing a phoenix, Japanese ivory netsuke, 19th century.

Tengu mischievous and boastful winged demonic spirits, either semi-human with excessively long noses and the wings and claws of giant eagles, or completely bird-like. Notable for their fury and threatening behaviour, they are often associated with swordsmanship in Japanese mythology.

Tiamat Mesopotamian female dragon, described as a huge, bloated creature signifying the primeval watery chaos, slain along with her army of monsters by the god Marduk (*see also* **Mušhuššu**, **Qingu**).

Tianlu Chinese deer-like creature.

Tian wu *see* **Wu**.

To Burmese lion-deer.

Triton son of the Greek sea-god Poseidon and the sea-goddess Amphitrite, human from the waist up but with the lower body of a fish or dolphin. He is often depicted blowing on a twisted conch-shell, by which he could stir up or calm the seas (*see also* **Mermaid**).

Tsenahale huge eagle-like, man-devouring beasts defeated by Nayenezgani, a hero of the Navajo of Arizona.

Tua guardian spirit of the Iban warriors of Borneo, most commonly a snake such as a python or cobra but occasionally a wild cat or deer.

Typhoeus *see* **Typhon**.

Typhon hundred-headed winged monster (also called Typhoeus), son of Gaia (Earth) and Tartarus, father (by **Echidna**) of **Cerberus**, the **Chimaera** and the **Hydra**, whose body ends in a snake's tail and whose eyes and mouth blaze fire. After challenging Zeus he is subdued with a thunderbolt and imprisoned under Mount Aetna in Sicily.

Unicorn *see* chapter on Unicorns (*see also* **Kirin**, **Qilin**).

Urisk part human, part goat, found in lonely places in the Scottish Highlands, especially near waterfalls (*see also* **Glaistig**).

Uroboros border design from the Book of Durrow, Northumbria, 7th century AD.

Uroboros 'the tail-devourer' (also called Ouroboros), representation of a serpent or dragon biting its own tail, usually appearing in northern European art in the form of a circle and used to symbolise concepts such as completion, totality and perfection (*see also* **Jormungandr**).

Urubutsin 'vulture-king', tricked, according to the Kamaiura tribe of the Amazon region of Brazil, by the sun-god Kuat in order to wrest the light of day as ransom in return for its freedom.

Usumgal serpentine monster mentioned in Sumerian poetry, used as a term of praise and as a metaphor for a god or king.

Vermilion Bird of the South mythical Chinese bird (*see also* **Phoenix**).

Vision Serpent Maya image of a rearing, undulating serpent, usually with a single head and prominent snake markings, from whose mouth are belched forth gods or noble humans; often portrayed within clouds of smoke rising from a burning blood offering (*see also* **Xiuhcoatl**).

Vritra dragon-deity which, in Hindu myth, causes drought by withholding water in its body until slain with a bolt of lightning by Indra, god of rain, to bring the monsoon.

Vucub Caquix monster-bird (also known as Seven Macaw) which presides over the murky twilight world following the flood in Maya myth. It is defeated by the Hero Twins in the sacred epic *Popol Vuh*.

Wakonda thunder-bird and lightning motif, Great Lakes area, 19th century.

Wakonda mighty thunder-bird of the Great Lakes tribes of Native Americans, which creates thunder by flapping its wings.

Werewolf lupine creature, usually the result of human metamorphosis.

Windigo immensely strong, vicious monster of Algonquin Native American myth, man-like in form, which feeds on human flesh.

Wishpoosh huge lake-dwelling beaver-monster of the Nez Percé tribe of the north-west Pacific coast and forest, vanquished in a titanic struggle by the trickster-god Coyote.

Wititj great python of the Australian Aborigines, whose spit forms the rain clouds of the first monsoon of the season.

Wu Chinese celestial spirit with a tiger's body, eight feet and tails, and eight human heads (also called *tian wu*).

Wyvern two-legged dragon with wings (*see also* chapter on Dragons).

Xanthus one of the two immortal horses of the Greek hero Achilles (the other called Balius), offspring of the **Harpy** Podarge and the West Wind, which is given the gift of speech in order to forewarn Achilles of his forthcoming death.

Xiuhcoatl Aztec fire-serpent or turquoise snake, with a segmented body and snout which turns sharply backwards; associated with fire and solar heat and with the Central Mexican god of fire, Xiuhtecuhtli (*see also* **Vision Serpent**).

Yale black or tawny animal the size of a hippopotamus, described in Pliny's *Natural History* as having two long horns that can be moved to face in any direction.

Yali composite leonine beast, often appearing in architectural decoration.

Zaltys harmless green snake revered by the Indo-European Balts (Lithuanians, Prussians and Letts) as a symbol of fertility. The Aitvaras, a flying zaltys which gives off light, is thought to bring wealth.

Ziz in Hebrew myth, the largest of all birds, which, when flying, darkens the light of the sun.

Bibliography

General

AELIAN, *On the Characteristics of Animals*, trans. A. F. Schofield, Cambridge, Mass., 1959

AMEISENOVA, Z., 'Animal-Headed Gods, Evangelists, Saints and Righteous Men', *Journal of the Warburg and Courtauld Institutes*, XII (1949), 21–45

ANDERSON, M. D., *History and Imagery in British Churches*, London, 1971

BARBER, R. W., and RICHES, A., *A Dictionary of Fabulous Beasts*, London, 1971

BERNHEIMER, R., *Wild Men in the Middle Ages*, London, 1952

BORGES, J. L., and GUERRERO, M., *The Book of Imaginary Beings*, London, 1970

BROWNE, Sir T., *Pseudodoxia Epidemica*, in *Works*, ed. C. Sayle, London, 1927

BUNT, C. G. E., 'The Lion and the Unicorn,' *Antiquity* IV, 1930

CLÉBERT, J. P., *Bestiaire fabuleux*, Paris, 1971

COOPER, S. C., *An Illustrated Encyclopaedia of Traditional Symbols*, London, 1984

COSTELLO, P., *The Magic Zoo: The Natural History of Fabulous Animals*, London, 1979

COTTERELL, A., *A Dictionary of World Mythology*, Oxford, 1986

CTESIAS, *La Perse, L'Inde*, trans. R. Henry, Brussels, 1947

DEBIDOUR, V.-H., *Le Bestiaire sculpté du Moyen Age en France*, Paris, 1961

DENNYS, R., *The Heraldic Imagination*, London, 1975

DESSENNE, A., *Le sphinx: étude iconographique. I. Des origines a la fin du second millenaire*, Paris, 1957

DRUCE, G. C., 'The Medieval Bestiaries: their influence on Ecclesiastical Art', in *J Brit Archaeol Assoc*, N.S. XXV (1919), 41–82, and XXVI (1920), 88–106

FARKAS, A. E. (ed.), *Monsters and Demons in the Ancient and Medieval Worlds*, Mainz, 1987

FARSON, D., and HALL, A., *Mysterious Monsters*, London, 1978

GOULD, C., *Mythical Monsters*, London, 1886

HART, G., *Egyptian Myths*, London, 1990

HICKS, C., *Animals in Early Medieval Art*, Edinburgh, 1993

HUBER, R., *Treasury of Fantastic and Mythological Creatures: 1,087 Renderings from Historic Sources*, New York, 1981

JAMES, M. R., *The Bestiary*, Oxford, 1928

JANSON, H. W., *Apes and Ape Lore in the Middle Ages and Renaissance*, London, 1952

KLINGENDER, F., *Animals in Art and Thought to the End of the Middle Ages*, London, 1971

LLOYD-JONES, H., *Mythical Beasts*, London, 1980

LUM, P., *Fabulous Beasts*, London, 1952

MARLE, R. van, *Iconographie de l'art profane au Moyen Age et à la Renaissance*, The Hague, 1931–2

McCALL, H., *Mesopotamian Myths*, London, 1990

McCULLOCH, F., *Medieval Latin and French Bestiaries*, Chapel Hill, 1962

MODE, H., *Fabulous Beasts and Demons*, London, 1975

PLINY, *Natural History*. trans. H. Rackham and others, Loeb Classical Library, 10 vols, 1938–62

ROWLAND, B., *Animals with Human Faces*, London, 1974

SCHIFFLER, B., *Die Typologie der Kentauren*, Frankfurt, 1976

SOUTH, M. (ed.), *Mythical and Fabulous Creatures: A Source Book and Research Guide*, Westport, Conn., 1987

WHITE, T. H., *The Book of Beasts, being a translation from the Latin Bestiary of the Twelfth Century* (Cambridge Univ. Library MS Ii.4.26), London, 1954

WITTKOWER, R. W., *Allegory and the Migration of Symbols*, London, 1977

Dragons

ALLEN, J., and GRIFFITHS, J., *The Book of the Dragon*, London, 1979

CREEL, H. G., *Studies in Early Chinese Culture*, London, 1938

CURATOLA, G., *Draghi*, Venice, 1989

DALLEY, S., *Myths from Mesopotamia*, Oxford, 1989

DE VISSER, M. W., *The Dragon in China and Japan*, Amsterdam, 1913

HARTNER, W., 'The Pseudoplanetary Nodes of the Moon's Orbit in Hindu and Islamic Iconographies', *Arts Islamica*, vol. v, pt. 2, 1938, 114–153

HOULT, J., *Dragons: Their History and Symbolism*, Glastonbury, 1987

JAMESON, A., *Sacred and Legendary Art*, London, 1850

KRAMRISCH, S., *Manifestations of Shiva*, Philadelphia, 1981

RAWSON, J., *Chinese Ornament: The Lotus and the Dragon*, London, 1984

STANFORD, H., *Royal Beasts*, London, 1956

ZHAO, Q., 'Dragon: The Symbol of China', *Oriental Art*, vol. XXXVII, No. 2 (Summer 1991), 72–80

Unicorns

AUDEN, W. H., *Collected Poems*, ed. E. Mendelson, London, 1976

BENEDETTO, L. F., *Marco Polo, Il Milione*, Florence, 1928

CAESAR, *The Gallic War*, trans. H. J. Edwards, London, 1917

ETTINGHAUSEN, R., *The Unicorn* (Studies in Muslim Iconography), Washington, 1950

FOURNIVAL, R. de, *Le Bestiaire d'amour*, ed. C. Hippeau, Paris, 1860

FREEMAN, M., *The Unicorn Tapestries*, New York, 1976

NAUMANN, H. 'Mon Seul Desir, La Dame à la Licorne vor dem Zelt des Aubert Le Viste', *Archives Heraldiques Suisses*, vol. CVI, 1992, pt 2

PETRARCH, *The Triumphs*, trans. E. H. Wilkins, Chicago, 1962

Physiologus, trans. M. J. Curley, Austin, Texas, 1979

RILKE, R. M., *Sonette an Orpheus*, in *Poems 1906–1926*, trans. J. B. Leishman, London, 1936

SANFORD, E. M., 'Honorius Presbyter and Scholasticus', *Speculum* XXIII (1948), 397–425

SHEPHARD, O., *The Lore of the Unicorn*, London, 1930

SPENSER, E., *The Faerie Queene*, London, 1955

STERN, C. M., *Unicorn, Myth and Reality*, London, 1977

THURBER, J., *The Thurber Carnival*, London, 1953

TOPSELL, E., *The Historie of Foure-footed Beastes,* London, 1607

VON ESCHENBACH, W., *Parzifal*, trans. H. M. Mustard and C. E. Passage, New York, 1961

Griffins

AELIAN, *On the Characteristics of Animals*, IV, 27, *see* 'General' section

AESCHYLUS, *Prometheus Bound*, 802–7, trans. H. W. Smith, Loeb Classical Library, 1922–6

AETHICUS of Istria, *Cosmographia*, III, 2, 5 and IV, v, 2, in *Ethicus et les ouvrages cosmographiques intitulés de ce nom*, ed. M. D'Avezac, Paris, 1852

ALBERT, St, *De animalibus libri XXVI*, XXIII, 24, 46, ed. H. Städler, Münster, 1916–20

ALDROVANDI, U., *Ornithologiae, hoc est de avibus historias libri XII*, X, 1, Bologna, 1599

ALDROVANDI, U., *Monstrorum historia*, Bologna, 1642

Alexander Romance, The: *Historia de preliis: Der Alexanderroman des Archipresbyters Leo*, ed. F. Pfister, Heidelberg, 1913

Archaeology, 47, no. 6 (November–December, 1994), 52–9

ARMOUR, P., *Dante's Griffin and the History of the World*, Oxford, 1989

ARRIAN, *Anabasis Alexandri*, v, 4, 3, trans. P. A. Brunt, Loeb Classical Library, 1929–33

AYZAC, F. d', 'Du symbolisme du griffon dans l'art chrétien du moyen-âge', *Revue de l'art chrétien*, 4 (1860), 241–63

BENJAMIN of Tudela, *Itinerarium ex versione Benedicti Ariae Montani*, Leipzig, 1764

BISI, A. M., *Il grifone: Storia di un motivo iconografico nell' antico Oriente mediterraneo*, Rome, 1965

BOLTON, J. D. P., *Aristeas of Proconnesus*, Oxford, 1962

Book of the Thousand Nights and One Night, The, ed. J. C. Mardrus, trans. P. Mathers, London, 1947

BOURAS, L., *The Griffin through the Ages*, Athens, 1983

BRENDAN, St, 'Navigatio Sancti Brendani Abbatis' from Early Latin Manuscripts, ed. C. Selmer, Notre Dame, Indiana, 1959

BROWN, R., *Remarks on the Gryphon, Heraldic and Mythological*, Westminster, 1885

BROWNE, Sir T., *Pseudodoxia epidemica*, III, 11, *see* 'General' section

BULWER LYTTON, E. G. E., *The Pilgrims of the Rhine*, ch. 12, London, n.d.

CARROLL, Lewis, *Alice's Adventures in Wonderland*, chs 9–12, London, 1972

CAXTON, W., *Caxton's Mirrour of the World*, ed. O. H. Prior, Oxford, 1913

CHAUCER, Geoffrey, 'The Knightes Tale', in *The Canterbury Tales*, London, 1906

CHIERICI, J., *Il grifo dantesco*, Rome, 1967

DANTE ALIGHIERI, *Purgatorio*, XXIX, XXXI, 112–26, and XXXII, 19–90, in *La Divina Commedia*, ed. U. Bosco and G. Reggio, Florence, 1979

DELPLACE, C., *Le griffon de l'archaïsme à l'époque impériale*, Brussels and Rome, 1980

Ernestus, seu carmen de varia Ernesti Bavariae ducis fortuna, auctore Odone, in E. Martène and U. Durand, *Thesaurus novus anecdotorum*, Paris, 1717

FLAGGE, I., *Untersuchungen zur Bedeutung des Greifen*, Sankt Augustin, 1975

FRUGONI, C. Settis, *Historia Alexandri elevati per griphos ad aerem*, Rome, 1973

GIORDANO of Pisa, Brother, Sermon 50, in *Quaresimale fiorentino, 1305–1306*, ed. C. Delcorno, Florence, 1974

Greek *Physiologus*: Peters, E., *Der griechische Physiologus und seine orientalischen Übersetzungen*, Berlin, 1898

GRIFFIN, M. I. J., *Frank R. Stockton: A Critical Biography*, Philadelphia, 1939

HELGAUD de Fleury, *Vie de Robert le Pieux (Epitoma vitae regis Roberti Pii)*, ed. R. H. Bautier and G. Labory, Paris, 1965

HERODOTUS, *History*, III, 116, and IV, 13–15, 27, trans. A. D. Godley, Loeb Classical Library, 1921–4

HILDEGARD of Bingen, St, *Subtilitatum diversarum naturarum creaturarum libri IX*, VI, 1, in *Patrologia latina*, ed. J.-P. Migne, vol. CXCVII, col. 1287

HUGH of St Victor (attrib.), *De bestiis et aliis rebus libri IV*, III, 4 and 58, in *Patrologia latina*, vol CLXXVII, cols 84, 116–17

ISIDORE of Seville, St, *Etymologiarum libri XX*, XII, 2, 17 and XIV, 3, 7 and 32, in *Patrologia latina*, vol. LXXXII, cols 436, 497, 501

JEROME, Jerome K., *Three Men on the Bummel*, ch. 10 Bristol, n.d.

JOHN of Genoa (Joannes Balbus), 'Arimaspi' and 'griphes', in *Catholicon*, Mainz, 1460; reprinted Westmead, 1971

JOHN SCOTUS ERIGENA, *De divisione naturae libri v*, III, 39, in *Patrologia latina*, vol. CXXII, col. 738

LINDSAY, V., *Collected Poems*, New York, 1946

Mandeville's Travels, ed. M. Letts, London, 1953

MICHOVIUS, Mathias, *Tractatus de duabus Sarmatiis Asiatica et Europiana et de contentis in eis*, I. 'De Sarmatia Asiana', II, ch. 5, Augsburg, 1518

MILTON, John, *Paradise Lost*, II, 943–7, in *The Poetical Works of John Milton*, ed. D. Masson, London 1890

NECKAM, A., *De naturis rerum libri II*, XXXI, and *De laudibus divinae sapientiae*, IX, 121–26, ed. T. Wright, London, 1863

NICOLAUS PERGAMENUS, *Dialogus creaturarum*, 87: 'De grife tyranno', in *Fabelbücher des Mittelalters*, ed., J. G. T. Grässe, Tübingen, 1880

NIGG, J., *The Book of Gryphons*, Cambridge, MA-Watertown 1982

NONNOS, *Dionysiaca*, XLVIII, 383, trans. W. H. D. Rouse, Loeb Classical Library, 1940

ORIGEN, *Peri archōn libri IV*, IV, 17, and *Contra Celsum*, III, 27, in *Patrologia graeca*, vol. XI, cols 379–80, 953–4

PAUSANIAS, *Description of Greece*, I, 24, 6, trans. W. H. S. Jones, Loeb Classical Library, 1926–35

PETRUS RIGA, *Aurora Petri Rigae: Biblia versificata*, ed. P. E. Beichner, Notre Dame, 1965

PHILOSTRATUS, *The Life of Apollonius of Tyana*, III, 48, trans. F. C. Conybeare, Loeb Classical Library, 1912

PLINY: *C. Plinii Secundi Naturalis Historiae libri XXXVII*, VII, 2, 10, and X, 49, 136, *see* 'General' section

POLO, Marco, *Il Milione*, ed. D. Olivieri, Bari, 1928

POMPONIUS MELA, *De chorographia libri tres*, II, 1, ed. G. Ranstrand, Göteberg, 1971

REANEY, P. H., *A Dictionary of British Surnames*, 'Griffin', London, 1961

ROSS, Alexander, *Arcana Microcosmi . . . with a Refutation of Doctor Browns Vulgar Errors, and the Ancient Opinions vindicated*, II, 20, London, 1651

Scientific American, The, 271, no. 6 (December 1994), 60–69

SIDONIUS APOLLINARIS, *Poem XXII*, 64–71, in *Poems and Letters*, ed. W. B. Anderson, Loeb Classical Library, 1936

SIMON, E., 'Zur Bedeutung des Greifen in der Kunst der Kaiserzeit', *Latomus*, 21 (1982), 749–80

SOLINUS: *C. Iulii Solini Collectanea rerum memorabilium*, 15, 22, ed. T. Mommsen, Berlin, 1864

STEELE, Sir Richard, *The Guardian*, no. 60, London, 1747

STOCKTON, F. R., *The Griffin and the Minor Canon* (1885), in *The Penguin Book of Western Fairy Tales*, ed. J. Zipes, Harmondsworth, 1993

STOCKTON, F. R., *The Great Show in Kobol-Land*, London, 1891

STRABO, *Geography*, XIII, 1, 16, trans. H. L. Jones, Loeb Classical Library, 1917–32

Suda, The, 'Abaris', in *Suidae Lexicon*, ed. A. Adler, Leipzig, 1928–38

THOMAS AQUINAS, St, *Summa theologica*, Ia–IIae, Q. 102, art. 6, ad 1, ed. de Rubeis, Billuart and others, Turin, 1922

VASARI, Giorgio, *La Vita di Michelangelo nelle redazioni del 1550 e del 1568*, ed. P. Barocchi, Milan and Naples 1962

VIRGIL, *Eclogues*, VIII, 26–8 and *Aeneid*, VI, 851–3, in *Virgil*, trans. H. R. Fairclough, Loeb Classical Library, 1974

WEGNER, I., *Studien zur Ikonographie des Greifen im Mittelalter*, Leipzig, 1928

ZIEGLER, K., 'Gryps', in *Paulys Real-Encyclopädie der classischen Altertumwissenschaft*, ed. G. Wissowa and W. Kroll, Stuttgart, 1912

Sphinxes

CURL, J. S., *The Egyptian Revival*, London, 1982

DEMISCH, H., *Die Sphinx*, Stuttgart, 1977

DESSENNE, A., *Sphinx iconographique*, Paris, 1957

FISCHER, H. G., *The Ancient Egyptian Attitude Towards the Monstrous (Monsters and Demons in the Ancient and Medieval Worlds)*, Papers presented in honour of Edith Porada, ed. Ann E. Farkas *et al.*, Mainz, 1987

GARDINER, Sir A., 'Some Personifications II', *Proceedings of the Society of Biblical Archaeology* (46th session), 1916, 83–94

HASSAN, S., *Le Sphinx, son histoire à la lumière des fouilles récentes*, Cairo, 1952

LEHNER, M., 'Reconstructing the Sphinx', *Cambridge Archaeological Journal*, 2(1), 1992, 3–26

SIMPSON, W. K., 'Egyptian Sculpture and Two-Dimensional Representation as Propaganda', *Journal of Egyptian Archaeology*, LXVIII, 266–71

Half-Human Creatures

ALCIATUS, A., *Emblemata cum commentariis*, Padua, 1621, reprinted as *The Renaissance and the Gods*, no. 25, New York and London, 1976

ALPERS, A., *Maori Myths and Tribal Legends*, London, 1964

ATWOOD, M., 'Siren song' in *You are Happy*, New York, 1974

BACON, Francis, *The Wisdom of the Ancients*, tr. Arthur Knight, London, 1619

BAER, E., *Sphinxes and Harpies in Medieval Islamic Art: An Iconographical Study*, Jerusalem, 1965

BAUR, P. V. C., *Centaurs in Ancient Art: The Archaic Period*, Berlin, 1912

BEAGON, M., *Roman Nature: The Thought of Pliny the Elder*, Oxford, 1992

BENWELL, G., and WAUGH, A., *Sea Enchantress: The Tale of the Mermaid and Her Kin*, London, 1961

BENNETT, A. G., *Focus on the Unknown*, London, 1953

BERMAN, R., 'Mermaids' and 'Sirens', in M. South (ed.), *Mythical and Fabulous Creatures*, Westport, Conn., 1987, 133–45 and 147–53

BINYON, L., *The Sirens: An Ode*, Chelsfield, 1924

BISSCHOP, E. de, *Tahiti-Nui*, London, 1959

BLAMIRES, A., PRATT, K., and MARX, C. W. (eds), *Woman Defamed and Woman Defended: An Anthology of Medieval Texts*, Oxford, 1992

CAMOENS, L. de, *The Lusiads*, trans. W. C. Atkinson, Harmondsworth, 1952

FRERE-COOK, G. (ed.), *The Decorative Arts of the Mariner*, London, 1966

DALY, M., and CAPUTI, J., *Webster's First Intergalactic Wickedary of the English Language*, London, 1988

DETIENNE, M. *The Gardens of Adonis*, trans. J. Lloyd, Brighton, 1977

DOUGLASS, N., *Siren Land* (2nd edn), London, 1923

duBOIS, P., *Centaurs and Amazons: Women and the Pre-History of the Great Chain of Being*, Ann Arbor, 1991

FARAL, E., 'La queue de poisson des sirènes,' *Romania* 47, 1953, 433–506

FORSTER, E. M., 'The Story of the Siren' in *Collected Short Stories*, vol. II, London, 1986

GARDNER, W. H., and MacKENZIE, N. H., *The Poems of Gerard Manley Hopkins*, London, 1967

GREENBLATT, S., *Marvelous Possessions: The Wonder of the New World*, Oxford, 1988

HALL, E., *Inventing the Barbarian: Greek Self-Definition through Tragedy*, Oxford, 1989

HOLZE, E. A., 'Sirens and their Song' in M. DeForest (ed.), *Woman's Power, Man's Game: Essays on Classical Antiquity in Honor of Joy A. King*, Wauconda, Illinois, 1993, 392–414

HONEYCOMBE, Gordon, *Selfridges: 75 Years. The Story of the Store, 1909–1984*, London, 1984

KASTNER, G., *Les Sirènes: Essai sur les principaux mythes relatifs à l'incantation*, Paris, 1858

KEARNS, E., 'Indian myth', in C. Larrington (ed.), *The Feminist Companion to Mythology*, London, 1992, 189–226

KING, H., 'Producing woman: Hippocratic Gynaecology', in L. Archer, S. Fischler and M. Wyke (eds), *An Illusion of the Night: Women in Ancient Societies*, Basingstoke, 1994, 102–114

LAMPEDUSA, G. di, 'The Professor and the Siren', in *Two Stories and a Meaning*, trans. A. Colquhoun, London, 1962

LARRINGTON, C. (ed.), *The Feminist Companion to Mythology*, London, 1992

LAWSON, J. C., *Modern Greek Folklore and Ancient Greek Religion*, Cambridge, 1910

LYCOSTHENES, C., *Prodigiorum ac Ostentorum Chronicon*, Basle, 1557

McCULLOCH, F., *Medieval Latin and French Bestiaries*, University of North Carolina Studies in the Romance Languages and Literatures No. 3, Chapel Hill, 1962

NAPIER, A. D., *Masks, Transformations and Paradoxes*, Berkeley and London, 1986

PADEL, R., 'Women: model for possession by Greek daemons', in A. Cameron and A. Kuhrt (eds), *Images of Women in Antiquity*, London, 1983

PAYNE, H. G. G., *Necrocorinthia*, Oxford, 1931

POLLARD, J., *Birds in Greek Life and Myth*, London, 1977

POLLARD, J., *Seers, Shrines and Sirens: The Greek Religious Revolution in the Sixth Century BC*, London, 1965

PUCCI, P., 'The Song of the Sirens', *Arethusa* 12, 1979, 121–32

RACHEWILTZ, S. de, *De Sirenibus: An Inquiry into Sirens from Homer to Shakespeare*, New York and London, 1987

ROWLAND, B., 'Harpies', in M. South (ed.), *Mythical and Fabulous Creatures*, Westport, Conn., 1987, 155–61

RUBENS, B., and Taplin, O., *An Odyssey round Odysseus: The Man and His Story Traced through Time and Place*, London, 1989

SMITH, J. C., and DE SELINCOURT, A., *Spenser: Poetical Works*, London, 1966

SYLVESTER, D., *Magritte: Catalogue of the Tate Gallery Exhibition*, London, 1969

THOMAS, K., *Man and the Natural World: Changing Attitudes in England, 1500–1800*, London, 1983

WALCOTT, D., *The Odyssey: A Stage Version*, London, 1993

WOODROFFE, P., *Hallelujah Anyway*, Limpsfield, 1984

YOLEN, J., 'The Lady and the Mermaid', in *Tales of Wonder*, London and Sydney, 1983

Illustration Sources

Illustrations are listed by page number, and objects in the British Museum (which also provided the photographs concerned) are indicated by the following departmental abbreviations:

CM   Coins and Medals
EA   Egyptian Antiquities
Ethno.   Museum of Mankind
GR   Greek and Roman Antiquities
JA   Japanese Antiquities
MLA   Medieval and Later Antiquities
OA   Oriental Antiquities
PD   Prints and Drawings
PRB   Prehistoric and Romano-British Antiquities
WA   Western Asiatic Antiquities

1 GR 1867.5–8.1048 (Vase E780)
2 *left* JA HG29
2 *right* JA HG236
3 WA 134322
7 British Library Royal MS 193XV fol.23
9 British Library Royal MS 2 BVII fol.2
10 MLA Sloane 1753
11 GR 1929.5–13.1
12 *above* MLA 1989.6–1.1
12 *below* Courtesy of Midland Bank plc
15 OA 1920.9–17.05
16 *above* OA 1973.7–26.140
16 *below* OA 1936.12–23.3
17 WA 122125
18 EA 10018/2
19 EA 1357
20 PD 1895.1–22.577
21 *above* OA 1900.10–11.1
21 *below* GR 1772.3–20.432 (Vase F148)
24 OA 1978.12–18.1
26 OA 1919.1–1.0157
27 OA 1968.4–23.2
30 JA Add.90 1934.7–14.01
33 CM 1950.11–9.6
35 © The Cleveland Museum of Art, J. H. Wade Fund, 44.492

37 MLA Slade Bequest S.947
39 MLA 1986.6–3.1
41 PD Pennant London Crowle vol. II, pl.172
42 PRB POA 201
43 Ethno. 94.634
45 British Library Add. MS 38122 fol.12
49 British Library Royal MS 28 VII fol.100
50 MLA 1975.4–1.1
51 Rolf Kreuder, Tann/Rhön, Germany
53 PD Hind A IV 4
54 *above* British Library Royal MS 12 FXIII fol.10v
54 *below* MLA 1856.6–23.166
55 Scala/Galleria degli Uffizi, Florence
56 Trustees of the Victoria and Albert Museum, 7131–1860
57 PD B47 (1834.8–4.43)
58 Rolf Kreuder, Tann/Rhön, Germany
59 Trustees of the Victoria and Albert Museum, A79–1936
61 CM E2512
62 Österreichische Nationalbibliothek, Vienna, cod. 1897, fol.24v
63 © Photo Réunion des Musées Nationaux, Paris
64 The Metropolitan Museum of Art, Rogers Fund, 1920, 20.53.3
66 MLA AF 3049
67 The Metropolitan Museum of Art, Gift of John D. Rockefeller, Jr, The Cloisters Collection, 37.80.4
68 PD RD 57 (1934.8–4.46)
71 The Metropolitan Museum of Art, Bequest of Lizzie P. Bliss, 1931, 31.67.12
73 WA 89148
74 GR 1897.4–1.927
75 GR 1856.10–1.19 (Vase E434)
76 GR 1805.7–3.1278
77 CM BMC 1181
78 PRB Corbridge Lanx

79 Michael Holford
80 CM Hill 22
81 Ashmolean Museum, Oxford
82 *top* MLA 1957.2–4.15
82 *below* MLA 92.11–2.1
83 British Library Harley MS 4751 fol.76
84 MLA OA24
86 British Library Royal MS 20AV fol.70v
87 The Dean and Chapter of Wells Cathedral (Misericord 64)
91 Scala/Palazzo dei Priori (Collegia della Mercanzia), Perugia
94 The Dean and Chapter, Hereford Cathedral
97 L'Arioste, *Roland Furieux*, Paris, 1879, Chant 10, p.103
99 MLA 1909.12–1.2
101 Lewis Carroll, *Aventures d'Alice aux Pays des Merveilles*, London, 1869, p.141
105 Griffith Institute, Ashmolean Museum, Oxford
108 British Library 07701 a15 p.112
109 The Metropolitan Museum of Art, Rogers Fund, 1931, 31.3.166
110 *above* EA 62494
110 *below* EA 54678
111 *Syria*, vol.26, 1949, pl. VIII, opp. p.195
113 British Library 1155. c.21 p.230
115 Diana Stein
116 British Library Ac. 2667 p.83
117 British Library Ac. 5206/2 p.227
120 British Library 145 g.16 p.7
121 British Library 07708 c.4 opp. p.171
122 GR 1889.4–10.1–5
127 British Library 60 g.8 pl.IV
129 British Library 744 fol.7
130 Christopher McCall
131 MLA 1909. 12–1
133 British Library 746 f.8 vol.2 pl.26
134 Trustees of the Victoria and

Albert Museum, C124/16–1979

135 *above* Deutsches Theatermuseum, Munich

135 *below* Henrietta McCall

139 WA 118801

140 GR Parthenon S. Metope 27

142 GR 1971.11–1.1

143 GR Vase E768

144 Ashmolean Museum, Oxford

145 Courtesy Museum of Fine Arts, Boston, Gift of Edward Perry Warren (Res. 08.34c)

146 GR 1958.7–21.1

147 GR 1843.11–3.31

149 U. Aldrovandi, *Monstrorum Historia*, 1642, p.337

150 GR Sculpture B287

151 John Rylands University Library of Manchester (Rylands Armenian MS 3 fol.108)

153 Photo Musée de la Marine, Paris

155 Bildarchiv Foto Marburg, Germany

157 OA 1869.5–3.2

158 Trustees of the Victoria and Albert Museum, 14.2697–1931

160 U. Aldrovandi, *Monstrorum Historia*, 1642, p.354

161 Courtesy of Selfridges plc

162 Ethno. 1942 As.1.1

163 British Library 459 d.4 vol. II pl. LVII (24)

167 Bridgeman Art Library/Ferens Art Gallery, Hull

168 Tessa Rickards (J. Black and A. Green, *Gods, Demons and Symbols of Ancient Mesopotamia*, London, 1992, p.14)

169 *left* PD E.2–373

169 *right* GR 1843.11–3.63 (Vase B213)

170 *left* Karl Taube, *Aztec and Maya Myths*, London, 1993, p.59

170 *right* GR Terracotta 616

172 *left* GR 1836.2–24.103 (Vase B194)

172 *right* GR 1861.4–25.46

173 CM PCG Addenda 7

174 *left* JA F747

174 *right* JA 1945.10–17.576

175 Edward Topsell, *Historie of Foure-footed Beastes*, 1607, p. 441

176 *left* GR Vase E441

176 *right* CM BMC Heraclea 28

177 *left* JA 1881.12–10.01771

177 *right* JA F1447

178 *left* CM 1987.6–49–270

178 *right* OA 1933.10–27.1

179 *above* OA 1920.9–17.051

179 *below* MLA 1982.7–1.1–3

180 *left* WA 124095

180 *top right* GR 1843.11–3.40

180 *below right* Eva Wilson, *8000 Years of Ornament*, London 1994, p.57

181 *left* OA 114

181 *right* Eva Wilson, *8000 Years of Ornament*, London, 1994, p.71 (after *Book of Durrow*, Trinity College Library, Dublin)

182 Eva Wilson, *North American Indian Designs*, London, 1994, pl.39

The drawings under the chapter titles on pp. 5, 6, 14, 44, 72, 104 and 138 are taken from Richard Huber, *Treasury of Fantastic and Mythological Creatures*, New York, 1981.

Index